INNOCENT IN ALASKA

The Story of

INNOCENT

Margaret Knudsen Burke

IN ALASKA

By John Springer

COWARD-McCANN, Inc.   New York

A PATHFINDER BOOK REPRINT EDITION
Complete and Unabridged

Printed in the United States of America

ISBN: 979-8-8691-1632-1

INNOCENT IN ALASKA

Chapter One

As I stood on the dock at Seattle that June evening, waiting for my friends Al and Lucy Boyd to appear in the milling crowd, the burnished arc of the sun sank into the Pacific among purple and ermine clouds. Save for the flocks of wheeling, shrilling sea gulls, the air was as clear as the Day of Creation and had the tonic quality of a powerful martini.

I looked at my watch for the tenth time in five minutes. On the dock, scrubbed, currycombed and dressed in their Sunday best, women and children stood about in clusters, tearfully kissing their menfolk good-bye. The passengers—miners, adventurers and tourists—thronged about me, wearing stocking caps and checked wool shirts. Dozens of longshoremen, stripped to the waist, sweating and cursing, fed cargo into a towering ship-to-shore crane that transferred it from stacks of crates into the hatches of the wooden ship that rode at the dockside.

It was seven o'clock and the *Yucatan* was due to sail at eight. I stood on tiptoe and peered over the heads of the mob, trying to spot Al and Lucy, but it was hopeless. I got my ticket out of my purse once more and admired its fancy lettering, closed my eyes, then opened them. It was hard to believe that I was not back home in Nebraska, dreaming.

Could this be I, Margaret Knudsen, about to sail for Alaska as the first woman telephone operator in the Territory? And was I really on my way to meet again the dark, handsome, rich man who, during our brief acquaintance, had already set the course of my life?

Somewhere in the throng on the dock were the Boyds, who —total strangers only a week before—had rescued me, a nearly penniless runaway from parental wrath, and bestowed on me the love and friendship that were to last for thirty years and who had been the means of my getting to Alaska. If I had known then what lay ahead—a maritime disaster that cost many lives, a week of hysteria and terror during which all our lives were in danger, two years of being miserably and gloriously in love, labor, anguish, the hardships and the triumphs of pioneering in a great new land—I could not have borne the prospect. But just now I was only undergoing the normal anxiety of the inexperienced traveler.

I had gone downtown ahead of the Boyds to do some last-minute shopping for clothes I thought suitable for my first sea voyage, having received Al's instructions to meet them on the dock near the bow of the *Yucatan*. I'd done quite a job on my going-away costume. At the age of eighteen I was less than five feet tall and weighed ninety pounds. And I was swathed in an oversized, too-long green plaid skirt and a cheap jacket, topped by my curly red hair, primly parted in the middle and ballooned out on each side by hair rats. I looked like a lopsided hayrick. As I nervously lifted the hem of the skirt to keep it from sweeping the dock, I craned my neck as far as it would go. At least the Boyds should have no trouble spotting *me* in the crowd.

I looked again at my ticket and at the ship. It was the *Yucatan*, and the day was June 7, 1904. Every shout and whistle made me jump.

Then there was a smell of pine behind me and a hand like an iron clamp on my arm and Al Boyd said, "We're a little late. Come on, we're going home!"

It seemed only a few weeks ago that I'd even heard of Alaska for the first time. I had been sitting at my switchboard in the

Yellowstone Telephone Company's branch in Denver, on my last day there, when Mr. Peavy, the manager, stopped at my side and introduced me to Will Burke.

"This is Miss Knudsen," Mr. Peavy had said. "Miss Knudsen is one of our *talented* operators." The compliment did not quite conceal the disapproval he felt at my having resigned the week before. "This is Mr. Will Burke, of the Northern Commercial Company in Alaska."

Save for his shirt, the whiteness of his teeth, and a thick gold watch chain that corralled his flat stomach, everything about Will Burke was black, or nearly so. From his shiny, benchmade boots to the top of his head, his over-all complexion was that of a wolf's mouth, and the thin mustache that stabbed across his upper lip served to accentuate the piratical swarthiness of his face.

I uprooted a couple of dead plug lines, got off my stool and took Will's fingers, but my grip lacked enthusiasm. I felt as if I had drawn a grizzly for a partner in a square dance. The day had been a rough one; a Shriners' convention was assembling in town, and relaying their messages through the switchboard all day had stove me up. I was sticky with perspiration, one of my hair rats had slipped its moorings, and one of my cheap shoes was pinching my little toe.

"It's a pleasure," Will Burke had said. His voice was soothing—a round bass—and his smile, though crooked as a dog's hind leg, was white and pleasant. Stepping forward, he bowed toward me. This act of courtesy increased Mr. Peavy's good humor. According to Mr. Peavy, the smile and the dulcet tone were more important than termite-free telephone poles, strong wire, or windbags on long-distance calls. He had spent the last two months trying to infect me with the Yellowstone hurrah.

"Remember, Margaret," he told me, "that you're a member of the Grande Dame's family. I refer to Mother Yellowstone. You've got a lot to live up to. When you meet people—*smile!* When you answer the board, put over the *glad* voice. Make 'em think you're wife, sweetheart, mother and sister or pal, all rolled into one."

At this point he intimated that the company considered asking for raises a singularly shocking discourtesy and an offense comparable to the infamous demands of some labor leaders for employee vacations with pay. Anyone so insensitive to Mother Yellowstone's feelings could expect his loyalty to be questioned. That was the sole reason for my resignation.

Will released my hand. I smiled and tried to get across the glad voice, at the same time making a pass at my rebellious rat and shifting my weight from my shrieking toe to the other foot.

"I'm losing one of my flock," Mr. Peavy said. "Try to talk some sense into this young lady, Will."

Ignoring the suggestion, Will took a gold case from his pocket, offered a cigar to Mr. Peavy, took one himself and lit both of them.

"May I," he said pausing. "Do you mind if I smoke?"

I was mildly surprised; no one had ever asked my permission to smoke. I began to look with new interest on Will Burke's good looks and easy manners.

"Margaret," Mr. Peavy said, with a *tchk-tchk* look, "thinks she'll be happier in Los Angeles." Mr. Peavy's sanctimonious tone made me sore as a boiled owl.

"I'm going too," I managed to say.

"Good for you," Will Burke said. "There's nothing like a change of jobs to bolster up the spirits. When are you leaving?"

"Tomorrow on the train. And nobody's going to stop me."

"I'd hate to be the man who tried," Will said, chuckling. "On the Shriners' Special?"

I nodded, still peeved at Mr. Peavy, who, however, seemed a little crestfallen at having failed to enlist Will Burke as an ally. "Yes. My cousin is going with me."

"Indeed. A lady?"

"No. My cousin Arthur—Arthur Williams."

"I'm glad to hear it. I'm taking the same train. Those holiday excursions can be entertaining. Perhaps we could have dinner on the train. With your cousin, too, of course."

"Well, I guess—"

"Good. I'll look you up en route." Bowing, he turned, and followed by the deflated Mr. Peavy, rounded a corner in the hallway and disappeared.

My hand went to my hair again and I found myself a bit short of breath. Contact with spit-and-polish bravos at that time in my life had been only through the medium of books and the few magazines my father had approved, and now that my snit at Mr. Peavy had vanished I suddenly felt green as a gourd and tacky as all get out. I wondered the usual things. Was he rich? Married? How old? I guessed his age at thirty. Actually he was thirty-seven.

But I didn't learn this until after we were married at Fort Gibbon, Territory of Alaska, two years later.

He was a beaner all of his life. Like Alaska, there never was anything like him.

At the date of our first meeting in Denver he already had the Territory by the ear, since the Northern Commercial Company's interests reached into every phase of Alaska's social, political or economic existence. He set the price structure for buying and selling, named his own law-enforcement officers, had a big voice in shipping, and on those rare occasions when he spoke loud enough for Washington, D. C., to hear, people listened.

The man never lived who could put the blade into him in a business deal or a poker game. He made $4,000,000 out of the Territory and encouraged others to try for the high score too. In fact he succeeded so well with me that on my twentieth birthday I was worth $24,000.

Naturally such a man would have plenty of friends and as many enemies. Yet in all the years we were married I never knew him to cheat or do a deliberately unkind or uncharitable thing to anyone, unless given the best of reasons.

On the contrary, he would lean over backward to slip a scarecrow aborigine a few extra dollars for his furs, hides, minerals or game. When he interested me in the sickness and poverty of the Indians of Nome and I went out to raise a rehabilitation fund, he started me off with $1,000 and committed himself to a similar contribution each year. More, he helped me put the arm on more than one reluctant humanitarian. He never docked the pay of a sick employee and would fight a blizzard twenty miles to look in on one. There was hardly a friend or acquaintance in Alaska who hadn't owed him money at one time or another.

Ordinarily he was quiet and pleasant. However, he could

turn with the suddenness of a killer wolf. He was well read and spoke not only fine English, but Spanish and French as well. Given cause, he could put a kind of mockery or sarcasm into his voice that left you squirming.

He usually rode his emotions with a tight rein, and so far as I can remember he never lost complete control of his temper. But when he found it necessary to knock a man down or beat a dog, it was carried off without malice or anger. To him it was a job to be done as efficiently as possible and with a minimum of feeling.

He was incurably restless and his capacity for work was almost unbelievable. His ambition for making money never flagged and his love for the Territory never waned. I am sorry that he did not live to see the Alaskan star in the flag.

As I look back I believe that there were four factors that helped keep our marriage strong. I have already mentioned three of them. I, too, could never stay put. I also wanted money, loved the Territory, and was willing to work for both. The other was childhood environment. Will and I came from similar backgrounds.

At the railroad station next day as I waited to board the Shriners' Special, my background was still very much with me in the persons of Mr. and Mrs. Anderson, who had driven me to the train, and their six stair-step children. During my two-month stay with his family Mr. Anderson had treated me like a bonbon.

Having grown resigned, he once told me, to the husbandly regimentation demanded by a big family, to dinky profits, high wages, green lumber and the insatiable upholstery appetites of mice and rats, I was a breath of spring to him. Mrs. Anderson's attitude had been no less complimentary and gratifying. I owed them a lot.

Old friends of my folks in Blair, Nebraska, they had helped me escape from a town and an environment that I had begun to despise at an early age. I was born during a blizzard, and—so family history had it—didn't quit howling until the storm gave up. In the ensuing eighteen years I found nothing to change my mind about the whole shebang.

The town itself was a kitchen midden and hodgepodge

of rambling, barn-painted houses, barns and storm cellars, a community hall, four churches, a blacksmith shop, two general stores and a livery stable, all ingeniously interlaced by a network of narrow, rutted, sun-baked roads that led off to the outlying farms or to the only Danish college in the United States, four miles out.

When a girl outgrew the pigtail-and-marble-shooting set, she could choose, for entertainment, between square dances, pie suppers, husking bees, prayer meetings or skull ramming. If she chose to work for money, her opportunities were likewise electrifying. She could become serf to a general store or pick up after a pastor.

My people were Danes and so was everyone else on the reservation, most of the elders having come from the old country. My father Nels was the town blacksmith. Aided by a kid named Karl Frandsen, he did his clanging and blistering in a shed next to our house. To my mother Hansena and my four brothers and sisters, the incessant uproar was a way of life. But I never got used to it. To this day the tinkle of a bell makes my head ache.

Father was convinced that his children were born with wild streaks in them, and his program of reformation was long range and diversified. This included standing in corners, extra chores, bed without supper, and denial of the privilege of fetching his slippers—all for misdemeanors—and the thump and the peach oil for major crimes. The thump usually was reserved for sloppy stoking at table, laughing in church or languishing underfoot when a customer approached. Father administered it by cocking his middle finger against his thumb and releasing it against an offender's skull. Upon contact it had the power to bring on a temporary cross-eyed trance.

Peach oil was also applied externally. Its benefit was derived from a switch cut from a nearby cottonwood tree. This remedy was reserved for fibbing, or something equally malodorous such as illegally making off with a brother or sister's personal merchandise. I got a dose of it as late as my seventeenth birthday. I had denied attending a box social topped off by an after-dinner kissing bee.

All in all, I had been about ready to call for the hemlock when Mr. Anderson, a gaunt man with the expression of a Saint

Bernard, and his well-insulated wife Anna arrived in Blair for a visit. By that time I had learned to operate the town switchboard, at eleven dollars a week. And, over the objections of my father, I parted my hair in the middle, wore rats, dusted my nose with cornstarch and had hidden more than $100 in savings in my room.

I'll never forget, to my dying day, the pleasure it gave me when my turn came for the Anderson hug.

"Margaret!" Mrs. Anderson said. "What a pretty girl you've become! Why, it was only yesterday that you were downright peaked! How you've filled out!"

Two back-yard talks later I had a case won. Mrs. Anderson, seconded by her husband, agreed with me that a visit with them would do me a world of good, and Father retired to scratch and pant. But it would be only for three months, he ruled. My vaporings grew so during the next week that I lost my appetite, forgot where I'd stashed my savings, and packed and repacked my trunk a dozen times.

My excitement was short lived. Denver offered about the same brand of taffy pull as Blair. True, my wages at Yellowstone were a dollar a week higher. But the Anderson chaperonage matched that of Father's at his level best, and upon my first sneak appearance at a square dance emporium I was promptly apprehended, so turned to reading for entertainment. By the time Cousin Arthur showed up I had nearly foundered on romantic tales and was so disgusted with reality that it was ten years later in Alaska before I returned seriously to the wick and the kerosene.

Good old Arthur.

A pink-faced man with a cowcatcher mustache and a fine belly, he had come to Denver to launch one of his periodic attacks against the local Wanamaker's. He was a salesman for an Eastern notions firm, a classy dresser, had a nose for good whisky, a gift of gab, lived in unmarried splendor at a Los Angeles hotel, and was my father's favorite nephew. *His* father had been one of the designers of the liner *Titanic*.

Arthur's sister, Cletus Varney—the widow of Clyde Varney, an insurance salesman—also lived in Los Angeles. Arthur considered Los Angeles the cat's pajamas. Those balmy breezes, black-eyed *señoritas*, high-toned theatres and saloons, couldn't be beat anywhere in the world.

That convinced me. I decided to move on. Every time Cousin Arthur came over I worked on him to take me to Los Angeles, and one night—when his breath proclaimed he'd been busy with Old Blabbermouth—I got him on the back porch and convinced him. Since the Andersons wouldn't parole me on their own, I had to go another twenty rounds, by mail, with Father. But a note of invitation and assurance from Cousin Arthur finally won him over. I was to mind Arthur and Cletus, though. I would get a job and live with Cletus too. I wasn't to gallivant around with sports and I was to be home by the first of September.

Now I was on my way. As I turned at Mrs. Anderson's sniffle I'm afraid the smug look on my face wasn't too well concealed.

"All ab-ooo-rd!"

Breaking Mrs. Anderson's wristlock, I grabbed my bag, smashed at my hat, got a grip on my purse and started for the first coach.

"Good-bye! Good-bye, dear friends! Take—"

The rest of my farewell was washed out by the train whistle.

Inside the coaches it was bedlam, but as I entered the first car my sorrows went out the window. As I passed through the second and third sections, looking for my Pullman berth, it became apparent that everyone aboard knew everyone else and was making the most of friendship. Shouts and laughter trailed in my wake and came from up ahead.

Having forgotten both Will and Arthur for the time being, I finally located my berth, racked my hat and bag, and sat back to view the scenery as we moved out.

I had barely rearranged myself and lifted the window shade for a wider view when Will walked up.

"Miss Knudsen." He smiled as his hat came off. "There are so many people here, I'd about given up finding you."

"Well, I—I'm here." I was happy to see him. But his sudden appearance had jolted me. Maybe it was his change in dress. I don't remember. Anyway, he now wore a brown doeskin suit with a double-breasted vest, and his boots glistened like wet gold. Whatever the reason, I had nearly bolted from my seat when I looked up, and I felt like a fool.

Smiling more widely, he eased himself into the seat beside me, and, pulling a gold watch from his vest pocket, snapped open the case, read the time and tucked it back. "After twelve," he announced. "What say to a look at the train and some lunch?"

As he rebuttoned his coat I noticed a yellow blob—about the size and shape of a lopsided prune—dangling from the chain that stretched across his middle. My curiosity overcame my manners.

"What's that?"

"What?" Will's eyes flicked ahead, then back to me and finally followed my pointing finger. "Oh."

Flaring his coat again, he took out the chain and watch and handed them over. "It's a nugget. Gold. One of my friends found it up Cleary Creek way."

I had never seen raw gold before and I didn't know Cleary Creek from Adam's off ox. But, hefting the nugget in my palm, I felt an unaccountable excitement. I couldn't have explained the feeling then. But I have since been able to recognize, and correctly diagnose, the infection. Indeed, I've been afflicted with the malady for most of my life, and to this day I never set eye on a piece of gold—ornament or otherwise—that it doesn't temporarily wake me up and make my fingers throb. The condition I refer to is popularly known as "gold fever."

As I turned the nugget over in my hand I was sure it was worth a million dollars.

"It—it's beautiful!"

"Yes," Will agreed. "Gold is always beautiful. The most beautiful thing on earth." He took it from me, and grasping the fob between the thumb and forefinger of his right hand, he held it stationary and level with my eyes.

"Look closely," he suggested. "And tell me what you see."

On one side the nugget bore a startling resemblance to a coach-and-four, down to and including a driver, spoked wheels and a baggage rack.

"Why—"

"Yes," Will said, grinning, "but it's not unique in the Territory. In their formative stages all metals take strange shapes, especially gold. I've seen Alaskan nuggets that looked like cats, dogs, people, trees and even foreign palaces. I saw one once that looked like a dinosaur. Its detail was so pronounced that it might have been made by an amateur metalsmith." Pocketing his watch, he rearranged his chain and fob and rebuttoned his coat. "Now, shall we be off?"

Poorer than a church mouse for eighteen years, I considered money-making the most stimulating of conversational topics. Now here was a man with a fortune on his watch chain, and he wanted to eat rather than talk about gold. But I was soon distracted by the social whirl around me. We made our way through the train which consisted of eight Pullman coaches with two baggage cars converted into a bar and diner, both of which the Shriners were now storming. Elsewhere the happy buckoes had poker games going at every third seat and were belting the horn as if they expected a prize to pop up in the bottom of every bottle. The aisles were littered with sawdust, paper cups, cigar butts, empty bottles and a sprinkling of well-trodden plug hats. The band, which had started out determinedly as an ensemble, had been so put to rout that its members were now scattered throughout the train, each the master of his own request program.

Even assisted by Will's line bucks, I felt like I'd spent the winter sorting wildcats by the time we reached the first baggage car, which was the saloon, and we stopped to catch a breath. In spite of my squashed hat and battered shoes, I found it easy to return Will's amused grin. It was only my second time on a train; the first, my trip from Blair to Denver with the Andersons, had been about as exciting as watching a tree grow. Now I was beginning to have fun.

Inside the saloon car the Shriners, glasses in hand, packed the bar six deep, gabbling, howling and back thumping with high good humor. We had nearly made our way through a roiling purple cloud of cigar smoke and a brace of merrily chiming spittoons when a yell nailed us.

"Hey, Chickabiddy!"

Huffing, grunting and champing at a short Havana cigar,

Cousin Arthur edged through the crowd, leading a buxom, good-looking chestnut blonde with a milk-fed skin. As he hove to, the stogie fell unheeded from his mouth. It took no specialized background to determine that Arthur had been perfuming his breath with his favorite mash; and his companion, who wore a smartly tailored dark blue suit and clanked with diamonds, had evidently been his ally in his assault on the bottle. Arthur introduced her as Mrs. Winter, the wife of a friend, and I introduced Will.

"I been lookin' all over f'r ya," Arthur said.

"You were supposed to meet me at the depot."

"Was I? Guess I musta got my wires crossed. Buy ya a drink?" he asked Will.

Will declined, saying we were ready for the feed bag, and we pushed on into the diner. I didn't see Cousin Arthur again until we got off the train in Los Angeles.

For an improvised eatery the second baggage car took the prize. A waist-high, black-walnut bar, no doubt a refugee from some nobby European saloon, ran along the left-hand side from door to door, and—save for a ten-foot service space in the center —was burdened with porcelain and silver platters heaped with coleslaw, potato salad, macaroni salad and green salad; crocks of baked beans and boiled eggs; gloves of pickled pigs' feet and veal tongue; pickled beets, pickled onions, spiced and smoked frankfurters, and a sturdy trencher of assorted cold meats; bowls of sauces and relishes, and cartwheels of brown, black, white, yellow and blue cheese.

Behind the bar three Negro knife artists with flaring white chefs' hats and starched smocks were busy slashing at beef roasts, pork roasts, turkey and ham. A fourth, at the far end, divided his efforts between browning a platoon of squab spitted over a charcoal burner and sawing slabs from basketballs and builders' blocks of French bread, rye bread, whole wheat, pumpernickel, Italian twist and German *schwarzbrot.*

Across the car a long table creaked under a load of assorted pies and cakes, a tray of French pastry, vanilla, rice and bread puddings, and a scuttle of prune whip; several wicker baskets of hard candy, boxes of soft candy, and enough shelled nuts, of one species or another, for a hundred years of squirrel life.

A huge coffee urn squatted beside the door at the back, and a great icebox stood near it. A fifth, grinning caterer staffed both with masterful aplomb, pouring coffee and serving the varied flavors of ice cream from two-gallon buckets in the freezer.

After we had stacked our plates we decided to eat on the observation platform. Bucking the Shriner line encumbered with delicatessen seemed a hopeless proposition, but after a few minor collisions we managed to get outside.

It was a lovely sunshiny day, and the cheerful clack of the wheels as the train rocketed across the red, brushy Colorado prairie filled me with a sense of high adventure. I fell upon my heaped plate with the appetite of a snow-bound wolf, and in the next half hour ate so much that my corset, laced to eighteen inches, nearly cut me in two. While Will returned our plates I had a chance to gulp and groan at leisure, and when he finally returned an hour later, explaining that he had been detained by a talkative and bibulous friend, I was once more breathing easily.

It was then that the sun, throwing longer shadows on the rear of the train, exaggerated the gray at his temples and the tiny swatches of wrinkles at the corners of his eyes.

I well recall my disappointment. True, I wasn't interested— whole hog, anyway—in romance at the time. Money and independence, both of which had eluded me so far, were my big interests. But it seemed so unfair.

Here beside me was the handsomest man I had ever seen, a polished, considerate, exciting man—and he had to be gray and wrinkled! It was a pretty howdy-do. It looked as if everyone I had known or ever would know was either old, knuckleheaded or against the gold standard. Oh well, maybe he was married. But that thought didn't console me either. In fact it made me uneasy, if anything.

"A penny."

"A what?" I looked up to find Will's eyes on me, amused but kindly, and my own dropped in embarrassment for my lengthy and impolite preoccupation. But the nugget on his watch chain again saved the day.

"Oh. A penny—for my thoughts." I pointed to the fob. "I

was thinking," I lied, "about Alaska. You promised to tell me all about it. Remember?"

He took his time in answering. "It's a hard country to describe and yet it's an easy one," he replied at last. "What, specifically, do you want to know about it?"

"Well, anything," I stammered. "How about working? Can a girl get a job up there? Or get into business?"

"If you're getting the gold bug," he said slowly, "I'd quickly take something for it. To me, there's no place on earth like that country. It's a land of tremendous, snow-capped mountains, lush prairies, foaming rivers, thick forests, rich mines, aurora borealis, terrifying storms, wild animals, good food in season, thick furs, ocean-going freighters, Indians, Eskimos, air like wine, and what the Ned Buntlines of this age call the Midnight Sun. But it's a country for strong men who can take a licking and ask for a rematch. Which means it's no country, yet, for a woman. Especially," he said, smiling, "for pretty little girls with red hair, blue eyes and a fudge-making background."

That last crack did not contribute much to our budding friendship.

"Fiddlesticks!" *Background* was the reason that I was on the dodge! "I'm going to Los Angeles—and get a job too! I'm not asking anyone to help me! And don't think your precious Alaska scares me either! Nothing does!"

"Whoa!" Will held up a hand placatingly. "Ear yourself down. I didn't intend to hurt your feelings. I was merely trying to explain."

"All right." I managed to avoid biting my lip too hard. "Aren't there any women up there?"

"If you mean white women," he replied patiently, "there are a few. In the main, however, they boil down to a handful of wives of various businessmen and the dance-hall girls. In the latter case it's a tough way to make a living." He took another cigar from his case, bit off the end, and fired it.

"We need women—wives and mothers—as much as we need the gold or industry in Alaska. The country will be a state one day. And only the homemaker can bring it about. The United States Government is pretty much of a domestic corporation.

22

A predominantly bachelor population is not favored as a recommendation for statehood."

"Well, if that's what you want, why don't you let some women in, then?"

"It isn't that we don't want them. We do. And we need them desperately. But look at it this way. We're young, raw, primitive. Where—to a man—Alaska is real country, it's just the opposite to a white woman. Where to me the living conditions mean little—the sun and wind, the cold and shacks, soon become horrors to a white woman. So we need time to get ready for them."

I was still a bit nettled. "How did you know about my background?"

"It's written all over you," he said, laughing. Then his brows arched in mock alarm. "Put that knife away! I take it back!"

My dander came down again. "I didn't think it showed."

"Not—" he said, chuckling, "to the unworldly. I'm something of a kindred spirit, you see. I come of much the same stock and neighborhood—the background that's so easy to recognize in your personality and bearing."

"Blair? Blair, Nebraska?"

"No. But not too far removed from Nebraska." Taking the cigar from his mouth, he leaned forward, tapped the coal against his boot heel, and sat back with a noisy sigh of satisfaction. "I was born and spent a good part of my youth in Burlington, Kansas."

His full name, he said, was William Stark Burke. His mother was of French descent and his father predominantly Irish. His father had been a successful lawyer and county judge in Burlington for many years preceding Will's birth and those of his two younger brothers. On Will's fifteenth birthday Burke *père*, who had been favorably regarded as a lawgiver outside of his own bailiwick, was appointed to a Federal bench in Washington, D. C. Consequently he had abandoned the family ranch on the outskirts of Burlington and had moved his wife and brood to the nation's capital. Will had loved the ranch and the sweeping, sere plains of Kansas. Two years later, following the combined attacks of Washington humidity and quarrels with his father, he ran away.

"The little money I had, gave out in a town called Tismalheepish. In Nebraska," he recalled.

"Dismal Seepage?"

"No!" He laughed. "Tismalheepish. It's an Indian name. But it might as well have been named Dismal Seepage, considering its size and location and living conditions."

"Is that where you lived? Before you went to Alaska?"

"Not exactly. There were a lot of junkets sandwiched between my hitch in Tismalheepish and my citizenship in Alaska."

"Well, why did you leave?" My curiosity, by then, had me by the throat.

"The reason was love," he said. "Unrequited love. The girl's name was Kolb. Clementine Kolb. She was the blond daughter of a hardware-store owner, and the most devastatingly beautiful creature that I had seen, at that juncture of my life."

Will had snared a job, shortly after his arrival in Tismalheepish, with a hog rancher and his wife—Marion and Maude Hefflefinger. He soon proved himself pretty good as a chore-boy and pig slopper, and the childless couple began to regard him with parental affection. This included prideful introductions around and even concessions such as driving the mare and buggy. He met Clementine at a Halloween dance in the school gymnasium and was smitten; at first she had seemed to like him, but when she began to show an interest in the son of the mayor and dismissed Will, he left her house in such anger and disappointment that he threw the whip at the Hefflefinger mare. She ran away with the buggy and flung it broadside at a Mexican railroad hand's shanty behind the Tismalheepish roundhouse.

As Will picked himself up he heard the starter whistle from a loaded stock train beyond the depot, and hesitated no longer. One glance at the smashed buggy, the trembling mare, the chewed-up shanty and the angry Mexicans, and he was a goner. He jumped a boxcar and was on his way.

Broke again, he joined the army in Chicago and was assigned to what in this day would be known as the Signal Corps. He saw service in Germany, France and Spain and briefly in the Far East. During his hitch he learned a great deal about telephone installations and systems and also became interested in boxing. In his last year he won the heavyweight championship of his division.

Discharged in 1892 in New York City, he was looking for a job when he passed Jamey McCracken's old White House Gym, then located at 154th Street and Madison Avenue. He decided a workout would do him no harm, and so he went in, rented ring togs and got into action with the skipping rope, pulleys and punching bag. As he came from the shower he was collared by a character named Foxey McBean.

Foxey, it developed, made his living from the bumps, lacerations and contusions dispensed and received by a stable of three pugs. Currently, European audiences were hot for fistic contests, and he intended to take his troupe over there. But he needed a good combination trainer and sparring partner for them. Will had looked good in workout. The job paid $200 a month, feed, water and expenses.

Will took it and enjoyed it from the start. It was a novel way of making a living. He was moving through Europe at a fast pace, but slowly enough to permit his study of languages, foreign customs and history. It had been something of a disappointment when the tour ended.

Back in New York once more, he went to work for the Cosmopolitan Communications System, Incorporated, and studied business administration through one of the numerous night courses available to company employees. Two years later he was eastern division manager for the organization, with headquarters in Seattle, Washington. Then the Northern Commercial Company made him a proposition that he couldn't turn down, and he was on his way to Alaska.

"My only regret," Will concluded, "is that it didn't come sooner. You couldn't get me out of there now."

I felt a glow start at my feet and work up to my head. But the reason had nothing to do with his last remark. It was related to the philosophy behind the old saw, "Misery loves company." In short, I was as comforted as a drunk is to see a fellow squiffy in the next cell. Here was a person of education, taste, sophistication, worldliness—and probably rich as dirt—and he had been born in Kansas! He had run away, too, and it had paid off!

"Why, you're a hick—just like me!"

He laughed so loud and long that the knot in his cravat sagged.

"I surely am, and I'm proud of it. In fact most Americans who have built anything constructive were hicks," he said when he could talk again. "It has to be like that, because of the natural laws of evolution. In a few years you and I will be considered hicks by a newer and more advanced civilization. Certainly I would rather be a hick than some of the moth-eaten, tradition-ridden, do-nothings I've encountered in some aristocratic circles during my wanderings. Wouldn't you?"

"Well—well, I never looked at it that way before. I . . ."

I shivered, surprised to find it had grown dark. I felt sleepy and decided to go to bed, so Will escorted me to my berth, snagged the porter, and slipped him a five-dollar bill. Then, after telling me where to find him in the morning, he said good night and left me.

I was so weary and depressed that I could not sleep, and the slowly dwindling hilarity of the Shriners gave me little chance. So I dressed, took a blanket, and made my way back to the observation platform, where Will found me asleep in a chair the next morning.

"Margaret—er—Miss Knudsen! I was worried. I looked all over for you. Are you all right?"

"Yes. I'm all right." He was as neat as a bandbox; I must have looked as crummy as a worn-out Indian blanket. "And you can call me Margaret, if you like."

Will brought breakfast to the platform, and after I had cleaned up a plate of ham and eggs and two cups of coffee I felt stronger.

A few minutes later we pulled into Cheyenne, Wyoming, and stopped for the first of the Shriner receptions that took place that day. Alerted in advance by their Denver brothers, the local Shriners of every major town en route spit on their hands and put on a show for the visitors. As we ground to a stop, a band burst forth with a deafening blast, while the city magnificoes and cheering onlookers gave an earsplitting ovation. Then followed dancing on the station platform, with the townspeople joining in. While Will went off to look for cigars

I stood on the platform and watched the dancing. I suddenly heard a laugh that sounded something like a jackass eating cactus. When I looked around I attracted the attention of a beefy Shriner who was being the life of the party. He immediately asked me to dance, and since I loved to dance and Will was not there, I accepted. When the dance was over he showed no signs of leaving my side, and gradually began to impart to me the idea that we should set a spell together when the train started again. Since I'd never been mashed in my life, I did not know how to dodge his loop and stood there like a rabbit in a snare, wishing I'd never left the train. Then Will appeared and read the situation at a glance.

His face took on a peculiar expression I was to see many times in later years. His smile remained intact, but his eyelids drooped and he stared steadily at the man. The Shriner took the hint and ducked off.

By the time we rolled into Los Angeles I was so weary that my eyes were crossed. I had still not found Cousin Arthur, and to make matters worse, I had lost Cletus' address. Will advised me to wait on the depot platform until I spotted Arthur while he went to look for a hansom cab. Plug hats dented, collars hanging, suits crumpled and mustaches drooping, the Shriners limped dejectedly off the train while I waited for Arthur. Soon he showed up, swaying slightly, a bit disheveled, but full of spunk.

"Musta got my wires crossed," he explained when I said I'd expected to see him before we got off the train. Will appeared, greeted Arthur, and led us to a cab, asking the cabbie to drop him at the Plaza Hotel. He got my address from Arthur and asked permission to call the next day. Then Arthur and I crawled out to Hollywood, and it was dark before we reached the imposing stucco house. It was clear that Cletus was not at home. Arthur showed me to a room upstairs and went looking for a drink. Numb and aching, I closed the door, fell in the bed, and was out cold as soon as I landed.

Chapter Two

"BREAKFAST!"

At first I thought that the roof had caved in, and as I opened my eyes and sat up on my bed I wasn't sure it hadn't landed on me. My eyes were gritty and puffed, my mouth was dry as an eel in a flour barrel, and my head felt like it was going through a spring thaw.

"Chickabiddy! Shake a leg! It's nine o'clock and I'm starved!" Cousin Arthur liked to believe that his voice was commanding. Actually it was only loud enough to break windows and tumble walls.

"Aw—all right. Coming."

"Get a move on. Cletus is in the kitchen and rarin' to go."

Standing up, I swayed for a moment, then finally got on course and eventually in front of a mirror that was bolted to the top of an old-fashioned chest of drawers across the room. The sight that looked back at me was not calculated to represent the latest in fashion and grooming. Having slept in my clothes, my hat resembled a flapjack sitting on a fence post. My rice powder was caked and grainy, and from the drape of my blouse and skirt I could have been either coming or going. Excursion trains, I decided at that point, were not what they were cracked up to be. However, a hot tub and a change to clean clothes soon put me in business again, despite the fact that my convalescence was cut short by Arthur's persistent trumpeting and blowing.

Downstairs I discovered that Cletus hadn't changed a particle, physically, since I had seen her five years before on her last visit to Blair. Which means that she was slim, dark, pretty and in a dither. As I stepped over the sill she turned and let out a squeal.

"Margaret! Baby duck! I'm so happy to see you! Why, I can't believe it! You're a grown lady! How are the folks? What fun we'll have visiting. Oh—" Limping to the stove, she scraped up a brace of burned cakes from a smoking skillet and tossed them into a big woodbox on the opposite side. "For pity's sake! I'm always doing that!"

Aside from the red in his eyes, Arthur was his usual dapper self. But that was as far as his niceties went. For the first time in my life I had run into a man with a bad hangover. Hunched over, he grabbed a knife in one hand and a fork in the other, butted them on the table, and let loose an exasperated sigh.

"Well, where is it? Git it on! I gotta git to the office sometime today!"

Then I learned something that I should have remembered later. This involved Cletus' aversion to spirits and malts and to patrons of the grape, large and small, male and female, here, there and everywhere. Slamming platters of flapjacks, fried eggs and bacon on the table, she stood at Arthur's shoulder, and while he shoveled doggedly she lit into him from every angle about his drinking.

He was tons overweight, she snapped. That meant fat around his heart, and all on account of whisky. His liver probably was eaten up, too, and the reason he was always taking bicarbonate of soda was because drink had ruined his stomach. Also, he was a different man when he was guzzling. For one thing, his memory went bad after the first drink. If he hadn't been at it yesterday, she wouldn't have had to stand around at the depot waiting for us, only to learn—an hour later—that we had gone.

Moreover, what would Margaret's folks think if they knew

he had been swilling in my company? Was this any way to act before a young girl? And on and on she went until Arthur made his escape.

Then Cletus softened a bit and showed me to my real room —not the hole that Arthur had taken me to last night! Then she went to arrange for my trunk to be delivered from the station.

The room was large and pleasant, had a row of windows toward the east, and was carpeted with throw rugs, furnished with a fat double bed, and decorated with religious prints. After my trunk had arrived and I had unpacked I took another hot bath, then went out to look at the house that was to be my home for three months at least—and I hoped longer. It was built of lumpy brown stucco, with a low, flat red-tile roof, and consisted of six bedrooms, three bathrooms, a small living room, a kitchen and ample closet space. Run up at the turn of the century when Coronado-Moorish was the last word in domestic architecture, it boasted a sunken nave entrance flanked by wrought-iron guard rails leading to a lawn patio with a rock-garden centerpiece choked with flowers, shrubs and fungus growth.

"Like it?" Cletus said as I came back into the house.

"I love it! I'm going to love Los Angeles! It's so warm—it's so full of people with money—beautiful people—clothes, carriages, theatres, and food . . ."

Cletus' smile was replaced by a forbidding expression that told me I was not quite free of herd riding in spite of having escaped Blair and the Andersons in Denver.

"Yes, and there's a lot of trash too!" she snapped. "The godlessness of this city is worse than Gomorrah—or that other Bible town—I can't remember the name. Just you take care! After all, you're still a chickabiddy, as Arthur would say!"

I began to feel that I had made the mistake of falling from the frying pan into the fire, and started to flare up—especially about that "chickabiddy" business. Then I remembered that any surplus sass might send me packing, and I buttoned my lip in time. I was saved by the ringing of the telephone, and Cletus returned from answering it to say that it was for me.

It was Will. He wanted to know if he could call for me at

seven to take me to dinner—with, of course, my two cousins. I answered for all three of us, without thinking, and assured him we would be ready when he came.

I hung up to find Cletus' mouth looking like a pucker on a gold-dust poke. I had already observed the expression before, so I sailed into the explanation I knew she expected of me.

"That was Will. Uh—Mr. Burke. He wants to take us all to dinner some place."

"Oh?" Cletus' enthusiasm couldn't have been less pronounced if I had invited her to stand in the rain and watch a village fire drill.

"He's awfully refined, and all. You'll like him." I told how we had met in Denver and how kind he had been to me on the train. "Arthur likes him too," I added.

I stumbled a bit there.

"Arthur!" she snorted. "He likes everybody. The bigger the scamp the better." Then she put her arm around me and said, "Honey, I don't want you to think I'm an old fuddy-duddy, but we have to be careful, don't we? You know how your folks are. And this is such a big town. But, shucks, we'll go."

I was dressing for dinner when the telephone rang again. This time it was Arthur. He told Cletus he was leaving for Seattle on business immediately. "He can't come to dinner," Cletus yelled upstairs. "He's leaving right away."

"All right," I yelled back, "you and I'll go."

I dressed, brushed and shined my shoes, got into a white blouse and my best two-piece bib and tucker, and belabored my hair rats into position, realizing all the time that I was looking forward to seeing Will again with growing excitement. The thought sobered me, and I wondered if I could be falling in love with him. It had never happened to me before, so I had no way of judging myself. Certainly he was attractive, a gentleman, a man of the world, educated and interesting; he had been kind and courteous and he was by all odds the handsomest man I had ever seen. But somehow, beyond all that, he frightened me. Was it because he was too good-looking and too plausible? No, that wasn't it. I suppressed the thought and went downstairs.

Cletus was waiting, and her get-up took some of the wind out of my sails. She was naturally good-looking, and her black hair and untouched brows were set off by a pearl gray, ankle-length satin gown with a sequin belt, and topped by a rope of pearls. Her gold rings and bracelet glittered with real diamonds. But she took my mind off her appearance in an instant; I felt a heart-to-heart talk coming on, and I was only saved by Will's knock on the door.

He was so handsome and slicked up that he was scary. Got up in black, as he had been in Denver, he glittered like a pewter dollar. You could have powdered your nose in the shine of his boots. As he stepped forward into the light you could see that his shirt buttons were diamonds. His straight black hair had a roach that would have outclassed that of an Iroquois warlock, and no barber had ever done a better job on the mustache of a grandee of Old Spain. I lost a shoe, knocked one of my rats galley west, and nearly stuck a thumb in my eye.

"Will, I'm pleased to meet—I mean I want you to meet—" I choked, blinking at Cletus. Then, noting that I had cracked a bit, Will gave me a quick glance and picked up the pieces.

"Mrs. Varney, your cousin and Arthur's sister," he murmured, smiling.

Cletus helped take me off the hook, too, although in a different way. She put out her hand. But her face, as Will stepped close, turned to stone. Then I caught the drift. He was not drunk, but he had evidently powered his journey from downtown with a pop or two of Wild Turkey and the essence was reported by his breath. Her reaction wasn't lost on Will. As he straightened up he grinned like a cat and his eyes went around the room.

"Where's Arthur?" he asked. "Or have I got my wires crossed again?"

Cletus frigidly explained that Arthur had had to leave suddenly for Seattle.

Inside the hansom cab, which Will had kept waiting outside, he told us that he had arranged dinner for us at the Westminster Hotel at Fourth and Main streets, and had got tickets for a new play at the Avalon Theatre nearby. I seconded Cletus' grunt of approval with what probably sounded like a whinny, and settled down to enjoy the evening. I'll never forget it; it was like tearing into a steak after a season of hominy grits.

The Westminster was then an oasis of waving palms, glittering chandeliers, rich carpetry, mirrored floors, romantic string music, snowy napery, gleaming silverware, cut glass, handsome men and beautiful women. In short, it was something I had dreamed of a thousand times before—a slice of heaven that in the past had always vanished with the ringing of an alarm clock, a rooster's yammering, a dog barking, or an anvil clanging under the blows of my father's hammer.

Seated at our table, a waiter standing to the left and one to the right, I began pinching myself—an operation I was not aware of until later when I wondered where all the black-and-blue marks originated.

"What do you ladies say to some champagne?"

I couldn't answer him. I was so enthralled by the wonders about me that I could only nod my head. Cletus, however, was in possession of *her* faculties.

"I do not drink."

"Not even wine?" Will smiled.

"Not even wine."

"Of course you won't mind if Margaret and I enjoy a bottle," he murmured, and signaling a waiter, he ordered our drinks and dinner.

I still remember what that champagne did to me. It was my first drink of anything stronger than coffee and it went down so easy and tasted so good!

Two glasses later I was dancing with Will when the enormity of my offense struck me and I missed three steps before I recovered from the wallop. I had been guilty of the unthinkable, for a lady. I had taken a drink, and in public, of all places! My father, if he ever discovered my slip, would lock me in my room for life! And Cletus—good grief and stars above us!

"Will." I couldn't keep the quiver from my voice. "I don't know what's got into me! That champagne, I mean. If my folks ever found out, I'd be done for! And Cletus—you don't know how she feels about drinking!"

If I expected sympathy from him I was up a stump. He

laughed so loudly that several people glanced in our direction.

"Margaret, you enchanting child. When will people like you—those who want love, life and laughter—realize that you can't have your cake and eat it too? There are many worlds within this world, and convention need not be violated to fit a baker's dozen of moral standards. Look about you. There are women drinking here tonight. Most of them, I'll warrant, are decent people. Los Angeles society, my dear, is somewhat different from that of Blair, Nebraska."

I was startled to discover that he was right. Every table had wine buckets, and there were women at nearly every table.

"You see," Will went on, "no one needs to become a drunk to enjoy his liquor, just as no one need be a puritan to observe the laws of common decency." He was serious now. "Girls like yourself are needed in the movement, now afoot, to emancipate women completely. Girls and women from the dry-bone great Middle West, those who have the courage to demand from men the equal rights of human beings—who have the courage to fling down the gauntlet. In brief, to demand that what's good for the gander also is good for the goose—and make their rebellion stick."

"Why, Will!" His remarks, which would have been considered heretical in the parlors of Blair, were no less shocking to me, steeped as I was in the tradition that a nation's strength lay mainly in the bravery of its men and the idiocy of its women.

"Don't say it." Will smiled. "I know it by heart already. A woman's place is in the home. Motherhood is woman's greatest reward. Well, I'll agree in part. But that's as far as I'll go, and I'll wager there are plenty of other men who feel the same as I do. You mark my words—one of these days women will refuse to wear those strait jackets you call corsets. Their dresses will be short enough to be comfortable and charming. They'll cut their hair, as men do. They'll be permitted to drink in saloons, and a lot of them will become engineers, doctors, scientists and even construction bosses. Someday we may even have a woman for President of the United States."

"Oh, Will!" I laughed. This was stretching it too thin. "You don't mean a word you say!"

"Don't I?" he drawled. "Well, we'll see. Meantime, you keep driving for that goal you were talking about, back there on the train. And have your fun, while you're at it. You can be a good girl and still be a free girl—a human being unfettered by the dragons and witch burnings of exaggerated puritanism, fruit cups, ankle-length tents, callused knees from unanswered prayers, a husband who insists on being served first at table, and a passel of kids you can't afford."

By this time my head was buzzing pleasantly. Coupled with Will's exciting presence and his electrifying opinions, the champagne had made the world a great place indeed. As he seated me at the table, following the dance, I automatically reached for the bottle. He was *so* right!

We didn't make the theatre, and I recall very little of the remainder of the evening. I remember Will's amusement when we ran out of wine and I asked for more; I recall trying to imitate the poised, casual postures of the women about me; Will's dark, smiling face above me on the dance floor; snatches of the dinner courses; Cletus' pouter-pigeon disapproval; my conviction that I was living inside a rainbow; Will's lazy conversation in the hansom on the way back; and accepting his invitation to dinner on the following night.

But I recall the next day very well. It marked the occasion of my first and last hangover. I spent most of that horror in bed, moaning and groaning by turns, sweating like a convict in Death Row, and unable even to keep water on my stomach. Once my heart slipped into gallop and it scared me out of a year's growth. I was sure that my Maker was calling, and I was about to have Cletus haul in a medic when the thumping tapered off. But after that I rested easier.

It was late afternoon when Cletus thawed sufficiently to remind me of my date of that night with Will and to explain in detail her stand on fast men, hooch and dancing cheek to cheek. However, she concluded, if I was abandoned enough to accept Will's company and his disgusting addiction to liquor, she would chaperone. It was little enough to do for a relative upon whom such evil days had descended.

At the moment I was so sick of Cletus *and* the hangover that I would have curtsied to the Devil, had he offered a kind word.

I crawled wanly from bed, staggered to the bathroom, scraped off my nightgown, and stayed in a hot tub for an hour. Somewhere in the wilds of my trunk I found a watered-silk green dress, dragged it downstairs, pressed it, bucked my aching body into it and generally got myself decked out for the evening. Then, while Cletus dressed, I pulled a chair to a window overlooking Mercade Drive and stared out with dim, unseeing eyes.

To my gasping relief, Will was punctual. Bowing himself in, he greeted Cletus pleasantly, inquired gravely after my health, and escorted us to his hansom. He had us driven to an Italian restaurant on Cahuenga Boulevard, commandeered a table near a three-piece string orchestra, and further outraged Cletus by spiking his conversation with Latin phrases and pouring down two drinks before ordering our meal. When we had packed in the last crumb, he took us to a play. Midnight saw us catching a cancan vaudeville downtown, where the costumes elevated Cletus' eyebrows from forbidding to thundercloud proportions. But Will either didn't mind her reactions or he ignored them. His deep voice continued to soothe and entertain me. His finesse as host was faultless. Once home, after accepting his invitation to lunch the next day, I felt very nearly human again.

Inside, however, my hide was nailed to the wall, even before I had shucked my coat and shoes.

"After tomorrow," Cletus began ominously, "we'll be seeing no more of that man."

"You mean Will?" The heavy meal and the hour, coupled with the final, wearying ravages of my hangover, had put me in a spot where it was difficult to say boo to a goose—at least with any spirit.

"I'm not talking about his brother!" Cletus shrilled. "He drinks. On top of that, he means you no good! Oh, don't think I haven't been watching him—the way he looks at you! He isn't fooling me! Him and his fine manners and diamond shirt buttons!"

"Cletus!" I was awake now.

"Don't Cletus me! I'm no namby-pamby! But I'm responsible for you! I know that young girls have to have fun. But it should be clean and wholesome, such as church socials and square dances and the like. Not times spent in places where women dress shamelessly and your beaus drink! He isn't pulling the wool over my eyes! Put that in your pipe and smoke it!"

For a moment I could only gasp. Then her resentment hit me between the eyes. Suddenly I was mad, and thus was born my first aggressive rebellion against the wheeze that Father knows best, even if he is as out of step with the times as flintlock rifles or modern Mexican plumbing.

"I won't listen to any more," I told her. "Will Burke is the first person to make me feel like I was somebody—like I amounted to something! Besides, he's too old for me! You're just being silly!"

"Oh? Well, you listen to me, Miss Uppity! He just seems old to you because he's a mature man and you're nothing but a baby! He's young enough for you in his mind!"

"I don't care. He's leaving in a week, and I'm going to see him all I please!"

"Very well." Cletus' voice went cold. "But it will have to be the two of you. I refuse to go out in his company again. I can't stand men who drink and dress like gamblers."

There was more to our quarrel than this. It was nearly one o'clock in the morning before we ran out of wind and snarled off to our respective rooms.

Next day, when I told Will about it, he smiled, then grew serious. Naturally I had skipped the part involving Cletus' appraisal of his attitude toward me, but he caught the drift anyway. He could read between lines faster than anyone I have ever known.

"She isn't too far off," he said. "I am fond of you, Margaret. Very fond of you." He leaned across the table at the Plaza Restaurant, where we were lunching in downtown Los Angeles, stretched out his arm, and my hand disappeared in his palm.

"I must leave for Alaska tomorrow. So I shan't see you again this trip. However, I wonder if I might write to you?"

"Oh, of course. I want you to, Will." The prospect of his leaving depressed me. This was puzzling too. How could a girl look upon one man as brother and beau, with a slice of father mixed in?

"Good. Now will you do something for me?" He drew a card from a pocket case and wrote on it, then handed it to me. "If you ever need help, will you get in touch with the man whose name and address I've written on this card? He's an old friend, married to a great girl, and you can trust them implicitly. Will you do this for me?"

"Yes, surely. But I don't see—"

"Never mind," he interrupted, "nobody ever knows when he might need a friend, even the most self-sufficient of us. Otherwise I'd ask you to contact me. But I'll be hard to track down, that's why I ask you to contact Al and Lucy Boyd if you need anything. Promise?"

"I promise." It was hard to keep back the tears—at finding a friend like Will, then losing him.

"Well, that's that." He took out his watch. "I've got a couple of appointments, then I've got to pack. Do you mind if I put you in a hansom instead of escorting you home?"

Will handed me into a cab and gave the driver a bill. Then he stuck his head inside and said, with a crooked smile,

"Give 'em the dickens and keep your powder dry."

"Don't you want me to see you off at the train?"

"I don't know which one I'll be able to catch, but I'll try to call you before I go. *Au revoir*."

At home old Stone Face Cletus was stonier than ever, and I still squirm when I think of the boredom of the next two days. I spent most of the time downtown, buying a few clothes and other knickknacks in preparation for job hunting. When my attempts at conversation failed to pry forth more than a grunt out of Cletus, it dawned on me that I'd better move out. So I decided to look for both a job and a room on Monday. But this plan never developed.

On Sunday afternoon it transpired that Cletus had dealt me a lick below the belt. The light came in the form of a telephone call from Blair. It was Father. He had received Cletus' letter. It appeared that I had gotten out of hand. I had betrayed his trust. I'd been out gallivanting with a man who drank and I'd even drunk myself. What were daughters coming to these days? If I wasn't home by noon next Friday he'd come out and get me.

I spent the next two hours in my room, trying to figure out what had hit me, my stomach feeling as empty as an abandoned shack. After months, even years, of sweating and conniving, I was virtually back where I'd started. It wasn't fair.

I didn't realize then, naturally, that Cletus had done me the greatest possible favor in writing to my folks. Her one little note set me up for a life that has been a good one; one I'd live over again, including all the heartaches and illnesses and financial ups and downs. At the moment, however, I could have wrung her neck, and that pleasant thought cleared my mind. I began to plan.

To start with, one thing was clear: I would not go back to Blair; I would live in a cave and eat rocks first. But what to do? I couldn't stay in Los Angeles. Even if I moved out, leaving no address, Father would find me eventually. I knew only one trade—telephone operator, and there weren't many of us in those days. I would have to move somewhere else—where they had telephones. San Francisco? Portland? Seattle?

I came out of the vapors in a hurry. Arthur was in Seattle. So were Mr. and Mrs. Boyd.

While I was packing, Cletus tried to get an oar in, but I told her nothing. No doubt she thought I was going to a furnished room in Los Angeles. After getting nowhere, she withdrew in a huff.

With my trunk checked, my ticket paid through to Seattle, and with exactly $42.16 between me and a charity ward, I boarded the smelliest, worst-lit, slowest, loudest, rudest train I've ever been stuck with, and took off.

Chapter Three

THE train lumbered, groaned, belched, jerked and staggered its way to San Francisco for the better part of a day and a night. After a three-hour layover in a dense fog—most of which I spent drinking coffee or walking up and down the platform in a cindery, wet breeze—I got on an even worse train that sighed, slumped and plodded another night and day before it reached Seattle.

Seattle, that Wednesday night in June, was a mermaid's dream of home. The rain was coming down as if someone had dynamited a dam, and as soon as I got off the train, looking like a bedraggled pullet, I was soaked to the skin. I found a hansom cab at the edge of the platform and asked the cabby if he knew of a cheap, respectable hotel near the station.

"You a workin' girl?" he asked, getting down from his perch to crane his neck at me.

"Yes."

"An honest workin' girl?"

"Yes."

He turned his head off-wind and spit, then said, "All right. Bunch of office girls live at the Puyallup Hotel on Pike Street.

I'll take you there." He slapped the reins, and the horse started. "Better be honest, though. The cops in this town is tough."

In a few minutes I was standing before a scarred desk super-intended by a bald little Milquetoast whose bulging eyes and steel-rimmed specs gave him the look of a frog in a Mason jar.

"You a workin' girl?"

"Yes."

"An honest workin' girl?"

I could have screamed. "I'm a telephone operator. From Los Angeles."

He pushed a ledger toward me and handed me a pencil. "Sign. Put yer last address too. That'll be three dollars. For the week." He handed over a key and two towels.

"Is there a bath? In the room?"

"Whattya want for three dollars? There's two baths on every floor. One says Wimmen and one says Men. You furnish yer own soap too. And don't ast me is there a bellboy. This is a friendly hotel. We figger everybody should be able to find their own room."

I found it, on the second floor, a cubicle with ragged wall-paper of poinsettia design. There was room enough for a bed adorned with brass knobs and furnished with a mattress petite enough to reveal six inches of springs on all four sides. A wounded bureau slumped against the opposite wall. The wood of the floor showed through the rug in several places, and an overhead gaslight brought the wallpaper design into relief and revealed another cheering motif in a picture of a Russian farm hand at twilight, sickle in hand. I sat in a chair looking out of the window into the rain and cried for an hour. Then I remem-bered Cousin Arthur and called the hotel he usually stayed at, the Northern. He was not even registered; the clerk remem-bered he'd wired, saying he was stopping over in Portland, Ore-gon, for a week.

By two in the morning I'd given up trying to sleep and I had to talk to someone—even Froggy, down in the lobby. So I went down the death-walk stairs and slumped on a horsehair sofa which was suffering from mange. Froggy came over and slumped into a barrel-backed chair nearby.

"Can't sleep, eh? Always that way, the first night in town. All

them wagons in the street and them foghorns in Puget Sound.
'Scuse me."

Turning his head, he yanked out his upper plate, unfurled a handkerchief and wrapped it up, then set the package on the writing stand.

"Things never did fit. Keep filin' off the bumps. Only makes new ones. Wouldn't wear 'em at all 'cept for the trade. Have to keep up a front. Father's like that too. He was a farmer back in Ioway. When he died I sold the farm. Went inta the livery-stable business with part of my money. Went broke pretty quick. Went back to farmin'. Wasn't the same. Taste o' the city did it. Come out here ten years ago. Married my wife. She owns this hotel. She's bugs. Nice rain, ain't it? Good fer crops."

Froggy's reminiscences about the old farm did the trick and set me off again. I didn't wail out loud; I just shed enough tears to inundate the fields around Blair, Nebraska.

"What in Tophet?" he said, and got up to pat my shoulder. But he only succeeded in knocking my purse from my knees and spilling the contents all over the floor.

"I'm just homesick," I sobbed, and bending forward, started to pick up the junk on the floor. My eye lit on the most reassuring sight I've ever seen. It was Will's card and it read: AL BOYD, 216 MARQUAND AVENUE, QUEEN ANNE'S HILL, SEATTLE.

Froggy must have thought I had escaped from an asylum. Snuffling and giggling, I knuckled my eyes, saw through the window that dawn was breaking, and, clutching the card in both hands, headed for the wall phone at a gallop. I had only one thought and it sang in my mind: Where Will had friends I had friends. He'd said so in so many words.

The impossibility of the hour never occurred to me. The long, horrible train rides, the hotel, the rain, the prospect of no money and no job in a strange town, the menace of parental wrath—all had been enough for one night. I cranked the phone, got the Boyds' number from Information, and did a little tap dance while the call went through.

Lucy Boyd answered. Her voice was more like home and Mother than home and Mother would have been; it had the same effect on me, and I greeted her just as I would have if I'd been calling Blair, Nebraska.

"It's me."

"Who?"

"Me, Margaret."

She gave a lazy, melodious laugh.

"Margaret who, dear?"

"Why, Margaret Knudsen."

"Oh, Margaret Knudsen. Will Burke's little girl. He's told us about you. Of course. Where are you?"

"At the Puyallup Hotel, on Pike Street."

"Puyallup Hotel. Just one minute, my dear." The receiver thumped against the wall; then she was back at the phone before I'd had a chance to feel foolish at the way I'd announced myself.

"Margaret—Al will be down to get you as soon as he's dressed. Pack your things. We want you to stay with us—at least till you find a suitable place. He'll be there in about fifteen minutes."

I don't know whether Froggy thought I was the victim of a white slaver, the wayward daughter of a rich father, or a simple nut, but he should have been reassured when Al appeared a few minutes after I'd been sitting with my packed suitcase in the lobby.

Al came through the door as if he'd pushed the storm aside to be first in line—a short man, with thick, gray hair and bushy eyebrows over a lively red face and light blue eyes. He looked at Froggy, then at me, and smiled—a smile as wide and white as Will's—like a doting older brother.

"Hello, honey. Ready?"

I don't remember much of the ride to the Boyds' house, except for the carriage lurching over the cobblestones and a feeling of security as I slumped against a rough shirt that smelled like pine. I don't remember much of what their house looked like either, except that there was a fireplace loaded with burning wood, a lot of bright colors, and a statuesque brown-eyed woman in an Indian-woven housecoat, and some good coffee. I tried to sit up and talk and to show how grateful I was to be rescued. All I remember clearly was Lucy's saying, "Come on, papoose, you're headed for the blanket."

44

If there's such a thing as love at first sight, I was smitten with
it before the next day rolled around at the Boyd home, and my
opinion of them never changed to the days of their deaths,
twenty-eight and thirty-two years later. To me and to thousands
of others, they were and always will be Mr. and Mrs. Alaska.

Al was thirty-nine and Lucy was twenty-seven when I first
met them, and they'd been married for nine years. Their marriage had a tremendous influence on me; their serene, well-
bred love, their respect and friendship for each other, inspired
me in coping with the trying moments in my own long, wonderful marriage. Each permitted the other his complete individuality in every respect, from habits—good and bad—to
preferences in dress and food. And they even maintained a
single standard of independence within their own home. Their
infrequent arguments were always in good taste, without name-
calling or personal rancor. Consequently they succeeded in
sharpening their intellects and broadening their imaginations
so that their differences helped rather than hindered their
progress and success. They worked and lived together with such
dignity and purpose that they eventually became the most popular and best-known couple in Alaska; and their hard work
and dedication brought them financial rewards too. In later
years they turned over their interests almost exclusively to
charitable enterprises and civic ventures, and their generous
gifts of time and money contributed a great deal to the growth
of America's last frontier. From the time they took me into
their warm hearts and loving home through the rest of our long
friendship, they were models and guides and a point of sanity
in the hectic and bewildering days I was to go through in
Alaska.

Before the fire in their comfortable living room I began to
learn something about my new-found friends. We had finished
a delicious steak dinner, touched up by a bottle of good wine.
It was chilly outside and still raining. Al, in slippers and smoking jacket, was puffing at a fat briar pipe, his feet stretched toward the blazing fireplace; Lucy, cross-legged on the floor, was
working on an embroidery hoop. I was sunk sleepily in a chair,
sipping Turkish coffee.

"You got here in the nick, honey," Lucy said, looking up from her needlework. "Another week and we'd have been on our way home."

"Home?" I came out of my hibernation in a hurry. "You mean you don't live here?"

Lucy laughed. "This is our house. Our home is in Nome. In Alaska. We come Outside once a year on business. The rest of the time the house is closed."

My face must have reflected all the alarm and despair I felt at being abandoned again. "Oh lordy!"

"Don't you worry, Margaret," Al cut in, "we'll get you settled before we leave. It may take ten days yet to finish my business. But we won't have any trouble finding you a job. We have connections."

Alaska, I thought, and Will's descriptions of it came to my mind vividly. I thought again of the lump of gold on his watch fob.

Al himself was, he told me, a veteran of the gold rush of 1902. Owner of a high sense of honor and a delightful sense of humor, he was a builder of everything from bridges to birdhouses. Like Will Burke, he was a worker. He lacked Will's polish—he was rough and hearty—but he had the same ready fists, big heart and indomitable drive.

A native of Nebraska, he was the only child of a railroad brakeman. His mother had died shortly after his birth, and like many a child from a motherless home, he had learned early that it's best to knock 'em down first and argue later.

Between hitches at keeping house, odd jobs and ducking the constabulary, he had managed to get through high school. Then he took a job as a digger with the local telephone company, where he was relatively happy. His enthusiasm for the telephone did not rub off on Boyd *père,* who thought the newfangled janglin' and clangin' thing was a fizzle; no future in 'em. But two years later Al was a lineman and had finished a mail-order course in electronics. When his father died, leaving him with no relatives, he found that the small town had begun to pall on him, so he sold the shack and went on the bum. Like Will, he had traveled extensively and had worked at every conceivable kind of job en route.

46

In the spring of 1898 he turned up in Seattle, where he took, in turn, short cracks at bartending, wiring houses for an electrical firm, working as a fisherman aboard a salmon-fleet purse seiner, and as a concrete man for a construction and shipbuilding organization.

At the home of friends, over a heaping plate of food and a churn of homemade Finnish wine, he met Lucy, a native of Seattle and secretary to a prominent lawyer in Tacoma. One look at Lucy's brown eyes, chestnut hair and splendid form, and Al's feet stopped itching. Since Lucy's people had moved to Chicago two years before, he had no trouble with the parental-consent problem—at least from a nose-to-nose standpoint—and he lost no time in spreading his snare.

Married three months later, Lucy quit her job and they bought their home in Seattle and began to bank some money. However, when Alaska's second big strike hit the front pages Al got the fever, and for a week he could talk and think of nothing else. There was gold up there, girl, gold! A little luck, and they'd be set for life! The other day a guy had said . . . on the other hand, what's a job . . . and. . . .

At the end Lucy laughed, slapped him on the back, told him to have at it, and went back to her dictation pad and typewriter. But her amusement soon turned to astonishment. Where she had expected a wild-goose chase and felt that it was needed to salt him down, he was actually bringing in the sheaves.

True, he had set no world afire as a miner, or even as a prospector. But that was to be expected. Arriving in Fairbanks—a new town reared by virtue of the strike on Cleary Creek—he ran into a situation that has scuttled more than one poor bloke in Alaska's golden days. Although the pay dirt of 1902 had pretty well petered out, the mob there was still so crazy and thick that people were cutting cards for breathing space. Claims had been staked for miles around, and the streams were choked with glassy-eyed panners.

Al, however, was a different breed of cat from the babes in the woods who used to get the fever, and he lost no time in honking and vaporing over the development. A shrewd look around showed three elements apparent in the economic structure of the town.

First, money was too plentiful to balance the law of supply and demand. Second, labor was at a premium. Third, commodities—save for the bare staples—simply didn't exist. Briefly, it was a seller's market of almost limitless scope, and he set out immediately to get his feet wet in it.

For a start he found what he wanted in a haywire combination sawmill and woodyard at the edge of a belt of scrub timber to the north. Run by a whiskered, ancient fellow named Scotty Packard, it consisted of little more than a couple of whipsaws, several rickety sleds, an assortment of tools, a jumble of sticks that passed for lumber, some sod hovels, a half-dozen Indian laborers—all blessed with families of two to twelve, and a couple of wolf dogs. Al sold Scotty on the idea that he could sell something beside "burnin' wood" and guaranteed to triple the production of the plant in a month if Scotty would give him a free hand and 50 percent of the profits. Scotty was skeptical but he had nothing to lose, so he agreed.

Then followed months of bone-splintering labor. One problem was the weather. Except for four months of the year— roughly June to October—logging and milling were out of the question. The rest of the time was nearly all blizzard. Then, there was no heavy equipment: no planers, bandsaws, trucks, cats or cranes. Summer and winter, land hauls were made by dog team, shoulder pack, mule or watercraft. Dogs were too light for timber, and there was no fast water nearby. That left mules.

But that possibility didn't exist either. The animals were scarce, their services were spoken for months in advance, they were worked to the limit, then shot before winter, since there was no forage to keep them through the winter and not enough cargo space to ship it in. It was easier to bring in new mules each summer with enough feed to last them until fall, then destroy them. (I myself was to see more than one tough-bearded character cry like a baby as, rifle in hand, he led his mules out onto the ice.)

Al was forced to cut, bark, trim and process the lumber within the belt itself, using sledge and wedge to split the trunk, and hacking it with ax and adz until it resembled a board. The best he could expect to get out of a unit of timber was about 20 percent in salable lumber. The shiftlessness of the Indians and the ruins Packard called equipment only added to his headaches.

However, the Indians began to change their philosophy; the tools took on a little more shine; and chairs and tables began to appear in Fairbanks. The 400-odd sod huts and shacks, saloons, dance halls and restaurants were sporting wooden uprights and supports, and patches of new lumber gleamed from the sides, bows and sterns of scows, barges and small boats lining the banks of the winding Tanana River nearby. Al was soon spending more time refusing orders for lumber than taking them, as he was still disgruntled to recall, and the situation was as galling to him as a pair of barbed-wire suspenders. Here, for the first time in his life, was the chance to get ahead, and he was helpless to cut the color. In a town of more than 1,000 people—most of them with money to burn—he stood like a starving man equipped with a fork in the middle of a soup storm. Moreover, his position was the more discouraging for the restrictions imposed by the shipping firms that served Fairbanks by way of Nome, St. Michaels and Fort Yukon, to the north. That is to say, he could have shipped in unfinished lumber from Seattle, except that these people demanded and got full complements of cargo before they played ball. As of that moment, Al's finances had not reached a point where he could splurge for a full consignment of any commodity.

Of course his frustration was not entirely the outgrowth of his inability to expand in the lumber business. In the last essence it stemmed from a change of heart involving the country itself. Where, a few months before, he had set out to seek gold, his premise had taken a reverse spin. In short, Al was a born builder, and as such the willy-nilly, pell-mell hunger for color faded into insignificance for him when compared with the opportunity and satisfying rewards he saw in helping to mold an empire.

Alaska's towering, ice-girt mountain chains, its rushing white-water rivers, hundreds of miles of forests and lush foliage, countless lakes, creeks and streams, ocean fronts, endless reaches of bleak, frightening tundra, teeming caribou herds and the hundred and one other species of wildlife—its Indian and Eskimo tribes and the over-all clean, raw grandeur of a last great frontier—had put him in the country's pocket.

This was man's meat, tough, hard and revitalizing. This was living; this represented ambition and challenge, while his earlier years had been given to security and complacency. Here he would bring Lucy and build their home as they would build for the Territory, and here they would live out their lives.

He got his foot in the door on a cold, blustery night two weeks later. He was playing poker in a tent-covered shack called the Monte Carlo, with three newly made friends, all miners, when Will Burke came in and asked to join the game. It ended around midnight, and the miners threw in their hands, leaving Will and Al winners by about $700 and $400 respectively. By the time they had put a few drinks under their belts they parted company with liking and a well-grounded respect for each other. Will had shown an interest in what was referred to as Scotty Packard's Sliver Store. He came around the following day and made Al a proposal: to buy out Scotty and go into a fifty-fifty partnership in the lumber business; Will would put up the money for a shipload of lumber and some new equipment. Once Will learned that Al liked the country and intended to make it his home, he had no misgivings about going into business with him.

Scotty resisted; he intimated to Al that Will Burke was becoming too big and too smart an operator to be universally beloved in the Territory: between his company, the Northern Commercial, and his private deals, he had a stake in nearly every enterprise in Alaska. There were those who scoffed at Will's ideas of the country being a state some day, with judges and police, churches and schools and hotels. But Scotty finally agreed to part with his interests for $5,000. Will agreed, insisting on a duly witnessed bill of sale; then placed an order for a cargo of lumber and set up banking arrangements for the new firm. He also turned over his own cabin to Al, and promised to send Lucy up on the next boat from Seattle.

This was only the beginning of Al's association with Will. The second of their business ventures got started in the spring of 1903, shortly after Al had received their first shipload of lumber, a small planer powered by a donkey engine, a new bandsaw, chains, whipsaws and other equipment, and was doing a land-office business with the mill. When Will came back to Fairbanks in the spring he hardly knew the place; there were so many new buildings that he said he felt as if he'd been gone ten years. True, most of them were saloons or dance halls, but there were new stores, a twenty-room hotel, and a new loading dock on the waterfront. Churches and schools, too, would come in due time.

Right now, he told Al, what Alaska needed were communications. Nome was a seaport with a stable population which would grow; the population would increase as people returned from gold strikes in outlying areas. There was no quick means of communication between the Nome, St. Michael and Fort Gibbon area and the hundred-odd gold camps in the region.

Will did not believe that all the gold in Alaska was in the ground; he envisaged a permanent and growing community, thriving on industry and commerce.

Al was inclined to brush off the idea as impractical: to set up such an operation as a telephone company would cost $1,000,000. How would you dig holes in the gummy tundra, let alone in ground frozen iron hard most of the year? Where would you get the labor? Where would you get enough poles? To ship them in would cost a fortune.

"Don't need poles," Will said, grinning like a man with an ace up his sleeve. "A few years ago the United States Army Signal Corps strung telegraph wire all over this area. They've already done the work for us; the lines and poles are there. Four months ago, when I got this idea, I contacted Colonel Ralph Demeter in Washington, D. C. He's the corps' trouble-shooter. Last month I got his answer. We have the go-ahead. We can cut into their lines anywhere we like."

In short, Will explained, the only expense would be wire, telephone unit receivers and labor. They'd ship in the necessary equipment and keep their fingers crossed on the labor question.

Thus the Nome Telephone Company was born. Al was to head for Seattle on the next boat, set up an office to handle the affairs Outside, order enough wire and manual equipment to handle 2,000 customers over a three-hundred-square-mile area;

then beat it back to Nome, hire all the labor he could get and go into business. If he needed any help, aside from labor, all he had to do was ask the Signal Corps.

"What about the mill?" Al wanted to know.

"I know a husky, smart young Swede in Fort Yukon. He's a former logger and millworker. He couldn't find gold in the United States Treasury. He'll jump at the chance to work for us. Name's Ivar Jensen."

Al still couldn't see where he fitted in, despite his experience as a telephone man.

"Things have been moving a bit fast for me, Will. No offense intended, but I'd like to know why this interest in me. You're putting up the dough. I haven't got any. Where do I stand? And why?"

"That's a fair question. I've reached a point where I need associates. Not labor. Associates. Up here, they're hard to get. One out of a thousand is interested in something more than panning for gold. I figure you'll make a good man for me. That honest enough? I'm ready to split the mill and the telephone company profits fifty-fifty—if you produce. The same goes for anything else we might set up to make money."

"And if I don't produce?"

"You're back where you started."

"You'll have lost money."

"I'll get it back."

"But you don't know anything about my background."

"Not interested."

Al tossed up his hands, then dropped them, palms down, on the table. "Needless to say, I'm about as lucky as a man can get. Anything else?"

Will swiveled in his chair and faced Al squarely. "Yes. Just don't forget who's the boss."

So far as I can recall today, Al never did. If there ever was a hot word between them or a challenge issued to Will's authority, I never knew of it in all of their years in business together. Perhaps Al recognized Will's genius for trading, early in their association, and decided to let well enough alone. To be honest, he had every reason to do so. His fortune was made from the moment he met Will, and he was never embarrassed to admit his superiority of direction, any more than I was ever embarrassed to boast of the fine talent and character of my husband. Come to think of it, the nature of their arrangement nearly put the sword to my introduction to Alaska.

"So," Al said as he finished telling me about the Nome Telephone Company, "all I have to do now is arrange for some supplies. And hire an operator."

I was so impressed by Will, so enchanted by the vision of Alaska that Al's story evoked, that I nearly missed this cue.

"Operator?" I said vaguely.

"Telephone operator. I've been running the board myself. It's an old-style drop board. Ever see one?"

"No, I don't think so."

"Well, when a call comes in, a metal disc—depending on who's calling—drops over the plughole. This indicates the number. But now we're changing over to an electric board, so we've decided to bring in a competent electric-board operator. If we can find one."

Suddenly Alaska seemed to leap closer.

"Why—I'm—that's my kind of work," I stuttered. "Let me —I could . . ."

Al chuckled, sucked on his pipe, blew a smoke ring, then jabbed the bit back between his teeth.

"I'm afraid not, honey. This girl's got to be hired on a two-year contract. To insure that she'll stay. We'll need to choose her carefully. She's got to be a mature, well-balanced, single woman. A person who can live with inconveniences, the cold and the frequent spells of loneliness. There'll be times when our operator must be stationed, alone, in pretty dismal outposts. You see, she's got to be a fairly tough person. Not a pretty little doll with red hair and blue eyes and a snub nose."

I wanted to shriek and moan, all in the same breath—bump my head on the floor or tear up something. I wanted that job. Then Lucy, God bless her, took a hand in the game.

"Al, wait a minute. You could be missing a good bet. How do you know she wouldn't fit? Big things can come in small packages."

Al smiled. Then his face grew serious. "Margaret's size and

her looks were meant as a joke. I'm thinking of something else.
There's Will's wishes to consider. I'm not sure he would appreciate my hiring Margaret and bringing her into the Territory,
as it stands now. After all, she's Will's protégée. That could
make a difference."

Lucy dropped the embroidery hoop in her lap, jabbed the
needle into the cloth, and laid the piece aside.

"I say she should get the job if she can handle the board.
Maybe she's tougher than she looks. Why is it necessary to hire
a female dock-walloper? A horse face is no indication of courage or stamina or efficiency."

"Lucy, please. Will—"

"Piffle," Lucy snapped. "I'm not afraid of Will Burke! Even
if he has everyone else kowtowing to him!"

"I'm sorry." Al got up, laid his pipe on the mantle, raised his
arms above his head and stretched. "I'm for bed."

When he had gone Lucy rose, dropped her hoop on a chair,
and turned to me. There was a determined set to her mouth—
one I came to recognize as a storm signal of the first chop in
later years. "Don't stew, honey. I'm on your side."

When she had followed Al to their bedroom I went to my
own, and for the next two hours I tossed and turned, more convinced than ever that the world was a dreadful place and my
own life a frightful failure. But I could have saved myself the
discomfort. Lucy was a woman of her word. During the dark
hours she had got in some good licks in my behalf—a campaign,
so far as sleep was concerned, that dropped Al in his tracks.

"You both win." He grinned wearily at breakfast. "A man's
a fool who thinks he can whip one woman. Let alone two." He
reached for a piece of toast, forked half an egg into his mouth,
and winked at me. "After we eat we'll go to my office. I've a
little work to do there. Then we'll head for the Seattle Telephone Company. I'll ask George Adams, the manager, to seat
you at a board. If you can strut your stuff you're hired."

Three hours later I was an employee of the Yukon Trading
Company, the holding firm that Burke and Boyd had started
two years before as a parent organization to administer the affairs of their growing enterprises. As such, I was one of their 62

workers, 4 of whom were stationed at the firm's Division and Lennon Street office (now the site of a Seattle bakery) and the rest of them scattered all over Alaska. For my part, I was to become the contact point for a telephone line that now numbered 1,500 customers in the Nome area, served by about 1,000 miles of wire and the stumps, trees and fence posts that functioned as poles. My contract called for a salary of $200 a month, free board and room, no vacations, two years on the job, no regular hours, the promise to conduct myself at all times in a moral and honorable manner and to be willing to serve, where needed, on committees and boards designed to improve the Territory, executively, judicially or administratively.

Back in the office, Al handed me the document and a pen. If I had been excited before, I was now at the jumping-off stage. "Where do I sign?"

"There." Al chuckled, pointing to the inevitable dotted line. "Shall I steady your hand? Or does it act like this all of the time?"

Two days later Al, guessing that I was short of cash, offered me a $100 advance on my first month's salary. I grabbed it. Armed with this bundle, I took a cab to the offices of the Northern Steamship Company and marched up to the ticket window.

"One way to Nome, please."

The fat little man in back of the stand sighed dolorously. "Which boat?"

"The *Yucatan*."

"Thought so. Everybody wants to go on the *Yucatan*. We ain't got a reservation left. *Yucatan*'s got a real restaurant on 'er. Everybody wants to git on the *Yucatan*."

At this juncture I wasn't feeling my oats as well as before. "But, how do I get to Alaska?"

"Ohio's headed out. Sister ship. No restaurant, though."

"All right. One ticket on the *Ohio*."

It was a genuine disappointment. Al and Lucy had told me that they were to sail on the *Yucatan* and had instructed me to book on the same boat. Now I would have to sail on another ship and without their company en route.

"Don't worry about it," Al said, the next day. "There are such things as cancellations."

There was one, a day or two later. Al checked on it and got me passage on the *Yucatan*. An adventuresome soul had caught the measles and couldn't make it. That was one of the many breaks I've had along the line. The switch probably saved my life.

Chapter Four

I FIND, looking back into a tattered diary, that it took the *Yucatan* twenty-two days, three hours and fourteen minutes, to reach Nome on my first trip to Alaska.

There were few conveniences aboard, no luxuries, and no entertainment, save for the card games—closed to the few women passengers aboard—and the knock-down-drag-out fights that broke out almost daily. With 600 people on an overgrown barge whose capacity was roughly 350, there was no room for cocktail-lounge soirees, water sports, deck shooting, balls and musicales, and other ocean-going diversions demanded by present-day mariners. But the food and drink were good, the society on the whole easy and pleasant, the cabins clean and the bunks fairly comfortable.

My debut as an ocean traveler was according to form. I can't recall ever making a trip—as a moppet or an adult—when I didn't get lost in the shuffle. Arriving on deck, I proceeded in several directions at once, with the result that at one moment Al and Lucy were at my side and the next moment they had vanished. On that day, on that ship, it could have happened to even the most seasoned *voyageur*.

There was barely an inch of space aboard that wasn't occupied by the roaring, waving throng or their mounds and hillocks of duffle. With a deafening blast from the ship's whistle, the *Yucatan*, lurching like a cradle with a broken rocker, began moving away from the pier into Puget Sound. As I turned from the rail, looking for the Boyds, I ran smack into a tall, thin, green-eyed girl about my own age.

"Oh, I'm sorry!" She acknowledged my apology with a smile and a shake of her head which caused her black shoulder-length curls to hide half of her face.

"I'll bet this is your first trip out."

"Why, yes. It is. Have you been to Alaska before?"

"I live there. At least, it's where I came from originally."

"Is that so?" My interest suddenly sprouted wings. "How wonderful!"

One of her sooty brows shot up, and she let loose an unladylike snort. "Is it? I'll take Seattle any time. I've been at the University of Washington for the past year. Art student. I'm going north for a short visit with my father in St. Michael. He's in business there. You visiting relatives?"

I told her of my association with Will and the Boyds. She told me she was Marie St. Denis, age nineteen, unmarried and hoping to finish her formal education at the university and then become a magazine illustrator in the States, preferably in New York City.

"So you know the Boyds? And Will Burke?" she continued.

"I surely do, I'm proud to say. They've all been perfectly grand to me."

"They're grand to everyone. Particularly the Boyds."

Something in her voice, perhaps the hint of reservation in regard to Will, made me curious. "Then you're a friend of theirs also? How long have you known them?"

"Since they arrived in the Territory." Her smile was a cross between irritation and resignation. "And bad cess to Burke."

"But I thought you said—or led me to believe—that you liked him?"

"I'm crazy about him. But he doesn't know I'm alive. The iron-jawed louse."

I didn't realize then that I could be jealous of Will. But to-day I know why I was relieved at her complaint.

The ship, now well into the Sound, was rolling strongly. Since I owned—then and now—the world's worst sea legs, I was making rough weather of it.

"Here." Marie cupped a helping hand around my elbow. "We'd better hit our cabins. Until we leave the Sound, anyway. The going should be easier at sea. Where are you staked out?"

"I don't know. But the number's here in my purse." Supported by her surprisingly strong arm, I managed to get out my ticket. "Number sixteen."

"Good," Marie said. "That's where I'm bunked. Me and a little squarehead who can't speak English."

"What luck!"

"Not so much luck." Marie grinned, tightening her grip on my arm. "If there are an even dozen females aboard, I'll eat my hat. That boils it down to two cabin reservations. You'd of had to draw one of them, since us unmarried critters of the sex must be stabled together on these old dinghys."

Getting to the cabins, which were located below deck, turned out to be something like hacking a path through a jungle with a putty knife. Every accommodation aboard had been taken, including the lifeboats, and the steerage also sheltered a dozen cows, six mule teams and several flocks of caged chickens. At the moment everyone was still topside, since we were but a few minutes out, and the picture was a blownup replica of the crowd and mood of my adventure aboard the Shriners' Special. Despite the frowns of the crew, bottles were at full and enthusiastic tilt. Wherever I looked, friendly clouts and scufflings were breaking out, and several quarrels were promising to hatch some busted beaks.

At virtually every step a heavy pack—hoisted from the deck and swung carelessly across shoulders—threatened to knock us for a loop. I was decked twice before we had made it halfway to the stairway. Then we spotted a knee-high coil of bull rope near a long, brass rail pointing to the steps.

"Jump in!" Marie ordered. "Let's let 'em thin out a little. I've only got one body. And my feet are already gone."

Seated on the rim of the coil, we finally twisted our clothes into shape again and daubed on fresh rice powder.

"Gee whilikins! These sourdoughs act just like the people did on a train I took a couple of weeks ago. From—"

"Sourdoughs?" Marie interrupted. "This rabble?" Eyes thoughtful, she looked the scene over once, then chuckled, reached over and patted my hand. "Do you know what a sourdough is?"

"Why, they're Alaskans—people going to live in Alaska. Will told me that sourdoughs were what everyone called Alaskans."

"No he didn't. You misunderstood him. A sourdough is a breed. He's a man who is only at home in Alaska. He's proud of it too. Proud of his guts to take cold, hunger, failure or fortune, at full gallop. In a sense, he's a trail breaker, a pioneer. And proud of these things, oddly, because he's proud of Alaska. That's the queer part of it. He couldn't be a sourdough in any part of the world except the Territory. He doesn't know it, but he's really a great citizen." She lifted her arm and waved a contemptuous hand at the scene on deck. "One, maybe two, out of this herd will stay in Alaska and really sink a pick in the ground. The rest of the fatheads will land in Nome or Fairbanks, get stupid drunk for a week, push the Indian and Eskimo women around, and spend another week looking for color—any place but where it is. Then they'll return to the States with their tails between their legs and spend the rest of their lives telling big stories of their adventures in the frozen north. You can buy my share of them for two bits. That goes for Alaska, too, come to think of it."

"Alaska too?" I felt as if someone had sneered at home cooking. "But you're an Alaskan!"

"I *was* Alaskan." She corrected me. She took her moody eyes from the crowd and returned her attention to me. Then her teeth sparkled again. "Don't let me snarl your traces, honey. I was just thinking to myself."

"But I don't understand. You say—"

"I said," she explained patiently, "that I didn't like Alaska. That has nothing to do with its people. The Territory is a cold, raw, cruel place to live. For man *or* animal. It's sure as shooting not for Mademoiselle St. Denis. I'm a perfume, hot-bath and silk-underwear woman. See the line I draw? I don't like Alaska. But I respect its true citizens."

"Then you aren't a sourdough?" I asked.

"In a sense," she conceded grudgingly. "I was born there, but I've been paroled to relatives in the States. Bet you don't know why we're called sourdoughs." She explained that sourdough is the staff of life in Alaska—a mixture of flour and potato water that rises, like bread dough, to twice its original size when it ferments. An Alaskan always saves a piece of it as a "sponge" or "starter" for the next batch; if he neglects to, he borrows a chunk of dough from the first miner or trapper he runs into. Usually the dough is baked on a shovel. Not too many Alaskans pack kitchenware on a thousand-mile trek.

I turned my head toward the crowd which was now thinning out. "What *are* these people, then?"

"We have a lot of names for 'em. The most polite one is cheechako. Most of the regulars pronounce it chee-chawker. It means something between a tenderfoot and a jackass."

For a moment I felt like both. "I guess I'll have to watch my step," I said meekly.

"Not so much. There are only a few things to remember. First, be honest—both with yourself and the people you meet. Don't put on airs. They'll see through you so fast it'll make you dizzy. Second, stick out a hand when and where it's needed. Make your word good. You can get a loan, ranging from five to twenty-five thousand dollars, by asking almost any friend for it. Money's cheap up there. But you'd better pay it back—on time. And don't expect to be able to run to a policeman every time your feelings are hurt. In most parts of the Territory there are none!"

"No law?" Here was a new one, and a development that was disturbing. "How can that be? Every place has to have police."

"The sourdough likes to handle things in his own way. Everyone up there must depend on his neighbor for help in dozens of ways. Soon or late, a rotten apple will get caught in weather to one hundred and fifty degrees below zero. No one tries to rescue him. So he just disappears. As an example of the code, lots of our people bank their gold in their woodboxes. No one would think of stealing it. In the years I've lived in the country I've never known anyone to put a lock on his door. Somebody might want to go in and cook up a meal. Or get warm while you're gone. Come on." Swinging her legs over the side of the coil, she stood up. "We can make it now."

With Marie breaking trail, we made it without mishap to Cabin 16. Opening the door, she said, "Your home for the next three weeks—if you're lucky. This kayak has been known to start for Alaska and end up in Itchy Brisket, Utah. The compass is made of the beard of a woman, the breath of a fish and the footsteps of a cat."

Stepping across the raised threshold, I came face to face with a pair of the most improbable people I've ever seen. The girl was blond-braided, blue-eyed and dressed to meet the most exacting standards favored by Scandinavian mothers for their daughters at smörgåsbord orgies or holidays. The boy at her side looked so much like her—save that he wore American clothes—that he could have been her twin. They were both so patently cornfed that, if they'd fallen into the hands of cannibals, they'd have been saved to serve up to visiting dignitaries.

Marie gave them a grin and they replied with beatific smiles. "The larger one," she said, "knows a few words of American. The cherub doesn't know applesauce from fat meat. I've tried her in French as well as English."

I loosed a few Danish gutturals at her, and instantly her face lit up and I was nearly swamped in the flood of words.

Her name was Greta Boerner and she had been married for a month to Lars, here, whose name was Boerner too. Lars—the swashbuckling rogue—had been a miner in Alaska for a year when suddenly he had heeded the mating call. So he had sailed for Denmark, and what do you think? He found Greta, of all people, working in a bakery in Copenhagen. His masterful electric personality and tender wooing had left her breathless and her folks helpless, and here she was—the luckiest girl in the whole wide world.

Moreover, she also had the most magnificent wedding gifts packed and stored in the ship's hold. These included a feather bed, blankets, her great-grandmother's quilt, pots and pans, a cradle for the babies that would come later, and a butter churn. Her father, a clockmaker, had given Lars a pip of a watch and a hundred kroner for a wedding present, and as for her gift to her husband—I just had to see for myself!

With that she hauled a cardboard box from beneath the lower of the three wall bunks, untied a mile of string around it, and displayed four shirts made of Danish wool. These, she added, were held in such esteem by Lars that he had instructed her to carry them in her arms until they reached their destination.

I recalled my mother's appraisal of Danish wool—that there was nothing like it—and my remarks on the fine tailoring and quality of the shirts were on the high, astounding side. My comments caused her cheeks to shine like candied apples. They were equally appreciated by Lars.

"She's goot voman." He beamed.

Ten minutes later, when she had run out of wind, she repacked the shirts and stowed them, and Lars went off to the cabin he shared with two other men.

Since Greta and I were tenderfeet, Marie assumed the role of housemother and assigned the bunks, giving Greta the lower and me the middle one, while she took the top, explaining, "I know how to ride these things in a heavy gale." Then she distributed towels and soap and showed us how to use the wall hooks which also served as clothesline anchors for the laundry we'd have to dry en route. The housekeeping arrangements completed, we set out in search of Al and Lucy.

On deck the crowd had regrouped for an impromptu entertainment; the crew had strung brass lanterns on ropes stretched overhead, and a dozen square dances—sparked by the squalling of fiddles—were under way. Only a skirt here and there showed the presence of a female; but that did not deter the whoopers and gallopers, and the sight of two half-soused bruisers dancing together made us erupt into laughter.

Marie found the purser and learned the Boyds' cabin number, and we jostled our way below to Number 23. Al opened the door.

"Hey!" Wrapping a hand around an arm of each of us, he

yanked us into the cabin, hugged Marie and planted a whopping kiss on her cheek, and yelled, "Hey, Lucy, look who's here!"

Lucy got off the bunk across the cabin, threw her arms about Marie, then stepped back to look her over.

"You lovely thing! How long has it been? A year, at least."

"Yes. Now I'm on my way back to submit to the heavy hand of devoted parenthood once more."

We all grabbed a stool apiece and sat down while Marie described our adventures on deck, our cabin arrangements and Lars and Greta. Then for two hours the three of them traded reminiscences of heroic adventures, hunting, friends and quick riches in Alaska, while I sat by with bulging eyes, wishing that someone had invented a quicker way of getting there than the *Yucatan*.

Finally Marie got up and said we'd take a look at the goings on on deck before turning in. Lucy bristled protectively.

"Do you think it's wise?"

"You old fogy," Al said. "Let 'em go. I'll look in on them from time to time. They'll be all right."

We agreed to meet at breakfast at seven, and Marie and I went up on deck.

At the foot of the pilothouse the crew had placed a number of long tables loaded with wooden trenchers of sandwiches. Blessed with the appetite of a giant, I fell to with enthusiasm and in no time was into my third ham sandwich and second cup of coffee.

Then, for the first time in my memory, I forgot my devotion to victuals while at table. Looking back, I still can't see why any eighteen-year-old farm girl wouldn't have fallen in love with Jack Bartlett at first sight. In fact, I see no reason not to be proud of it. It was a rich, troublesome, exciting, clean love—one that broadened me emotionally.

In any case, one minute I was munching on a sandwich with total concentration and the next I was looking up some six feet, three inches to meet the blue-gray eyes of a Hellenic god. His brows were gracefully arched, light brown and so symmetrical that they seemed to have been painted on; and the hair above them was a tangle of white gold. He could have hidden a dime in each of the dimples in his cheeks. The rest of him, covered by a green woolen shirt, brown drill britches and yellow calfskin boots, was drawn along the lines of a tall, straight oak, and he stood out among other men like the King of the Forest.

I dropped my half-eaten sandwich and all I could do was stand there, grinning foolishly and letting out a hiccup.

"Coffee?" His big-city accent didn't help my composure a bit.

"No. I mean yes. Cert—I'd enjoya—cuppa—"

"Coming up." He lifted his hand to a crewman at the nearest urn, and his gesture was one that left no doubt that he was used to being served efficiently and quickly and with a minimum of guff. A second later he handed me the cup, and his smile was a peach. "There you are."

"Thank you—very much." Then, to cover my embarrassment, I lifted the mug too quickly, scalded my tongue with the blistering stuff, and added to my cropper by spewing a fine stream at him.

"I've done that a time or two myself," he said, quickly. "Hurts, doesn't it?"

Anger at myself—a happy faculty that has rescued me more than once—got on my side. "That was a silly thing to do. Please excuse me!"

"No apologies needed. It's happened to everyone. This is some boat, isn't it?"

"Uh, huh."

"Where are you going?"

"Why—to Alaska."

"Naturally." He smiled. "I meant to what area?"

"Oh—to Nome. I'm going to work there. I'm a telephone operator."

"Is that so? A pretty little redhead goes to live in America's only jumping-off place. My hat's off."

"Pooh." I was on an even keel again and certainly enjoying myself. "I'm with friends. They live in Nome. I'll be working for them. They own the telephone company there."

"Wonder if they could use a lawyer too?"

"Lawyer?"

"I'm an attorney. An untried one, I'm sorry to say. But you've got to start somewhere."

Looking out over the water, he lifted his head, pulled in a deep breath and stretched, an exercise that caused his chest and arm muscles to swell and crack.

"Let's get away from this animal house." He pointed to a scattering of heavy chairs—obviously converted wooden barrels—on the opposite side of the deck. "How about over there? Okay?"

"That's a good idea. But, first . . ."

Reluctant to ditch Marie so abruptly, I looked around and finally located her rangy form at the end of the farthest table. With her back to us, she was talking to Al, who apparently was fulfilling his promise to ride herd on us. Before I could finish my sentence or attract her attention Jack's hand was at my elbow and I was across the deck and in one of the chairs.

"I'm forgetting my manners," he apologized as he sank down beside me. "But then, I progress daily from worse to impossible. I haven't introduced myself. I'm Jack Bartlett."

"Pleased to meet you. I'm Margaret Knudsen."

In the ensuing hour I learned all that I ever knew of Jack Bartlett's history. He was the son of Andrew Bartlett, a Scotch immigrant who had come to America with a fair education. Andrew had worked for a New York grocery store for two years, saved a little money, and then taken a successful swipe at Wall Street. On a trip abroad he met and fell in love with Anna Paula Kalenkov Kuwalski, the daughter of an impoverished Polish nobleman of minor rank, and married her.

Back in the States, however, the marriage sprang a limp. Anna Paula could not forget that she, an aristocrat, had married an American moneychanger, even if her father *did* need a quarter or two. Within two months she came to detest Andrew and to hate America and made no bones about her feelings.

By the time Jack was born as John Andrew Bartlett in New York in 1881, she had made up her mind. After his birth in June she packed up and returned to her people. Andrew sought to forget his grief and disappointment in repeated plunges in the stock market. But the fire had died in his arithmetic as well as in his heart. Soon he had gutted his financial reserves to a point where he was forced to dispose of his home and liquidate other holdings. He solved his earthly problems by committing suicide when Jack was ten.

An unwanted child by his mother, Jack had never seen or heard from her after her departure. To the day of Andrew's death, Jack's home ties had been reflected in the ministrations of a platoon of governesses, most of them on the spinster-strict side.

After Andrew's death Jack became a ward of the county, where he was the forerunner of today's juvenile delinquent. He took his first sly crack at the black bottle when he was fourteen, and by his eighteenth birthday he had slipped the barbed wire a dozen times, stolen everything from apples to arch supports, and become a good drinking man.

Upon his release at nineteen he found that he had exhausted his father's small insurance bequest. The county, an official explained, was entitled to restitution for monies expended in the process of treeing him from time to time. People who fled her motherly lap must pay the fiddler.

A two-year hitch in the United States Merchant Marine taught Jack to play cards, take a water-front dive apart when he was mean drunk, and that women of all races, creeds and color were receptive to his appearance and attentions. A lucky meeting with a beached, booze-bedazzled second mate in a Hong Kong gin trough excited in him a desire to study law. There was love, life, laughter and a lot of lettuce, in lip, the man—a disbarred attorney—explained in purple detail.

Jack had rounded out his high-school education, gone on to Columbia University and its law school, and six months prior to our meeting had passed his bar examinations.

These improvements, he added, had been brought about largely by his faculty for generally coming up with better than two pair when certain tables had been decorated with a centerpiece of beautiful blue chips.

While working as a law clerk in San Francisco by day and getting loaded to the hairline by night, he had heard of a new gold strike in Fairbanks and of the growth and riches of Nome.

Since his pay checks failed to compare for size with his hang-overs, he decided a change of venue was indicated.

"Not that I've had trouble lately," he said, "in shying away from the mule. But that's because I'm broke."

"Mule?" In those many-colored days I was stuck to the hubs by any idiom that hadn't come out of Blair.

"Liquor, kitten—whisky." He laughed. "I guess the experts are right. Just don't take the first one."

Jack's observation—voiced in a day when Alcoholics Anonymous was yet to become a part of history—sounded like a noise fresh off Weird Street. Contrary to most Midwestern families, the Danes—at least those of Blair—always enjoyed a home-made berry or grape wine with their meals, which frequently included breakfast. Even toddlers were permitted a short, watered slug on festive occasions such as Thanksgiving, Christmas or a good harvest season.

"One drink? How can that hurt you?"

"There's an old acorn," he answered soberly, "that fits some people. Something like, 'One drink's too many, and a gallon's not enough.'" Pulling a sack of Durham and papers from his shirt pocket, he rolled a cigarette, exploded a sulphur match against his thumbnail and lit up. "That should be enough of me. Let's hear about you."

That was a chance I jumped at. If there had ever been a time when I wanted to look, act and be somebody, it was at that moment, and I recall today—with some discomfort—that I threw into my story a good many silly stretchers. At the finish, in fact, I even tried to steal the clever description of Greta and Lars that Marie had given to Al and Lucy Boyd, including Greta's childish pride in Lars' shirts.

"They must be something to look at." Jack laughed. "What did you say they were made of?"

"Danish wool."

"Ah, huh. Is that supposed to be better than American wool?"

"Oh—yes—of course! Much better! And they have hand-polished bone buttons!"

"They must be expensive."

"Terribly!" It goes without saying that I didn't know what I was talking about. As I say, however, I was a hog in silk britches that night and determined to snatch every opportunity to rise and shine. "At least a hundred dollars!"

"Say! That's the kind of a wife to have. I suppose Greta keeps them under pretty heavy guard?"

"No, that's the looney part. She keeps them in an old cardboard box under her bunk."

Jack stood up, stepped to the rail and flipped his cigarette overboard. Hands on hips and legs widespread, he stood there for a dozen heart beats, staring out over the moon-gilded water. When he faced about again, his smile was that of a man who likes his world and his work. His eyes, sweeping the crowds behind me, were more peaceful than I was ever to see them again.

"Let's take a look around. You on?"

Thus began a program of fun and action that lasted for two days, highlighted by more dancing on deck, dinner with Al, Lucy, Marie and Jack, in the ship's big dining room, a smile from the captain—one Henry Emerson, a stooped, bearded cadaverous man whose piety impelled him to conduct church services personally every evening—a patting acquaintanceship with the cows in the hold, and rainbow-hued dreams at night.

There was only one note of disharmony. Marie didn't like Jack and she did not hesitate to say so.

"He's handsome, smart and has guts to burn. But he isn't worth the grease it'll take for the devil to fry him. He's mean and treacherous as a ridge-running wolf. He'll do anything, including murder, to get what he wants. Then he'll stomp on it or throw it away. He's utterly worthless. Anyone but a half-baked ninny like you could read him like a book. Keep your head and watch your step. Hear?"

As it transpired, her concern for me—during the next three days at any rate—amounted to so much foofaraw. Jack simply dropped from sight, without word or warning, leaving no trail or clue to his whereabouts. When he failed to appear for breakfast the next morning I wrote it off as necessary to some reasonable masculine enterprise and returned to my cabin and busied myself with laundry, bunk-making and other domestic chores. But when the same thing happened at lunchtime, I became both worried and shrewish. The dinner hour found me staring at Jack's empty chair, pecking at my food morosely and silently.

It is not comfortable to recall, baby though I was, the in-excusably awkward hour I must have inflicted on Al, Lucy and Marie, even if the racket in the dining room—as at any feeding time—was distracting enough to have hushed up the noise at a Chilkoot fish festival. In answer to their pleasantries I gave them grunts. Comment on the food, good or bad, got them a disinterested look. Once when Lucy mentioned a song she liked, I treated her to a rolling-eyed sigh to end all rolling-eyed sighs. Anyway, I paid for my bad manners almost immediately.

On deck Al suggested that we play cards in their quarters. After a last hopeless sifting of the assembled loungers—in the hope of spotting Jack—I agreed and dropped after them. But once inside I decided that my martyrdom had not been properly appreciated at table, and I refused to sit in. Then Lucy took a hand.

"What's the matter with you? You act like a sick calf."

I was on my feet before I knew it. "I don't see what you mean, Lucy."

"If you were my daughter, I'd whale you within an inch of your life. Acting so downright silly!"

"Lucy! How can you say that to me?"

"Because you've got it coming. You're not engaged to Jack Bartlett. Yet you're acting as if he owed you an explanation of his actions. Well, he doesn't, and you'd best remember it."

"You're saying that because you don't like Jack! Any of you! Marie in particular!"

"Marie doesn't speak for Al and me. He seems all right. But that's not the point. The issue here is with you and your crybaby attitude. You straighten up, miss!"

The bit scratchy lump in my throat was growing larger, despite some pretty hefty swallowing, and the tears arrived whether I liked it or not. "I won't stay here another minute!"

"Perhaps then you'd better go to your cabin. Maybe a good night's sleep will pound some sense into your head."

"Now, Lucy," Al cut in, "she's just—"

"You mind your own business!" Lucy snapped. "Margaret, go to your cabin!"

Nose dripping and eyes drowning, I stumbled outside and made my way forward. I would have been better off, however, had I stayed and taken my medicine. The woes of the day were not over. As I opened the door to my cabin a blizzard of guttural Danish staggered me, followed by a series of wails and cater-wauls that made a chump of my own snorts and heaves. Lars stood in the center of the room, lips puckered in anger, bawling Greta out to a fare-thee-well. She sat huddled on her bunk, hands covering her face, sobbing out choked, broken explanations.

Someone had pinched one of Lars' shirts. It was Greta's fault. She should have stood guard on them day and night. What kind of a wife was it who couldn't be trusted to protect her husband's property?

Greta found the strength to say that she had left the cabin for only a moment. She couldn't have locked the door; there was no lock. How could the thief have known of the shirts? She had told but two people of them. She had showed them to Marie and me. But Marie didn't have a young man aboard. So. . . .

That did it. I'd had enough for one day. My tears vanished on the instant and I kicked that big boob of a Lars through the door with a dispatch and verve that I recall with some pride to this day.

In spite of Greta's painful lowing in the night, I was a healed woman the next morning, for it was becoming clear to me that things were never so bad that they couldn't get worse, even at that sproutish age. At least I had escaped Blair, and that had been a major triumph in itself. Moreover, Jack would show him-self, and probably with a reasonable account of his absence. Cer-tainly it was a long swim back to Seattle.

Following their customary, lifelong good taste, neither Al nor Lucy referred to my deportment of the day before, and Marie—who had come in late from their card session—was still in her bunk. So things were clicking merrily again and we were at breakfast when we learned where Jack had been. The infor-mation came from our waiter, a round-faced, fiercely mus-tachioed Canuck, who wore his hair tightly glued to his skull and carried his trays with the finesse of a master in the art of juggling.

"You folk 'ave heard of ze stow'way? He was capture last night."

"Stowaway, what stowaway?" Al asked.

"A y'ong man call Bartlett. He come aboard and do not pay."

Al unfolded his napkin, spread it carefully over his middle, and chuckled like he had caught an urchin throwing a dead cat on an old maid's porch. "So that was it?"

"Stowaway? What's a stowaway?" I had a hazy idea of the meaning of the term, but wasn't quite sure. "Is that someone who gets on a ship and hides? So he won't have to pay?"

"That's it," Al said. Then to the waiter, "How'd they catch him?"

"He ask ze purser for employment. Ze purser take him to Capitaine Emerson. Ze *capitaine* say he mus' go in ze brig. M'sieu O'Brien save him."

"O'Brien? Who's O'Brien?"

"Ze man who own ze cows an' chickens. When he learn M'sieu Bartlett's misfortune, he go to ze *capitaine*. If M'sieu Bartlett will minister to ze cows and chickens, he will pay his passage. M'sieu Bartlett agree. So ze *capitaine* release M'sieu Bartlett."

"Where's Bartlett now?"

"I 'ave no knowledge. I 'ave not seen him. I repeat only w'at I 'ave ascertain from others."

"Okay." Al grinned. "Maybe he'll be along pretty soon."

But Jack continued to be a will-o'-the-wisp, and by the meal's end I'm not sure that his absence wasn't for the best. Somehow the term "stowaway" had an unpleasant ring to it—a suggestion that such a man was the type to sell cut whisky, add the date of the month to one's grocery bill, and charge for delivery service. Such a man might even borrow another's shirt without asking permission! Al stood up, tucked his napkin under his plate, lit a cigar and announced that he intended to look around for Jack.

"I won't be long. I'll just take a turn around the saloon and drop into the hold," he explained.

Lucy and I ordered a coffee refill apiece and were only halfway into them when Al appeared again, shaking his head and whooping like a schoolboy over his first Shetland pony.

"You'll never believe it. Never in a thousand years."

"All right," Lucy returned testily. "Why don't you try us? Did you find him?"

"I did. He's been playing poker all night with his benefactor O'Brien and several others. The game broke up as I walked in. He has won all the money in the game, including several thousand from O'Brien. Also, he now owns O'Brien's cows and chickens. O'Brien's so sore he could kill him."

This information carried a dash of cold water. Several days ago Jack had admitted to me that he was stony broke. His status as a stowaway bore out his contention. He had no friends aboard, save the three of us, and he hadn't borrowed money from us. How, then, had he got the stake with which to gamble? From O'Brien? Hardly. Surely there was no profit in backing an opponent. I had the answer before my face could turn any redder, and I flounced through the door with a single thought in mind. Lucky my family couldn't know that I had been associating with a thief! That shirt! He had stolen Lars' shirt, sold it for enough money to gamble with, and had made me a party to the entire disgusting operation! To make the situation worse, I found Lars in the cabin when I returned, and the silence with which I was greeted was earsplitting. But I wasn't asked to wait long for a turn of events.

I was barely inside when a knock sounded at the door and Jack, red-eyed from lack of sleep but wearing a pleasant grin, stood at the sill, the purloined shirt draped across his arm.

"Hello, kitten. May I come in? For just a moment?"

"Y-yes—surely." Swinging the door wide, I stood to one side, undecided whether to grow wings or hide.

"Here." Jack held out the shirt with one hand, and with the other indicated Greta and Lars. "Sorry to have swiped this. But I had to get a stake somehow. Anyway, I just hocked it. With the cook. It hasn't been worn. Tell them thanks. In fact," he ran his broad hand through his hair and blew out a tired breath, "I'll be glad to pay for the use of it."

Employing all the polite Danish phrases I could remember, I relayed his message. Unfortunately Lars wouldn't or couldn't be soft-soaped. Clenching his fists and drawing himself up, which caused him to be even more at a disadvantage to Jack's height, he spat out a naughty Danish answer and gave evidence of impending attack.

That was the worst thing he could have done. One sharp glance and Jack caught the picture, with or without translation. The smile left his face and he laughed, harshly and shortly. Then he did a cruel and senseless thing. Holding the shirt against his chest, he ripped off the buttons, one by one, wadded up the shirt and threw it at Lars' feet.

"Tell him," he snarled, "if he makes a move I'll beat his brains out."

Lars did not move, and Jack turned and walked out of the cabin. I sank onto a bunk, with my face in my hands. Lars and Greta tactfully withdrew and left me alone. Numb as I was, I knew one thing: I could never have anything to do with Jack again.

Yet such was his mercurial luck and reckless nature that the next day he was the hero of the ship, admired by everyone aboard.

Chapter Five

THE *Ohio,* sister ship to the *Yucatan,* went down some
150 miles out at sea on June 15, 1904, after striking an iceberg
of such awesome size and contour that, at our first sight of it, a
hush fell over the deck of the vessel; then a witless panic broke
out.

Since those melancholy days in which more than 300
passengers lost their lives I have often wondered if my imagination hadn't played me false in relation to the aspect of that berg.
But I think not. I recall the reaction of Marie St. Denis as she
stood near me on the after deck of the *Yucatan* and we watched
the slowly sinking *Ohio* and the mountain of ice that rode at
her stern.

"Look! Near the top! It's got a face!"

"I—I know! I see it. . . ."

There were others, too, who admitted later to the same impression. These included Al and Lucy Boyd, Captain Emerson,
Jack Bartlett and various of the *Yucatan's* sea-going sheep,
whose bleating for days afterward could have been heard by
the totally deaf a mile away.

"Look! Near the top!" Marie repeated.

"I—know!"

Adding more goose pimples to my fright, I remembered that I had been scheduled to sail on the *Ohio* and that—save for the paternal maneuvering of Al—I would have been listed among the scrambling figures on the deck of the crippled vessel or among those who slipped overboard from time to time.

"I must be having a nightmare," Marie whispered.

She wasn't. The berg had a *face*. High up near the top nature had fashioned a gargoyle in the ice—leering, malignantly smiling, neck bent forward, arms cocked and fingers hooked. If the scene was a grisly one, however, it was preceded by a preliminary setting that was fitting for its final gloomy curtain. One day we were sailing along over water with scarcely a ripple to its surface, enjoying the sun and gentle winds. The next, we were on deck, bundled to the ears with heavy clothing and refereeing the *Yucatan*'s passage through a white world of grinding, snarling ice packs. One evening we watched the sun go down on the skyline, and the next day it returned to glower for twenty-four hours on end.

"We're entering the northern circle," Jack Bartlett explained on a dazzling day about midnight. We were sitting in a couple of the barrel-stave chairs near the lifeboats.

A day or two before, Lucy had handed me a down-stuffed, fur-trimmed parka and several pair of woolen socks, explaining that a change of climate—depending on the ship's speed—could be expected soon.

Now, even with the parka and the blazing sun, I could feel the murderous stab of the Arctic wind as I sat there on deck, blinking against the sun's glare.

"Honey," Jack continued, dropping his hand on my shoulder. "That outfit really becomes you." He scraped his chair closer and to such an angle that he partly faced me. "Now that I've made a little bundle in chickens and cows—and added to it by raiding the sucker market—I've got something to say to you. How would you like—?"

That's when the condition of the *Ohio*, floundering among the ice floes about a quarter mile off, was seen by the lookout on top of the wheelhouse. Within the space of a shaved second everyone on deck was at the rail, staring silently and unbelievingly at the spectacle.

"You stay here!" A flick of Jack's hand dumped me back into my chair as I started to get up. "Don't move until I come back for you! I've seen featherbrained mobs in action before!"

He couldn't have called the turn better had he sized up the scope of a flood on its way to wipe out a town. The insanity began with a muttering, then moved up to a charivari of hysterical yells and shouts.

"That's her! That's the *Ohio!*"

"Sure is! Left Seattle a week before we did! Loaded to the gills with people an' baggage too!"

"Hit that iceberg, it did! No ship's got a chance ag'in 'em! Big as they is—most of 'em is under water!"

"Hey, look up there—up at th' top!"

At this point Captain Emerson, flanked by a dozen uniformed, grim-faced crew members, appeared on the poop deck, carrying a bell-nosed megaphone. Pressing its off end to his lips, he held up his free hand and began waving it, semaphore fashion.

"Your attention, please." His hoarse voice had a shiver to it. "Yonder is the ship *Ohio.* She has collided with the iceberg. Every one of you will be needed to aid in the rescue of those aboard her. Meantime, we are in no danger. I repeat—"

He might as well have saved his breath. Reflecting one of those freaks of human behavior that no one has ever explained logically, the mob began surging about, yelling, crying, pulling crazily at each other or dropping to their knees in prayer. More weirdly yet, a hulking, baldheaded man with a red beard, standing just beyond me at the rail, pointed to the lifeboats and let out a roar.

"The boats! Let's git at 'em, men!"

He was instantly joined by around twenty more of his own cut and jib, and heedless of the booming orders of Captain Emerson, they came on with a rush that knocked over my chair and swept me along with them. It may be that I have never been closer to serious injury or death than I was in the moments that followed. However, if such should happen before I take the thirteenth step, I hope there will be a Jack Bartlett nearby.

Crouched near the boats and trying to avoid being trampled, I heard the groan of timbers and looked up to see that the loons had unjacked one of the lashings and were working on the one up forward. The craft, a twenty-four footer, was directly over me and there was no chance—boxed in as I was—of getting away if and when it dropped. Above the clamor I could hear Jack's voice in some of the wildest cursing that ever battered the human ear. This was punctuated by a series of groans and thuds, and in another minute the churning legs thinned out. Jack was starting for Redbeard as I regained my feet, and the sight that followed didn't help to settle my stomach. Starting from the vicinity of his instep, Jack's punch must have driven every tooth the man possessed into his throat and nearly torn his head off. Then Jack was at my side.

"Hurt?"

Pinching and poking here and there, I discovered that—save for lost skin on my knuckles and forehead—I was still in one piece, even if my wind and dignity were gone. But I was almost paralyzed with fear. "No—I guess—not."

"Good. Come along."

Grabbing my arm, Jack urged me toward Lucy, Al and Marie, who had come on deck and were standing near the wheelhouse —and he played no favorites in roughing up anyone in our path. As we approached our group the captain's voice reached us again, this time backed up by a score of crew members carrying pistols and marlinspikes.

"Listen to this, you scum!" he bawled. "You've got one minute to get your bearings! After that we'll shoot the first one who makes a demonstration!"

Taking a watch from his pocket, he stared at the hands of the instrument while his men moved quietly through the crowd. This had the necessary influence. Within seconds the fools began thinking again, and by the time he had returned the watch to his vest the shouting had subsided and the stampede had slowed to a walk.

"All right." Lifting his hand, he rasped the back of it across his lips, pulled his cap down, and raised the megaphone. "We'll need at least two hundred of you to man the lifeboats—in relays. Each boat will be officered by an experienced crewman. Volunteers step forward, please."

Jack and Al were the first up, and a large body of men soon followed. After Captain Emerson had sorted out those with some experience as seamen and assigned them their duties, he summoned the ladies to the dining room and gave us instructions for serving hot food to the rescued and finding them cabin space. Lucy took charge of this, obtained from the purser the cabin numbers of all the women aboard, and began to round them up. Apparently they were all on deck, as we found none of them in their cabins.

Outside the passengers and crew swarmed over the decks like ants. Skeleton crews had put all but one of the lifeboats into the water when the first of a chain of mishaps occurred. Just after the last of the boats touched the water it cracked up on a jagged ice floe and dumped its crew into the sea; encumbered by heavy clothing, five of them were nearly trapped beneath the ice. But somehow they all managed to hang onto something until the last craft in line could pick them up. Lucy's face turned the color of skimmed milk as she saw Al in the bow of the lead boat.

"Don't worry, ma'am," Captain Emerson told her. "That other boat shouldn't have been put into the water at all—it was old and dried out. The others are strong enough."

Lucy and I returned to our search for women passengers, and an hour later we had run down three—Greta, who was huddled with Lars in his cabin, and two middle-aged sisters, both Alaskans. One was Emily Murchison, married to a Fort Yukon businessman; the other, Paula McLain, was a spinster. The women had been Outside to pay their annual visit to relatives in Des Moines, Iowa. Emily's husband had accompanied her as far as Seattle. There, confronted with the same problem that had faced me in the matter of sailing accommodations, he had been forced to a decision: either he must take a berth on another ship or displace Paula on the *Yucatan,* thus breaking up the sisters' yearly old-home spree and gabfest.

He had chosen the *Ohio.*

"All right, dear." Lucy, noting Emily's trembling chin, urged her toward the door of the dining room. "We can do without you. Why don't you go to the rail and wait there for him? He might even be on the first boat."

Greta was too frightened to be of any help, so we cut her loose, too, and the four of us split up and began taking inventory. On orders from Lucy, everything not nailed down was thrown outside of each cabin in order to provide as much sleeping space as possible. We had gone through about twenty of them when a yell from above announced the approach of the first boat. Low in the water and crammed with humanity, it was still about fifty yards out when we reached the deck. It was bouncing like a chip in the choppy waters, battered by the ice, and moving at a snail's pace. Jack Bartlett's head gleamed in the blinding sun as he stood in the bow, thrusting at the floes with a long pole. Men on either side of the craft bailed frantically with small kettles and cans.

The boat's arrival alongside was accompanied by a cheer that would have matched the roar of a volcano. But the ovation was replaced in the next moment by an opposite reaction. The ice-coated rope ladder hanging over the rail had no anchor, and, agitated by the rolling ship and the wind, it was whipping wildly.

The bobbing and bucking of the rescue craft didn't help either, and despite the efforts of the oarsmen and Jack's powerful stabs with his pole, the ice cakes kept drifting between the boat and the *Yucatan*. For two of the survivors, however, the suspense didn't last long. Ignoring the commands of the officer in the stern of the boat, a couple of men, their faces twisted with fear, clambered past Jack and leaped at the ladder. Both missed it by inches and disappeared under the ice. As usual under such circumstances, the herd instinct took over. Three more men began crawling forward. But this time Jack was ready for them. He waited until the first was within range, and, with a chop to the man's jaw, laid him out cold. The other two, one of whom was knocked down by the falling man, decided to take orders.

Then Captain Emerson arrived at the rail, took in the picture at a glance, and went over the side. His weight at the bottom of the ladder spelled the difference. Ten minutes later he was back on deck, followed by Jack and a group of the most miserable, exhausted creatures to be imagined.

"Hey! Honey!"

Jack's kiss put a bump on my lip that lasted for a week and his hug nearly broke my back. But I had no chance to speak.

Lucy, who had got the line of stumbling, half-frozen men started toward the hot food in the dining room, broke it up.

"Al?" she asked quietly. "He was in the lead boat."

Jack turned and nodded toward the open sea where a wedge-shaped speck could be seen about 500 yards out. "That's his baby, coming in. They had some trouble when we got there. Ice, mostly." Lifting his arms above his head, he crooked his elbows and his muscles cracked like stretched cables. "Yo-ho, ho, ho, and a bottle of rum!" he roared.

I glanced at him, then at Lucy, and it was obvious that she was as surprised as I. There was a happy grin on his face and his eyes had the expression of a man who has just had a glass of champagne in the apartment of a celebrated beauty. It was incredible, in view of the situation. But he was obviously enjoying himself!

"Jack!" Somehow his attitude seemed callous—even sacrilegious—particularly since more than one passing survivor would stagger or fall on his way to the dining room. I was cut off from further comment.

"Did you see a Mr. Murchison out there?" Emily Murchison's hand on Jack's arm was that of a dead woman's. "He's fat and short—and he's baldheaded."

Jack's grin vanished. His eyes, for one of the few times that I can recall, were warm.

"There are a lot of people out there. Murchison? Is—"

"He's my husband," she whispered.

Jack reached out, and his hands—gripping her arms—couldn't have been more gentle and reassuring had they been half their size.

"I'll bring him back. I'll look for him. You have my word."

Pushing her at me, he turned. Cupping his palms to his lips, he let out a yell. "Let's go! Next bunch. Over the side!" With another kiss that nearly caved in my teeth, Jack was off, trailed by a fresh crew. Then Al's boat arrived.

"Al." I thought Lucy would never let go of him. "It looks bad, doesn't it?"

"The *Ohio*'s going down. There's a hole in her side you could drive a locomotive through. The captain's missing—fell overboard maybe. The officers are still trying to maintain some order, but I'm afraid it's hopeless. The ship's crawling with madmen—"

"Any women aboard?" Lucy asked.

"Didn't see any. Looks like they loaded the lifeboats with women, and they just drifted off. Anyway, there're none in sight."

Just then Captain Emerson spotted Al and summoned him to give a report on what he had seen. Lucy and I went on with our work.

Thus began a period of hardship and heartbreak that lasted for two days and nights as the rescue work went on. The boats departed and returned with survivors, and the *Yucatan* was jammed until her sides groaned. Through it all we slept only in snatches filled with bad dreams, since the half-dead men, after being fed, were given the most comfortable accommodations in which to recover. The ship's doctor, a codger whose name I recall as McGill, found ample use for our few spare moments. We dressed wounds and nursed the broken bones caused by the impact of the iceberg and the subsequent mob rule aboard the *Ohio*. Later I learned that our rescue count amounted to 307 men. But it is possible that a bare three-fourths of them survived aboard the *Yucatan*. The others died with such regularity that it demanded the fulltime labors of two crewmen to sew their bodies in canvas, recite a short prayer from a ship's Bible, and throw them overboard. We were so tired that the sight of dead men and the sound of the splashes soon ceased to depress us.

It was during this time that Jack Bartlett became something of a short-term legend to most of us and a hero to some of us. Despite the remonstrances of Captain Emerson that he take a rest, Jack consistently refused. After his fourth trip out Emerson not only threw up his hands but swore Jack in as a temporary officer of the *Yucatan* to serve jointly with the second officer, Horrigan. In this job Jack's vitality, physical strength and almost senseless courage, soon erected a challenge to the other volunteers and inspired a change in morale that undoubtedly was responsible for saving many lives that would otherwise have been lost.

Time after time he left the security of his craft to jump on an ice floe that blocked his way, the better to use his pole to break a passage for his boat and those behind. Reports, which I heard and saw written on the ship's log at a later date, credited him with saving, singlehanded, the lives of eighteen men. Approaching one struggling weakly in the water, he would lean over the side, and, grasping the man by the hair and belt, yank and heave until he got him aboard.

Once when his boat was creaking with its overload, he pulled a stunt that almost caused my heart to stop. Seeing a half-frozen man on a jagged pack, he leaped from the bow, snatched him up, and started back. However, the ice was so slippery and rough that he fell twice before getting into position for his return. By this time the current had edged the boat too far off-side to be reached with even a long step, and the gap was widening each moment. It was apparent that he was practically marooned.

But his next move was characteristic of his magnificent reflexes. Raising the man chest high, Jack hurled him straight at the boat, where his body pinwheeled into the outstretched arms of the crew. Then Jack leaped into the icy water, his fingers closing on the rail, without an inch to spare. True to his word, he went all over the *Ohio* in search of Emily Murchison's husband, ignoring the fact that the ship could have gone down at any time, taking him along with it. To do this properly and thoroughly he ordered his crew to continue their operations while he interviewed survivors and shook down dark corners. Every time he came back to the *Yucatan,* he made a point of contacting Mrs. Murchison.

"Don't worry," he would reassure her. "We'll find him. It takes time to go over that ship. Now try to get hold of yourself. If you don't, you're going to be sick."

It was early afternoon of the third day when the inevitable happened, although a feeling of dread that the *Ohio* was near its end had been growing since morning. I was asleep in a chair in the lounge when a flurry of shouts and scurryings outside awoke me. I wasted no time in getting to the rail.

Since the boats were being winched aboard one by one, I knew, without being informed, that Captain Emerson had ordered an end to the rescue lest the small craft be pulled under by the suction created by the sinking ship. Then I saw Jack talking to Horrigan and Al near the wheelhouse. When I reached his side he filled me in on the developments.

"She can't last an hour," he said wearily. "Her hold's got more water in it than the rest of the ocean. Her stern's nearly submerged now."

"How many more are there aboard?"

"Couple hundred, maybe."

"Did you find Mr. Murchison?"

"No. Where's his wife?"

Looking about, I discovered her in her usual position near the lifeboats, watching the survivors as they moved along. I reached her just as the last man passed by, and led her, crying hoarsely, back to Jack.

"Did you find his body? Or—did anyone say anything —about him?"

"No." Lifting her chin, he took out his handkerchief, balled it and wiped the tears from her face. "But that doesn't mean a thing. He's probably adrift on one of the *Ohio*'s lifeboats. Emerson tells me he's wirelessed the Navy at Seattle. This area will be swarming with ice cutters before another day's gone by. So he'll probably be back in Seattle before you reach Nome."

Closing his eyes, he blew out a sigh. Then a gust of wind hit him, and, in his exhausted condition, he nearly fell. It took no second look to see that he was virtually out on his feet, and I got him headed for the dining room in a hurry. I pushed him into a chair and wasn't too ladylike to throw people right and left in rounding up hot coffee and sandwiches for him. But when I returned, his head was on the table and he was asleep. No amount of cudgeling could arouse him. I threw a blanket over his shoulders and went on deck again to see what I could do to help, and to sit out the deathwatch.

A few minutes later the *Ohio* quivered, lunged upward, then settled backward like a dog on its haunches—and died. As the last particle of her wood sank beneath the ice a groan swept over the *Yucatan*. I didn't realize that I was crying until Lucy walked up and took me into her arms.

"Don't, honey. You can't do anything about it."

"It's horrible!"

"Go back and sit with Jack. Or lie down in the lounge. You're so tired you hurt. Run along."

I turned, meaning to take her advice. But I had taken no more than one step when my plans were changed. Although the *Yucatan*'s motors had started, we weren't going forward an inch, and the reason became known when Emerson arrived once more on deck, megaphone in hand.

"The ship," he shouted, "is wedged in a heavy ice pack. Our crew will begin freeing us immediately. Do not be alarmed. We are not in danger."

Then the megaphone fell from his hand. Staring out to sea, his eyes bulged and his jaw sagged on its hinges. My own muscles turned to gelatin and my heart slugged my ribs so hard that I was on the verge of being sick. The iceberg, its gargoyle turned toward the *Yucatan*, was coming at us, its flaring skirt kicking the floes from its path as though they were children's blocks. Held motionless and helpless by the grip of the pack on the port side, the *Yucatan* looked like a sister ship to the *Ohio* in more than one way. Silence held sway on deck for a full minute. Then a burst of hysterical laughter came from a man standing farther front.

"Glory to God—an' th' Resurrection to come!" he shrieked. "It's chasin' *us* now!"

His outburst sparked panic again, and once more the *Yucatan*'s crew moved in, pistols and marlinspikes in hand. This time they were forced to use both, and the sound of gunfire and cracking skulls was punctuated by cries, prayers and splashes as one man after another jumped overboard in the frenzy of his terror.

I am not ashamed to admit that I went to my knees, and took a lot of comfort from it. I can't remember when I've prayed so hard or so long before or since in my life, and I've done a powerful bit of heavenly petitioning in seventy-five years. In fact I probably would have been on my prayer bones yet, as the saying goes, if Al hadn't come along, yanked me to my feet, and shoved me into the dining room where I managed to club Jack awake. In his shadow I felt a measure of composure return to me.

"What's up, honey?"

Upon hearing my disjointed, babbling account of the latest developments he pulled in his belt a notch, told me to keep calm and stay rooted, and flung himself outside. I could hear Captain Emerson reading the riot act from the poop deck again, even above the bark of the pistols, the snarling of the ice pack and the general hysteria.

"Listen, you fools! You can help save this ship—if you do as I say! Quiet! Quiet! Lie flat! On your stomachs! All of you!"

For a third time in thirty-six hours his commands found some customers, and the noise—after reaching a second crescendo—gradually leveled off. But as far as I was concerned, I couldn't have stretched out had I been plugged, dead center, by a slug from a Sharps fifty-six. Since I was somewhat prayed out and there seemed no other recourse to salvation, I found myself outside, back against the wall, watching a sight that brings on a chill when I think of it to this day.

There was no noise beyond that caused by the gnashing of the ice pack. Like myself, most of the several hundred people on deck had ignored Emerson's order to lie down, although some were on their knees, heads bowed. Every other eye was fixed on the glittering juggernaut that plowed its way toward us. The picture it presented was the more terrifying for the unswerving, relentless approach of the thing. Despite the speed of the current, its arrival seemed to consume a lifetime—an ageless period in which its gentle, rocking motion and its crouching gargoyle face were more representative of disaster and destruction than its size or the brutal ease with which it smashed and crumbled the big floes in its path. Then its bulk shut out the sky, sun and water. Waves, twenty feet high, slashed at the ship. The *Yucatan* wallowed about crazily, and in the next moment we were living in a world where hope was forgotten and abandoned.

Others may have had some occult vision at that point—a

fleeting, pictorial repetition of their past lives, the revival of long-lost ambitions, or glimpses of heaven. Some people, I'm told, go through those things when death is near. But if I did, the vision has since escaped me. I remember only that I gritted my teeth, braced myself, and closed my eyes. Then there was a rasping explosion and the ship's bells began ringing. Her motors started up at full throttle. When I looked, her stern had come hard about and her starboard side was banked solidly against the berg. At the same time the ice pack closed in, port side, with a grinding crash. The bells stopped clanging and the motors cut out. At that instant Jack came up, grabbed me by the waist, and hoisted me with a happy jerk above his head.

"He did it!"

"Did it—what?" I was still too far in shock to make any sense.

"Honey, you've just seen the finest exhibition of seamanship you'll ever see! At the last moment Emerson broke the ship loose from that pack and coasted it alongside the berg! I've never seen anything like it—and I've done some sailing! It had to be split-second work! He must have had less than two minutes to get into position before the pack closed in again!"

The captain mounted the poop deck again and waved the throng quiet. We were safe for the moment, he said, drifting toward the north curve of the Japanese current where the warm waters would break up the ice. If another berg should approach, the ship might be crushed and most of us lost; if that happened, we would have warning, and lifeboats would be launched, women and their husbands going first. Meanwhile, there would be no smoking. Cooking fires would be lit each morning for two hours only.

"In the name of charity and fellowship," he finished, "please share your warm clothing with others. Now let us pray together."

Folding his hands and bowing his head, Emerson began the Lord's Prayer. I started to my knees, then a glance at Jack's face hauled me up, ramrod stiff. I've never seen such a sneering expression of contempt, and his whisper—obviously not meant for my ears—was even more shocking.

"You crawling, weak-spined fool!"

Since that incident—which impressed me so starkly that it

could have happened yesterday—I have spent hours mulling over the fascinating, yet strange, perverse character of Jack Bartlett. I realize now that he was what the psychiatrists of today would call a victim of schizophrenia, or one afflicted with a divided personality. But I wonder if our modern psychoanalysts, advanced as their science has become, could have helped him. That he was tortured by his nature is a certainty, since he showed it by his actions on innumerable occasions.

Obviously he both hated and liked each side of his character, and this led to self-destruction of an extremely dangerous nature. He could be incredibly cruel, then kind, charitable and generous in proportion. But when this benign element rose to the surface he would grow inevitably vicious shortly thereafter, and would permit himself no credit in any matter, whatever it chanced to represent.

I got a taste of this two days later as we drifted along—cold, exhausted and watching apprehensively for the appearance of another berg or the formation of additional ice in the pack. He came to my cabin about ten o'clock in the morning, rapped, waited patiently until I had dressed and come out, then handed me a crumpled piece of paper.

"What is it?" I was in a mood that was short of being civil. Like the other women aboard, I was running out of legs and I had been in the bunk less than two hours.

"Read it. I found it in my jacket pocket a little while ago. I don't know how long it's been there."

Smoothing out the wrinkles, I held it up to see it better. It read:

DEAR MR. BARTLETT:

Me and my husband has always been together. God bless you for what you done.

Yrs. Respt.

MRS. EMILY MURCHISON

It must have been a full minute before the implication stabbed home. Then I could only stammer. "What on earth—"

"It should be clear. Is she with you? If not, where's her cabin?"

"I'll— Come with me."

Emily was not in her berth. Her sister Paula admitted that she had not seen her since the night before. Paula had not been alarmed about her sister's absence; we had been working like dogs and sleeping, more or less, where we fell.

"Come along, Margaret," Jack ordered. "We'll turn this note over to Emerson."

Five hours later the search was called off. Apparently Emily had slid over the side during the panic caused by the approach of the berg or a little while afterward. The news dumped the ship into an even deeper gloom, and there were a good many blurry eyes around, including my own, Lucy's and Marie's. Paula's case was particularly pitiful. The sisters had been very close, and Doctor McGill virtually kept Paula under guard and knocked out by sedatives for two days.

Then Jack added to my discomfiture and depression by voicing, for the first time in our association, one of his typical philosophies. We were drinking cold coffee in the dining room when I mentioned that Emily evidently had loved her husband more than her own life, or some such casual and superfluous remark.

"Probably. It makes no difference."

"No difference? I don't understand."

"She was useless. I have no sympathy for gutless men *or* women. They are inexcusable nuisances, hanging around and taking breathing room from worth-while people. They're better off dead."

"Better off? What a horrible thing to say! After hunting all over that ship for her husband, and all!"

"Your appreciation for my noble act makes me feel good inside," he returned, bitingly. "But I must be honest. It's a quality that has been almost forgotten. I boarded the *Ohio* because I wanted to see what she looked like in her death struggles, not especially to look for Mrs. Murchison's bum at all."

"But—but what about those men you saved? Why, you're a hero!"

Jack threw back his head and laughed until tears came to his eyes.

"Hero? That's rich!" Setting down his cup, he reached over, took both of my hands in his own, and bent his head closer.

"Margaret, let's get something straight. Right now. I wouldn't turn my hand to save the life of anyone on this ship except yours. Everything I do stems from selfishness—honest selfishness. In the case of the scum I'm supposed to have saved, I did it for the fun of it. That and nothing more. Selfishness has been my only motivation for anything I've ever done, good or bad. And so it is with everyone in this world too. Only a hypocrite disguises his motive with a cloak of saintliness. Give a gift, and you do it because you're selfish. You feel good about it. Smash someone's face, and you do it for the same reason. You're selfish enough to want to see him hurt. Society is as simple as that, the world over. That's all it amounts to."

Pulling out his tobacco sack, he rolled a cigarette and lit it in defiance of Emerson's dictum, blew out a lungful of smoke, and chuckled at the expression of incredulity on my face.

"Oh, I've learned about the gratitude of princes and the traditions and the sacred cows and the general stupidity and rotten conventions so revered by the saps of this century, Margaret. Far as I'm concerned, it boils down to a simple solution. I didn't ask to be born. I'll have nothing to say about when or where I die. Meanwhile I intend to live as I please. I certainly don't care what anyone thinks about it. And that includes the opinion of God himself."

"God?" I was so stunned by his blasphemy that my voice must have been less than a sick gulp. In fact I expected in the next instant to see him struck by lightning or to hear the cracking of the ship's timbers announcing a visitation of vengeance from above. Indeed, my surprise when neither happened had the effect of shivering me even more.

"Don't you believe in God?"

"Of course not." He laughed. "It's all a lot of superstition written down by sheepherders." Getting out of his chair, he craned his neck toward a big clock on the opposite wall. "Got to go baby my cows and chickens, honey. Be a good girl, and don't take any wooden bibles."

Shivering from the cold, bogged down from the soggy pancakes and sandwiches that were the current afternoon and evening bill of fare and miserable over Jack's attitude, I tried to muster enough git and go to make my bunk again. But I was so tired that I fell asleep at table, despite my conviction that the absence of heavenly punishment for Jack's words meant that a more terrible form of retribution awaited us. I guess the Lord is willing to make exceptions, after all.

I awoke on the heels of an explosion that made the first one —when the *Yucatan* was captured by the pack—sound like a popcorn burp. Dragging myself outside, expecting the end, I was almost blinded by the most glorious burst of sunlight that ever greeted the human eye. The iceberg was about fifty yards off, heading toward its own destruction. The ship was free of the pack. Its engines were going and its crew was trying to control a ruckus comparable in scope with those just past, but of another color. I could hardly believe our change of fortune until Jack came up behind me and began tossing me around like a rag doll.

"Hey, honey! We made the current! We're on our way—to Alaska!"

We were interrupted once more en route, this time by a school of whales pursued by three whalers, each equipped with an armory of harpoon guns. The *Yucatan*'s engines were quiet for three days while the water was clotted with the blood of the animals, some of which escaped wounded and attracted several killer-whale packs. These beasts, roiling about, teeth gleaming, churned the water to foam over a mile-wide area before the carnage was through. Then on the late afternoon of June 28 Jack and I were brought to our feet by the lookout's call.

"Land, ho!"

There she was, finally! The long, hazy, jagged coastline of Alaska! Curling his arm around my waist, Jack bent his head and put his lips against my ear.

"A new country, honey. Think we could share it together?" Then his eyes filmed over and his voice became a mocking drawl. "In holy matrimony, that is?"

Regardless of this offensive tone and attitude, I swear that my feet were a foot off the deck.

Chapter Six

DESPITE my delirium over Jack Bartlett's proposal of marriage, I felt about as much ecstasy for Nome, as we approached her, as an exiled European aristocrat with ulcers might feel for a Mission Street boardinghouse in San Francisco.

For one thing, I wasn't sure—as we floundered and wallowed toward shore in the *Yucatan*'s lighter—whether we would make it with whole skins. In addition to a sustained three-hour attack by waves that looked sky high, the water was a dirty gray and laced with debris near the beach. Since morning the sun had been boxed in by a heavy overcast, and now at noon the light was turning to an eerie blue, with the wind sharp enough to make a polar bear head for Tahiti.

Beyond a curving winnow of frothy scum at the water's edge, a helter-skelter scattering of weather-hammered lean-tos and shacks huddled in raunchy disorder, some resting on stilts to permit the ebb and flow of the tide beneath them.

An arrow's flight farther back, a more orderly yet equally bleak formation of rooftops pointed out the center of town, and, stretching as far as the eye would permit on either side, was a solid reach of gray, soggy, treeless, grassless tundra.

Our disembarkation from the *Yucatan* was as hectic and disorderly as the rest of the voyage had been. The seas were running high, and the captain ordered the ship to anchor ten miles out from shore, instead of the usual five or so that were the normal margin of safety for unloading along Nome's shoreline. We stood off, hoping for better weather, but when the ship's barometer offered no hope of improvement, Captain Emerson sent for a tug and lighter and announced that the women would disembark first, with the husbands of the married ones; after that the rest of the passengers would be put ashore in alphabetical order. Each person would be allowed to take one bag or suitcase on the lighter; heavy luggage would be unloaded with other cargo after the passengers were ashore.

When the captain had made his announcement, Jack leapt forward, cupped his hands to his mouth, and yelled, "Hey, Emerson! How about me?" He whipped his arm around my waist and hoisted me a foot off the deck. "I'm going to marry this girl as soon as I hit dirt. How about my going ashore with her?"

Emerson smiled, but got no chance to speak. Before Jack's last word was out, a friendly if rough gang of passengers was on us, pummeling him, kissing me, hooting at Emerson.

"Let 'im go with 'er!"

"Ye wouldna par-r-r-t them b'foor theer feerst ficht, noo, would ye, Captain?"

Jack's popularity was such that there was no resisting the appeal.

After silencing the mob by walking off, then turning back to the rail, Emerson said, "I think everyone would agree that your services on this voyage entitle you to special consideration. You may escort your lady ashore, and my congratulations."

We tried to get to the rail to watch the approach of the tug and lighter, but the friendly chee-chawkers mobbed us again, and we ducked into Al's and Lucy's cabin for refuge until it was time to board the lighter.

The tug was a trim little craft called *Yukon Beauty*, wearing a gorgeous coat of crankcase oil and creosote; but the lighter itself was right off Nome's nautical skid row, a big raft with

94

sideboards capable of holding fifty persons and manned by black-faced river rats.

Jack put his arm around me as the lighter moved shoreward and said, pointing ahead, "See that? That's our country. We'll run it, you and me. We'll eat and drink the best. We'll get married as soon as we hit Nome."

"Oh, Jack, I can hardly wait. But what about money? We're not even started yet."

"We're in pretty fair shape. I can squeeze out fifty dollars a quart for the milk from those cows, and maybe twenty dollars a dozen for the eggs. I've got enough cash from that poker session to set up my law office, and there ought to be plenty of work, if Nome is what I've heard she is." He was no more juvenile then I was over our prospects. Life, for both of us, in the past day or two, had seemed bathed in champagne and as rich as rainbow stew.

On the long low pier, constructed of the mutilated trees passed for lumber, another mob awaited us—creatures topped with wide, floppy hats or woolen caps and encapsulated the rest of the way in garish parkas or mackinaws, jeans or canvas pants, and square-toed thick felt boots. They waved, leapt and fired off a pistol or rifle now and then. It was hard to tell whether they had come to welcome or attack us. Packs of bushy-tailed dogs scrabbled and snarled underfoot; and ranks of blanket-draped figures with braided black hair stood right and left of the center of the crowd.

Everyone on the pier seemed to be trying to shake Al's hand or hug and kiss Lucy and Marie.

"Al! Y'old boar bear! Thought ye'd never git back!"

"Lookit, men! The Candy Kid! He's wearin' them oxford shoes without tops!"

"Wal, bust me in the chops, if it ain't that dirty-faced kid from Fort Yukon; and all growed up. Give us a squeeze, Marie!"

"Al? Who's the little redheaded beauty?"

Then it was my turn and their welcome was so honest, friendly and exuberant that introductions were abandoned and I forgot my grim first impression of Nome in a glow of appre-

ciation for its hospitality. Jack was also treated like a long-lost
relative, and to my relief he accepted with good grace the
friendly hugs and buffets I received. I had already learned that
he could blow hot with little or no prodding and that there was
no way of anticipating his reactions.

"Hey, you two-bit field hands! Lay off, will you? We're home
to stay. Now beat it!"

Al's booming voice, while pleasant, carried a rasp of authority. We were all tired, and several times since our landing I had
seen him glance at Lucy with concern. In addition to bossing
the *Yucatan*'s female crew through our danger period, Lucy
had handled more than her share of manual labor, and the
strain was evident in the droop of her shoulders and the lines
of her face. Jack caught the drift, perched me on his shoulder,
and waded into the knee-deep mud of the narrow, straight path
that led toward town. This gesture gave the celebrating sourdoughs an idea. In the twinkling of an eye Marie and Lucy were
shoulder riding uptown also. Then the town band went into
action.

This unit consisted of a cornet and a harmonica, fingered and
blown by a couple of pleasant fellows dolled up in derby hats,
denim overalls and rubber hip boots, who stood in the doorway
of a blocky shack at the edge of the town proper. The one with
the horn really had a set of bellows. The high notes of his "Gerry
Owen"—the marching song of the late General George Arm-
strong Custer—probably were heard by those still aboard the
Yucatan and even caused a slab sign overhead which read SIL-
VER KING SALOON to turn momentarily spastic.

We turned onto Main Street, Nome's thoroughfare—a civic
convenience that was distinguished by crooked boardwalks
on each side choked with dogs, Indians and other of the
local citizenry—and it boasted of more churned mud than
the paths that led off haphazardly to the shacks. Here our
respective bearers bucked us off on the walks and I got a
chance to look around.

Signs, some of them burned into the wood and others paint
gobbed, gave notice that this lucky corner of the world was the
home of the GOLDEN GATE HOTEL, the A.T. COMMERCIAL CO.,
ERICKSON'S RESTAURANT, THORNTON'S RESTAURANT, SUTTER'S

96

JEWELRY STORE, the *Nugget* newspaper, NORTHERN MERCAN-
TILE CO. CHILDBERG'S BANN, E.B. SWEETWATER CO. NAYTHING IN
CO., CHILBERG'S BANK, E. B. SWEETWATER CO. ANYTHING IN HARD-
WARE AND HEAVY EQUIPMENT. IF WE HAVEN'T GOT IT—YOU CAN'T
GET IT!, and the YUKON TRADING CO., a peaked-roof, slob of a
log structure that I learned later was a recently forged link in
the blossoming chain of enterprises being engineered by Will
Burke and Al Boyd.

So far as the fourteen saloons and two dance halls figure
in the panorama of that year, their printed messages ranged
from THE GREAT NORTHERN SALOON, THE NUGGET, THE MINER,
LA BELLE MARIE and LA BELLE CONTESSA, to a pipsqueak of
an eatery—THE HASH KNIFE—which sported a sign almost
as large as the place itself. For the rest, Nome looked as if
a cyclone had grabbed up a couple of lumberyards somewhere,
got tired of the load, and thrown it away in bunches.

"Not very inspiring, is it?"

Apparently Jack had misread my preoccupation with the
scene, and I can't blame him there. Surely the town was no
chamber of commerce pride and joy. Jack assumed that I was
down in the mouth, but just the opposite was true. I fell in love
with Nome *and* Alaska at that moment. I can find—even today
—no plausible reason for it. The country at that time probably
was guilty of the most impossible, if not improbable, civilization yet known to man. However, I felt suddenly as if I owned
every sliver of wood and gob of mud.

"Oh! It's—it's just wonderful!"

"What?" Pulling me around to face him, Jack looked down
and his expression suggested that he believed I'd gone potty.
Then he grinned and laid the back of his hand against my
cheek. "You've got to have a high fever. You're seeing things."

I was too far gone to appreciate any brand of humor, good
or bad.

"Jack! You can have your office in one of those buildings!"

"Sure, sure can."

"I'll make your lunch every day. That way we can save money,
and—"

"Indeed yes. That's very important."

"And when I get off work I can come down and help you—"

"Belay, girl!" Jack roared. "If we stand here yipping any longer, we'll lose Lucy and Al!" He indicated a spot up the street where flashes of Marie and the Boyds showed through the crowd as they fought to keep their places on the walk. "Come on! Lift your feet!" Grabbing my hand, he led off at a pace that had me flying at his heels like the tail of a kite. A few minutes under this head of steam filled the bill, and we caught them at what passed for a street corner, where Marie was in the process of taking her leave.

"The *Yale* will be blundering off for St. Michael in an hour or two and I've got to be on it. Papa frets when he's kept waiting. Meantime, I want to look up some friends."

She kissed Lucy, shook Al's hand, and turned to me. "You're going to fit nicely up here, little one." She gave my arm an affectionate pinch. "Just stay as sweet as you are." Serenely ignoring Jack, she jumped off the walk and began slogging diagonally across the street toward Erickson's Café.

"Whew!" Jack whistled. "I've been slapped down in my day. But never like that. What did I do to her?"

"Nothing." Al's voice was gruff and iced with an irritation he didn't try to conceal. "I like that kid. But she can be trying. It's one thing to have a mind of your own; it's another to be guilty of bad taste. Careful, now."

As we entered a path to our right he stopped and pointed ahead. Underfoot, a choppy ribbon of planking stretched past an uneven formation of shacks and disappeared around a pair of one-story, fortlike buildings about 200 yards beyond.

"Stay on these planks," Al cautioned, "otherwise you'll find yourself hock deep in tundra."

As we neared the structures it became evident that we were on the home plates of the N-C BOTTLING WORKS, and the CAR-MACK STABLES, and the latter sign gave Jack an idea.

"Al, I wonder if I can't make a deal to keep my livestock there?"

"Why not? They keep some mules. About a dozen, I think. Tell Jules Carmack I sent you over."

Ten minutes later, after making another fishhook twist, we stood in front of a roomy, rough-lumber cabin—which I eventually learned was the only one in Nome that was duded up with chintz window curtains. Grunting like a hog in clover, Al opened the door and herded us inside a room that had been dedicated to good living. Several nice prints were nailed to the four walls, a rack to the right was crammed with books, and in an opposite corner a small sewing table was loaded with fat folds of bright cloth in the middle of which nestled a yellow wicker sewing basket brimming with spools of thread and skeins of yarn. Animal skins covered the floor—lynx, caribou, bear and mountain sheep—and a paunchy couch near the bookcase set the style for the comfortable assembly of leather-covered chairs that hadn't been designed for speed either. To the left were two more rooms. In the first was a bed burdened with blankets, and in the second a square black Yukon stove, hemmed in by kettles, skillets and pots and pans.

Without ceremony, Al fell into the nearest chair.

"Man," he breathed gratefully, "sure, an' there's no place like home."

Lucy announced her intention of hitting the hay and offered to show me to my quarters first. Jack gave me a quick peck, then went off to make arrangements for quartering his livestock and finding himself a room at the Golden Gate.

The shack to which Lucy led me, up a short trail in back of the Boyd cabin, belonged to Jake Phariss, a friend of theirs who'd taken off for the Cleary Creek gold strike and expected to be gone a year or more. Until he came back I could call the place my own. There wasn't much to it, aside from a potbellied stove and a woodbox, a floor skin or two, a rocker and a chair, a bed and cupboard, and an assortment of kitchenware, but I felt as if I'd fallen heir to Mrs. Astor's country estate.

Lucy built a fire in the stove, and advised me to take a nap; then we'd go to the bathhouse and afterward to dinner at Thornton's Restaurant.

I tossed on the bed for awhile, thinking of ways to save money, planning my wedding—and wondering when I would see Will Burke. Each time I thought of Jack the shadow of Will fell across my mind. I don't suppose I allowed myself any explicit misgivings at that moment; I was still too deliriously in love to imagine that anything could go wrong. I had no sense of conflicting loyalties, yet some insistent fear must have nagged at me. I realized that I was too fired up to sleep and decided to take a walk. Passing back through the Boyd cabin on my way to the street, I found Al in the office and he beckoned me inside.

"Your trouble is easy to diagnose," he said when I told him I was too restless to sleep. "You're just sitting tall in the saddle. Happens to everybody at first sight of this country. Tell you what, there's nothing like a shopping tour to relax a lady, and you might as well start getting what you need now. Why don't you go over to our commissary and ask for Jim McLaurin or Andy Whipple and tell them I said to outfit you for fall and winter wear? You'll need a lot of stuff and knickknacks for your cabin too."

"But how do I pay for it? I only have a little money left."

"You pay for it out of wages, when it's convenient for you," he said, and told me how to get to the commissary.

The Yukon Trading Company, like other stores that Will and Al owned in Fairbanks, Sitka, Anchorage and Fort Gibbon, was operated as a sort of serve-yourself warehouse and stocked everything from cheese to horse collars. In Nome the floor space of the half-log, half-frame building was occupied by long tables that supported heaps of blankets, bolt cloth, heavy clothing, boots, bedrolls, tarps, iron kettles, pots and pans, eating tools, dog harness, rawhide whips, rope, paint, hatchets, long-bladed knives, and furs. Shelves around the four walls sagged under an overload of canned food. Picks, shovels, axes, heavy rifles and fishing poles had been stacked wherever a spot of ground showed itself. Flanked by two huge rolls of greased paper and spools of hemp twine, a short counter at the far end fronted a half-open door that let to a storage lean-to. As I entered the place a thin, semibald, blue-eyed fellow—perhaps three years my senior—charged in from the back, swept around the counter in the grand manner of a born floorwalker, and held up a finger. His smile uncovered a gold tooth in front, and he was decked out in a red woolen shirt, blue jeans and knee-length, lavishly beaded Indian moccasins.

"Good afternoon, miss. I'm Andy Whipple. May I help?"

I told him who I was, repeated Al's instructions, and met his outstretched hand with my own. Had he applied the same action that followed to a pump handle, he would have drowned himself.

A short time later, a stack of clothes was piled on the counter—several green- and red-checked shirts; a half-dozen pairs of heavy black pants; ten pairs of thick red socks; three pairs of felt boots; two pairs of beaded, hand-worked Indian moccasins for indoor wear; six suits of long underwear; a skin-tight silk parka to be worn over the shirt; a short-waisted blue mackinaw and an overall parka cross-stitched with red, green and yellow thread and hood-rimmed with wolf hackles; twelve pairs of mittens and an armload of fuzzy scarves of assorted colors.

Andy totaled up the bill—$106.19, a sum that staggered me. I still have the bill, yellowed, faded and ragged, and when I run across it I recall the thrill I felt at owning those duds. What did it matter if I was crushed with debt? They made me an Alaskan!

When I tried to cart off the load, I found I had bitten off more than I could chew, and I asked Andy if he could deliver the bundle.

"We don't have any delivery service for the lighter merchandise," he said. "However, in your case, we'll see what we can do—"

Going to the door, he squinted up and down the street. Then suddenly he began waving and hollering. Seconds later he was followed inside by a hulking man of fifty or so, whose clothes, from wolfskin cap to rubber boots, were caked with mud. A wide leather belt secured by a brass buckle circled his middle and imprisoned a hatchet, crowbar and a buckhorn butcher knife.

"Lady, here, needs some portage," Andy said. "My name's Andy Whipple. Yukon Trading Company. Can you give us a hand, sir?" He indicated the packages with a flip of his hand.

"Glad to. I'm Jack Pace."

"This is Miss Margaret Knudsen."

"Pleased, ma'am. Ready?" He tucked the parcels under his arms. "You lead off."

Naturally such generosity surprised me. You just didn't call in a stranger and ask him to become a beast of burden.

"Why, this is very nice of you! But I couldn't impose like that! It's asking too much!"

Mr. Pace's frown was one of bewilderment. Then he made an observation that summed up in twelve words the philosophy that has ruled the Alaskan brotherhood since the first white man set foot on that terrain. I never forgot the man's simple lesson.

"What's that got to do with it? You need help, don't you?"

Still shaking my head over the situation, I trudged ahead of him to the Boyd cabin, which now, in the murkiness of late afternoon, showed lights at the windows. At the doorstep Mr. Pace deposited my packages and held out his hand.

"I'd like to meet your folks, miss. But I'm a carpenter and there aren't too many of us around. I've been on the job for fourteen hours straight. I'm tired. Good luck." He touched his cap and slogged off toward town.

In the living room I found Al and Lucy up and looking as if they had never lost an hour's sleep in their lives. To their obvious amusement I opened my bundles and insisted upon admiring comments on every article I'd bought—not once but twice.

"All right." Lucy chuckled as the signs apparently pointed to a third exposition. "So you're a whale of an operator clothes-horse. Now you'd better put your stuff away. We'll be starting for the bathhouse and dinner soon." She left the room and returned to hand me a claw hammer and a fistful of nails. "You've no closet. That means you'll need to be pioneerlike. Now git!"

Back in my hut, I had only started when Lucy's voice sounded from her back door. "Margaret! Come here a minute. You have a caller."

"Caller?"

"Yes. Tall, dark and the devil's own."

For a second I didn't get the drift, I was so bemused by housekeeping. Then in a second I'd dropped hammer and nails and was flying down the path to the Boyds'.

"Will!"

He was standing in the center of the room as I rushed in.

"Margaret, my dear."

The ring of his voice brought back a hundred warm memories and suddenly I was feeling very much at peace with the world. Where my love for Jack Bartlett was like champagne, the sight of Will was the smell of pine needles and freshly peeled logs on a spring day, the caress of familiar clothes or a favorite chair, the luxury of fine music, good food, hot water and blazing fireplaces on cold nights—and the security of the earth itself. I couldn't have resisted my next move had it meant death at the stake. Running forward, I threw myself into his arms.

Then the door opened behind me and I was torn from Will's embrace and sent spinning into a chair. I looked up to see Jack standing at a crouch, about six feet from Will, his eyes glaring, his face wearing the set, foolish look of a man close to madness.

"What's this?"

I was so frightened that I could not muster the strength to make a sound. I think anyone would have been tongue-tied; and it had never fallen to me to provoke a fight between a berserk Viking and a black Irish giant.

Lucy had more alloy in her bones than I could find in mine. Moving quietly to my side, she reached down, hauled me upright, and curled her arm around my shoulders.

"Not hurt—are you?"

Since my answer came out a strangled gulp, I shook my head to indicate that I was still whole. Then Lucy turned, and walking up to Jack, she lifted her chin and practically spit in his eye.

"Before you make a bigger fool of yourself, Bartlett," she said, her voice dripping ice, "perhaps you should hear something. Will and Margaret are friends. That and nothing more. This is the first time they've seen each other for some time. Their actions are entirely excusable, if a brother's embrace of a sister is excusable." Then she took on Will, but in an entirely different tone and manner.

"Will, Margaret and Jack became engaged to be married on the trip up here. I ask you to forget this unpleasantness for that reason. After all, jealousy can be the root of a lot of trouble. I'm sure you understand."

Will didn't reply for a moment, and his face wore the look that I mentioned earlier. I mean that his expression was impassive and inscrutable and his eyelids dropped, unblinking. Then, while I held my breath, he smiled, stepped forward, and extended his hand to Jack.

"Sorry, Bartlett. I meant no offense. And my heartiest congratulations."

But his generous gesture only nourished Jack's senseless rage. Balling his fingers into fists, he crouched even lower and his eyes traveled over Will as if he were seeking a particular point to center his attack.

"Stow it, mister! I'm going to bust you up so bad you'll wish you had nine lives!"

Will moved back a pace or two, pulled in his belt a notch, and shrugged his shoulders. "Come and get me," he murmured.

Then I located my vocal chords, and although what followed was a series of screeches rather than coherent communication, it probably saved the day. Which is to say it transferred Jack's gorge from Will to me.

"How can you treat Will like that? He didn't do anything! You let him alone! You're acting crazy! I haven't seen him for a dog's age—and you come in here and—and make a fool of me —and hurt his feelings—and—you leave him alone!"

Straightening, Jack ran his hand through his tangled hair and faced me. "So, my devoted little bride-to-be is on the other side? Nice to know where I stand! Okay! Take him! You can have him! He'll need you—for a lot of reasons—when I run into him again!"

He wheeled and plunged through the door and into the path where his cursing and snarling probably caused a good many people to wonder if a lunatic asylum shouldn't be next on Nome's civic-expansion program. I can't recall when I've cried any harder. "This is terrible! I'm so ashamed! I don't know what to do! You've all been so good to me—and it's all my fault!"

But Will, bless him, merely chuckled, lifted me from the chair and rubbed down my face with his handkerchief. "Here, here! It's not your fault. No one can be responsible for the actions of others. Forget it, now. Hear me?" Lifting my chin, he gave me a smile and pinched my nose. "Welcome to Alaska.

You're going to live a happy life, make a packet of money, and raise all of your children to be telephone operators!"

"Then you're not mad at Jack?"

"Well, I don't like him too much right now. But I won't bear a grudge. Anyone can lose his head, though I hope he straightens himself out, for your sake." He winked, and pulled up the collar of his jacket. Turning to Al and Lucy, he said, "I'm sorry I can't have dinner with you people tonight. But I've got a sick Indian up the river and I'll have to look after him; I can't bring him into town. See you tomorrow at the office."

Unwilling to inflict any further tears on Al and Lucy, I ran to my cabin and flung myself on the bed where I cried through four handkerchiefs. Lucy tactfully stayed away until I could recuperate. Then she came in to suggest I get dressed.

I couldn't quite give up before one more display of temper. "I don't see why Al didn't take up for Will," I said.

"There was no need for it."

"But—in your own home. I'm not criticizing, but Will didn't deserve that—"

"Hang on, honey. Al wouldn't interfere in a fight between two men *or* two women. You don't do that up here. You let people slug it out on their own."

"Yes—but if Jack catches Will, he'll beat him up."

"Oh?" Lucy straightened my clothes a bit and began to pin up my disheveled hair. "Don't bet any money on it.

"Come on now, off to a hot bath and dinner."

I have often wondered why I didn't realize then that it was Will I loved and not Jack. I had gone to Will's defense at once. I had even upbraided Lucy for Al's hands-off policy. I had always been taught that a woman's loyalty belonged unquestioningly to her fiancé or husband; and certainly a girl should be proud as a peacock of a man as protective and possessive as Jack. Yet for all of this, it was Jack's treatment of Will that had hurt me.

But Al was hollering for us, and Lucy bundled me up to go out.

There was no plumbing in Nome so the residents took their

baths at public bath-houses. I'll never forget my embarrassment at my first visit to one of them. The one favored by the Boyds was located north and east of the main stem near Nome's dance halls, and it consisted of twelve shacks, all spurting steam through their chinks and fairly rocking from the activity within. A well-worn plank path ran between them, dividing them into blocks of six, and no signs were needed to indicate those reserved for gents and those at the disposal of ladies. The squeals, shrieks and titters that came from one side blended with the roars, shouts and amiable cursing from the other.

The arrangements inside the women's section included a small dressing room ringed by wooden benches. Irregular strips of planking in back provided a run-off for the excess water that squirted in every direction from a network of lead pipes plugged at the ends, drilled with holes and extending head high from the back wall. Lending a common touch, a dozen naked women scampered about, throwing water at each other and apparently determined to outdo each other in developing laryngitis from the giggles. Some of these were middle-aged, but the others were young and pretty, and it took no exhaustive study, even for a greenhorn, to recognize their professional station in life. I have always felt like a fool when stripped down, even before my doctor, and so it was that I immediately began to halt and stumble.

"Lucy, I can't undress before these people! I'll simply die! Those girls!"

"Simpleton!" she snapped, slipping out of her mackinaw and yanking at a boot. "Don't get prissy, miss! You want a bath, you'd better forget your modesty and shuck off."

"But before those girls?"

"They've got as much right here as you, Miss Prude! This is frontier country, not Blair, Nebraska, or Los Angeles or Seattle. These girls have their place. It's a lonely country for a man without a wife. They won't bite you either. They won't even speak to you unless you speak first. Besides, most of them are good people, aside from their profession, and they've proved it. There's been more than one man nursed through a sickness by one of these girls. And there are few prospectors who haven't accepted a grubstake from them. So I wouldn't be casting any boulders, if I were you."

Such a skinning smarted some, and I had it in mind to sulk a spell. However, since Lucy ignored me after the barrage and went to the showers, I decided to let sleeping dogs lie, and managed to get separated from my clothes. The luxury of the scalding water and soap gave me a great lift, and by the time we had finished and started downtown I was up to snuff, mentally and physically.

"Wow! Everybody and his pup are out on the town tonight," Al observed as we swung into Main Street. "But it's always like that when a boat comes in."

Everybody and his pup were right in the *middle* of town. If the street had been crowded with the arrival of the *Yucatan*, it now was practically convulsed with humanity, and getting to Thornton's Restaurant, about halfway downstreet, took nothing short of a fight.

The place itself was but a succession of partitions added to accommodate the need for expansion in a growing town, and patterned and furnished along the general mold of all cafés in early Alaska. It was big, rattle-boned, whopper-jawed and equipped at the far end with a long, unsteady bar behind which two gentlemen in fancy vests, peppermint-striped shirts and string ties, served pop-skull drinks. It enclosed tables packed so snugly that in passing one needed to travel crabwise. Its frontier aspect included a dirt floor, and the place smelled of tobacco smoke, whisky and fried food. Here again it looked as if everyone in town knew Al and Lucy.

We had only stepped in when the shouts and hail-fellows started up. In the next twenty minutes we were all pretty well roughed up, and with both the Boyds introducing me I found myself shaking with one hand, then the other. I don't remember half the people I met, since Nome in that era was composed more or less of a transient population—here today and gone tomorrow. But some of them were to become fine friends.

One of these was Charlie Thornton, the proprietor, a chubby, pink-faced fellow who eventually became a wealthy man by grubstaking some successful miners and investing wisely in Alaska real estate. Until his death in 1916 he made it a habit to visit Will and me periodically at one or another of our homes. He always stayed as long as he pleased and he couldn't have been more welcome anywhere in the world.

Another was Tex Rickard, who even then wore a zipper on his lip, had the heart of a tiger, and couldn't control a streak of generosity that bordered on folly. At that time Tex owned the Great Northern Saloon, a shack which he had ballooned and parlayed into a gold mine, and he was also distinguished for being the employer and gallant of the celebrated Cherry Malotte, the most astonishingly beautiful girl I have ever seen.

There was also Rex Beach, a New York dancer turned prospector, a lithe, sandy-haired, courtly bravo who with Barney McCready—then working as a bartender for Rickard—later bought the Great Northern. Eventually Rex returned to New York City, and—a man who boasted that he could turn his hand to anything—became a successful writer and made a fortune at it. I can testify that his novel *The Poilers* is authentic Alaska.

We finally got to a table. Perked up by the hot bath and the walk in the cold air, my palate was aching. From force of habit, as I sat down to order dinner, I thought of Jack and looked over the crowd, hoping to pick him out. But I could see him nowhere, and I began to feel a nagging remorse.

I could have been more understanding, I told myself; he had reacted to Will so violently only because he felt loyal and protective toward me. At the same time another thought struck me a chilling blow: I suddenly recalled that never at any stage of our courtship had Jack told me he loved me. His proposal of marriage on the deck of the *Yucatan* had been made almost mockingly, even offensively. There was none of the tenderness I had always associated with such an emotional occasion. But then, he loathed sentimentality, I reasoned, and had only covered his feelings by his brittle, offhand proposal. Still, I could not escape an uneasy feeling of doubt and frustration. I need not have worried for fear of not seeing him again that evening.

I was distracted by the arrival at our table of a stooped, watery-eyed man of about sixty, dressed in the usual Alaskan tenting and wearing a brass star on the lapel of his mackinaw.

"Steep!" Al said, rising to shake his hand, and nearly scuttling a waiter who had come up with an armload of plattered salmon, boiled potatoes, stewed tomatoes, coffee and sourdough bread. "How's the lawman dodge?"

"Tol'able quiet. 'Lo, Miss Lucy."

Al introduced me and kicked a vacant chair in Steep's direction, inviting him to have a meal with us.

"Nope. Thanks. Filled up an hour ago. But I'll set a minute. Fack is, I've some checkin' to do. Mebbe yew folks can h'ep. Lookin' fer a feller." Slumping into the chair, Steep dragged off his cap and stuffed it inside his mackinaw.

Then I could see what had prompted his odd name. He was completely bald and his head was cast in the general shape of an inverted ice-cream cone. Later I learned that he had a Christian name, but everyone found it unpronounceable, and so no one tried to tongue it, much less spell it. He had made his living by manufacturing bootlaces and leather belts before his appointment as deputy in the marshal's office. A year previously some wag had tagged him with the nickname, Steeplehead. The label, shortened to "Steep," had stuck, despite what he considered the dignity and importance of his office. But he never gave up trying to get himself addressed as Sergeant.

"Yew people come back on the *Yucatan*, didn't yew?" he went on. "Yew 'quainted with a young man name o' Bartlett?"

We all jumped at that, since Jack had been in such a beastly mood when he left the Boyd cabin. I had a sharp premonition of trouble—big trouble. "He's my fiancé. What has he done?"

"Suthin' purty serious, miss. Know whur I can find him?"

"Why, I don't know. But, please, what is it?"

Steep's evaluation of Jack's present position with the law proved to be on course, although it had its humorous facets. Pieced out with what Jack told me later and what I heard at his subsequent arrest and trial, I'm sure no one could argue that he had been unlucky the way it ended.

After he left us he had barged uptown, looking for either a fight or a frolic, and wound up in the Nugget Saloon where he had his first drink. A second and third followed, and since he had laid off the stuff for more than a year, the jolts hit him between the horns. He was ready for anything at this point and made off toward the Yukon House, downstreet, where the noise indicated that a good deal of partying was under way.

In transit, however, he observed a pair of good-looking women leaning from an upper-story window, greeting various men who passed below. He couldn't have known that he was looking at Mrs. John Elsen, the wealthy widow of a Canadian banker, and her friend Mrs. Jake Roberts, the leader of Nome's social set and wife of the town's outstanding civic pillar and politician. The ladies were in the Roberts' living quarters above Jake Roberts' own store, but Jack was yet to discover the difference between women leaning from windows in Alaska and those yelling at men from doorways in Hong Kong. So he took the obvious step for a man in his currently woozy and reckless state.

"Hello, girls. Just got off the *Yucatan.* You holding open house?"

"Well!" Mrs. Roberts laughed. "Another stranger in town!"

"Yep. And I could use some friends. May I come up?"

The reactions of the women can easily be imagined. Jack's application of the term "girls" to their matronly figures surely was not unwelcome, misinterpreted or not. Further, Alaskan social codes, as I have mentioned, permitted women a freer relationship with men—at least within certain bounds—and Jack's male beauty was second to that of no man's.

"We know about everyone else in town," Mrs. Roberts replied. "Might as well get acquainted with you. Bring up some champagne."

An hour later the three of them had tapped four bottles, and on the heels of Jack's tenth story they were about to crack another when a tubby, button-nosed fellow, dressed in a derby, peg-top pants and a knee-length topcoat, came in. Smiling pleasantly, he waddled to a wall closet and began peeling off the outer layers of his clothing.

"Hey!" Jack exploded. "What's going on? Who're you?"

"Me?" The man's double chin quivered from the force of his astonishment. "I'm Jake—Jake Roberts."

Tossing off his drink, Jack came out of his chair, set the empty globe on a nearby table, and pointed to the door. "All right, Jakie, beat it!"

"Me? Say, have you got bats in your belfry?"

"Probably, probably. But that's not the point. Just leave me and my, uh, ladies of the night alone and we'll have no trouble."

"Ladies—ladies of the—" Mrs. Roberts' outraged honk would have attracted the attention of a migration of wild geese three miles up. "You crazy—I'm—that's Jake! He's—"

"We're getting in a rut," Jack interrupted. "So that's Jake. I wouldn't care if he was Cornelia, the Mother of the Gracchi. Now, fatty, do you leave? Or do I launch you?"

"You're the one that's going to clear out!" Jake bawled.

That was all Jack needed. Scooping Jake up, he opened the door and hurled him down the stairs, legs and arms flailing and pockets emptying themselves of everything from lead pencils to peanuts and sen-sen.

"Now, girls," Jack said, returning to his seat and jovially rubbing his hands. "Let's get back to our champagne. I apologize for the interruption."

"Interruption?" Mrs. Roberts could only moan and stare at the door in shock and dismay. "That's my husband you just killed."

"Husband?" For all of his drink-befuddled condition, Jack caught the pitch and recognized the need for making himself scarce. "I'm off. I'll get him to a doctor if he needs it."

But such consideration, if laudable, was not required. Jack's display of informality had not set well with Jake, and he was at that moment reliving the incident with Steep in a wild and deafening manner, highlighted by the demand that Jack be hanged or banished to the ice fields.

"So," Steep concluded, pulling his cap on and standing up, "I'm lookin' fer him. If yew can lead me to him, miss, I'd be obleeged. Mister Roberts is purty miffed."

"I'll try." My backbone felt colder than a welldigger's nose in the Yukon, and my hands began to tremble. It wasn't difficult to forget Jack's recent insults to Will and me or his questionable manners at the Roberts' now that he was in serious trouble. "I'll go with you anyway."

As Jack had announced his intention of staying at the Golden Gate Hotel temporarily, we decided to shake it down first. Here we struck oil. Jack was sleeping it off in his room when we collared the room clerk, an unkempt old souse whose name I recall as Tom Rafferty, and had him roust Jack out.

"New boy friend?" Jack asked, indicating Steep. But there was no meanness in his tone, no sarcasm or resentment. Like a Nebraska dust devil, he could always blow himself out as suddenly as he blew himself in. "Where'd you get this one, and why?" He laughed.

Steep motioned us to a caribouhide davenport across the lobby. When we were seated he pulled up a wooden rocker and sat down facing us.

"Name Bartlett?" he queried. His manner was that of the big-time sleuth about to put the pump on a hardened, clever criminal. "Jack Bartlett?"

"That's me, Sherlock. What can I do for you?"

"Don't git smart," Steep said darkly, fixing Jack with what he probably imagined as a piercing glance. "I'll clink yew so fast yew'll think yew was rollin' downhill."

"All right." Jack chuckled. "Bang away."

"Whur was yew, say, couple hours ago?"

"Uptown."

"Whur—uptown?"

"The Nugget."

"See anybody? Any women, fer instance?"

"Are you," Jack roared happily, "asking me if I tangled with a couple of crows and set the husband of one on his ear?"

"So, yew admit it?" Steep mumbled sorrowfully, plainly disappointed to secure Jack's confession without recourse to the rack, thumbscrew or rubber hose. "Have to take yew in. An' it's my duty to warn yew—"

"Can it, old-timer," Jack interrupted. "I'm a lawyer, among other things. Now, what's the procedure in this prairie-dog village? Is my offense bailable?"

"Wal, can't say—yit."

"You can't say? What kind of a cop are you? What am I charged with?"

"Fer throwin' Jake Roberts outa his own house—yew know thet!"

"Okay, so I know that. What I specifically want to learn is

what local statute I have violated. Mayhem? Attempted murder? Assault and battery?"

"Told yew I don't know!" Steep sputtered. "Got to see Judge Scott first. He's the one thet decides!"

"Well, I demand to know what the charge is against me, before I submit to arrest. I told you I'm a lawyer. I know my rights." In Dutch or not, Jack obviously was having the time of his life, and troubled as I was, the growing, bewildered discomfiture of Steep was beginning to limber up my funny muscles also. Apparently Jack was working an angle in his own behalf. It soon took shape. "Now," he went on, "make up your mind."

"Don't have to!" Steep yapped. "I can pinch—any time I want!"

"Not me you can't."

"But I'm the law! Unner'stand? I'm the law!"

"True, very true," Jack agreed thoughtfully. "We must also remember there is such a thing as civil rights. You haul me in without charging me, and I shall have you jerked up on a charge of unlawful arrest, maybe even police brutality."

"Yew can't do it!"

"I surely can and I will."

"Wal." Steep grew cautious. "You sure about thet?"

"Sure as rain." Jack made a housetop of his fingers and studied the ceiling. "Tell you what. There's a way we can work this out. Since I'm a law-abiding man and a lawyer, I'll help you. Get a pencil and paper from that clerk and I'll make out a warrant for my own arrest. I'll charge myself with, say, simple assault. How's that, for a start?"

"Don't know." Steep floundered. "Could it be changed to suthin' wuss—if the judge wants?"

"Certainly."

"Be fittin' an' proper—all inside the law?"

"Absolutely. The procedure is known as a citizen's arrest. In this case I'm arresting myself. Aided, of course, by an officer."

"It's a deal." Loping to the desk, Steep took a piece of paper and a pencil from Rafferty, returned and handed them to Jack. "Write."

Shaking with laughter, Jack wrote out the warrant. It charged, in part, that "one Jack Bartlett, white, American, did willfully and maliciously take umbrage on this date with one Jake Roberts, white, American, in the latter's home, and in the ensuing altercation Jack Bartlett did make earnest onslaught on the person of Jake Roberts, an act that culminated in the person of Jake Roberts being violently ejected from his house by way of a stairway, such act to have caused the plaintiff, Jake Roberts, extreme mental anguish and physical lacerations and contusions," et cetera.

"Okay," Jack said, stabbing in the final punctuation mark. "Read it and sign it."

Steep took the document and held it up to the light. But before he had waded halfway through it a look of disbelief came over his face and a thin sweat broke out on his upper lip. "What's this?" he brayed. "I don't savvy any of it! Whut's it say?"

"It's legal language. Sign it, and take me in."

Steep's eyes rolled helplessly. Then he put pencil to paper with a pressure that looked as if he were trying to cut his initials in the table. "Wuss mess o' words ever was writ," he complained bitterly. Folding the square, he stuffed it into a pocket and stood up. "Come on. Peaceable, mind yew."

"Okay. But wait a second. Can I stand trial right away? If not, I want to arrange for bail."

"Yew can stand trial in fifteen minutes if yew want. Judge Scott likes to convict 'em quick. Quicker the better."

"He on the bench, now?"

"Probly. Sent fer him, soon's I went lookin' fer yew."

"Fine." Jack gave my cheek a peck and shoved me toward the door. "Get Al, honey. Ask him to come over to court. I want a friend outside, looking in. No telling what kind of railroads these rubes have on their books."

I was in the street in a second, for I needed Al's strong arm at that moment even more than Jack did. Despite the lightness with which Jack took Steep, there was a hard core to the old deputy's attitude that meant business. My people in Blair had taught me that jail was a disgrace. I recalled instances back home where men had spent the night in poky and had never again been able to hold up their heads. Al was so well-known that he might even be a friend of such powerful and forbidding characters as judges. I fairly flew through the mud.

Luckily I found Al and Lucy coming out of Thornton's on their way home. I gasped out the story of Jack's plight and repeated his request.

"You can bet I'll back him. Both of you come with me," Al ordered, swinging up the walk. "But I wouldn't worry, Margaret, Judge Scott's a fair man and a tolerant one."

Nome's courthouse, which was under Federal jurisdiction, was located a few blocks beyond the baths, next to a hutch with a sign that read CHURCH OF JESUS, OUR SAVIOUR. It could justifiably lord it over the town's other structures; it was larger, had a pitched roof with real shingles, and sported an American flag above its door.

The interior was lighted by gas lanterns. A seating capacity of possibly 100 was provided by benches that stretched the width of the room. A plank dais at the far end supported a table and two chairs, one for the judge and the other for witnesses. Six stools to the far right of the "bench" were reserved for the culprit set, and there was no jury box. Such a division of authority as that represented by a jury system was unthinkable to a judge of that era, except in a murder trial, and ranked with such foolishness as pardons, paroles and prison-inmate rehabilitation.

By the time we arrived Judge Vernon Scott, a shambling, weather-beaten man, was already seated behind the table, adjusting his specs, rearranging the coat of his baggy gray suit, and running his fingers through his kinky white hair.

The place was packed with entertainment seekers who evidently had been attending a prayer meeting in the church, but had deserted their pastor for Judge Scott's meatier, if less uplifting, program. The principals were present. Jack sprawled lazily on one of the stools. Mrs. Elsen and Mrs. Roberts, dressed fit to kill, sat stiffly on a front-row bench, sandwiching a red-faced and perspiring Jake. Warrant in hand, Steep stood stiffly before the bench.

We had barely taken seats when the judge raised the wooden bung starter which served as his gavel and took a tremendous cut at the table.

"Court is now in session. There will be no talking and no smoking. Steep, what is the case pending?"

"Jake Roberts versus Jack Bartlett, Yer Honor."

"The circumstances?"

"Wal, I got a warrant here. It says whut there is to say."

"A warrant? Who wrote it?"

"Him." Steep pointed at Jack. "He writ it. Says he's a lawyer. Told me I couldn't arrest him 'thout chargin' him with suthin' or other."

"What!" Scott choked, his mouth open and his Adam's apple going mad. "The accused—you mean—he wrote out his own warrant?"

"Yow. Thet's correct."

"By whose authority—in heaven's name?"

"How should I know?" Steep cried. "I don't unner'stand any o' this!"

Lifting his gavel, Scott brought it crashing down again. "Steep, are you drunk?"

"Yew know I ain't!"

"Why didn't you follow our usual pattern? Arrest the man on suspicion? You should know that I am the only person, under the jurisdiction of our local government, who is authorized to issue warrants and fix charges."

"Thet's whut I always thought!" Steep screeched. "But I ain't never tried to arrest a lawyer before! He filled me so fulla guff it was comin' out my ears! How'd I know he wasn't right?"

Scott whaled away at the table once more with his gavel. "Very well, Steep, very well. For the record, you may read it."

"Me? It ain't even in American!"

Leaning across the bench, Scott extended his hand and snapped his fingers. "Let me see it."

A few seconds later he smiled, then chuckled. Crumpling the document, he dropped it on the floor behind him, took a cloth from his pocket, and began polishing his specs.

"A citizen's arrest, eh," he said, addressing Jack. "And very professionally drawn. Even signed by our deputy marshal, giving the charge precedence over others of a more serious nature which could be presented later. All right, since you have named your own poison and I am bound by law to honor it, how do you plead?"

"Not guilty, Your Honor," Jack returned, rising to his feet and facing the bench, "and I further petition the court to find the charge of simple assault, as named in the warrant, a true and final bill. I make this petition on grounds that the plaintiff is not seriously injured and that there was no premeditation involved in the assault."

He had hardly uttered his last word before Jake Roberts was on his feet, waving a handkerchief to get Scott's attention.

"Your Honor!"

"Jake."

"Your Honor," Jake babbled, "I protest. Even the charge of assault and battery is insufficient. The indignity this man has visited upon my person! The embarrassment he has caused my wife and her friend."

"I've been embroiled in some crackbrained cases in my life," Scott interrupted gloomily, "but never one so palpably insane as this one."

"Your Honor, I was thrown—actually thrown—out of my own home! For no reason! And by a stranger, mind you!"

"Shut up, Jake!" Scott boomed. "Before you rupture yourself! I'll decide this case! Now you just tell me how badly you're hurt."

"Well," Jake groaned, "I'm skinned up. And I've got a knot on my head."

"Any bones broken?"

"No, I guess not."

"Very well." Scott took up his specs, saddled his nose once more, scraped his chair closer to the bench and addressed Jack again. "Mr. Bartlett, our judicial customs in Alaska differ considerably from the more decorous and more admirably detailed procedures in some areas Outside. Therefore I shall explain, since you are a stranger, that our marshal or his deputy generally acts as prosecuting attorney—with myself aiding in the interrogation of both sides. But you, as a defendant, are entitled to a lawyer. Do you want one? We have two in Nome. Both are very capable men."

"No sir," Jack returned. "I *am* a lawyer, as the deputy marshal has informed Your Honor."

"So be it. Under the law you are entitled to plead your own case, lawyer or not."

Hunching forward, he folded his hands on the bench, looked squarely at Jake and his ladies, frowned and pinched at his lower lip. He studied Jack's face for a minute, got up, took a turn around the bench and sat down.

"As there appears to be no premeditation involved here, or evidence of serious injury, the court will honor Mr. Bartlett's citizen's arrest on a charge of simple assault, a misdemeanor, although the procedure—in the instance of the warrant—is somewhat alien to our ordinary course of action. Steep, call Mrs. Roberts to the stand."

Under Steep's faltering questions, bolstered by Scott's precise interrogation, Mrs. Roberts told her story. She was followed to the stand by Mrs. Elsen and Jake, and at the end of testimony a storm of hoots, catcalls and laughter shook the courtroom. These demonstrations were quashed only by Scott's threats to clear the court. Several weeks went by before I discovered the reason for the crowd's lack of sympathy for them. A lot of people had been hurt by Jake's flair for greasy politicing and the social dictatorship of the two women, and they hadn't forgotten it.

But if the spectators had been delighted with the show put on by the Robertses and Mrs. Elsen, they practically tore down the rafters when Jack took the floor for his final argument. His defense was based on his inexperience with Alaskan custom and a sly reference to Jake's arrival on the scene in question. When he hinted that Jake's precipitous entrance had frightened him, a quick comparison of Roberts' squabby stature and Bartlett's brawny figure caused a dozen men to duck outside, holding their stomachs.

While he didn't conceal his admiration for Jack's courtroom technique and was obviously amused, Scott didn't see it Jack's way.

"Young man," he drawled at the conclusion, "my compliments. You should go far in your profession. I have seldom heard a more convincing summation or a clearer presentation of extenuating circumstances. But on the evidence here presented, I find you guilty. Five-hundred dollars fine or ten days in jail. I advise that you pay the fine if you can. Our jail is fit only for dog poisoners and suffragettes."

"Whom do I pay, Your Honor?" My heart nearly lost count at the sum levied, but Jack was grinning and there was a gleam of respect for Scott in his eyes.

"Give it to Steep. The marshal's office collects our fines. Anybody out there got a cigar?"

Jack plunked out the money, shook hands with Scott and Steep, and for the next ten minutes became a punching bag for congratulations and back slapping that was second only to the ones to which he had been subjected earlier aboard the *Yucatan*. Of course there were three people in the crowd who found it easy to abstain from the hurrahs. For instance, as he passed the Roberts and Mrs. Elsen, we both heard a large hiss.

"You dirty whelp!"

Jack stopped and looked about. Back stiffer than a banker's upper lip and face like a frozen pie, Mrs. Roberts stood near the door, arms folded and fronting for Jake, who looked like he wanted to cry. Jack's eyes traveled over Mrs. Roberts' form insultingly, from shoes to hairline.

"Shame, shame, Grandmother," he murmured. "Such language. At your age."

Outside we lost Al and Lucy when Jack suggested a cup of coffee before he took me home.

I had seen so much action and excitement for one eighteen-hour stretch that I was too tired to light into him, much as he had it coming. And the hurt of his intended infidelity lost weight with me when I considered that he could have been jugged for two, possibly three, years had Judge Scott been a judicial head-hunter. But the day was not to end comfortably or quietly.

The first sip of the hot stuff at a table in Erickson's crowded restaurant had barely gone down when a disheveled little riverman ran in, stopped short enough to plow up a cloud of dust, made a trumpet of his hands and began shouting.

"Mobright! Mobright! You here?"

His ruckus stilled the buzz of voices, and a square-jawed man, wearing the Northern Steamship Company insignia on his cap, left the men at the bar and rolled forward.

"What's up, Tod?"

"The lighter! The lighter—with them cows and chickens—it got away. Broke loose from the tug! Driftin off! Loaded with baggage too!"

"Broke loose? When— How th—?"

"Hey!" Jack was out of his chair by the time the pair reached the restaurant's swinging doors. But he was too late to stop them.

"They're talking about *my* cows and chickens," he yelled. "Margaret! You stay here!"

"No—no! My trunk's probably on it too! Oh! What happened?"

It was about eleven in the evening when we reached the pier. The tug was securely moored. But a small speck was spinning slowly in the distance. On dock the man called Mobright stood listening to a disjointed babble from a couple of his rats.

Jack threw me topside like a sack of spuds. Next he had a handful of Mobright's mackinaw.

"That's my stock out there! What're you going to do about it? *Wish* it back?"

"Your stock? I'm sorry, but there's nothing we can do now."

"Nothing you can do? Are you crazy? Get that tug going— go after it!"

"Not a chance. The current's got it, and this tug's a joke. Even if we could catch it, we'd run out of fuel before we got it halfway back. Then *we'd* be drifting off."

"Get the *Yucatan* after it!"

Mobright carefully disengaged Jack's grip and indicated the endless, gloomy reach of ocean with a nod. "See her any place out there? Half of her passengers decided to go back. So she left as soon as we pulled off the stock and the baggage and the mail."

"All right," Jack snarled, "but I'm going to sue that outfit of yours! For every penny it owns! And then some!"

"Don't blame you," Mobright said calmly. "Do the same myself, in your boots. I'll even let you know what caused it, when I find out."

"Why weren't *you* on the job? You were in Erickson's dump when it happened!"

"Man's got to eat," Mobright answered patiently. "Only takes three men to operate the tug. I went uptown to grub. That left Tod on duty. When I get it sifted over, as I said, I'll tell you."

"Easy come, easy go," Jack mused, as we sloshed back uptown. "This'll change our plans, for the time being. I'm sorry about your clothes."

"Pooh. Who cares about clothes? I'm sorry about those poor animals and chickens."

"Me, too, in a way. But I'm sorrier for us. Our stake's now the property of Father Neptune."

"Pooh. We'll get along. I've got a good job."

He stopped, took me in his arms, kissed me, then gave the death knell to my hopes. "I've got a few skins left—enough to set up a law practice. But remember this, my sweet. We don't get married until I can support you. If I can't support a wife— I don't have a wife."

I crept into bed that night with a chin that was hanging mighty low.

Chapter Seven

JACK rustled up enough furniture to knock the edges off a barren, dusty room above Eugene Chilberg's bank. He had his sign burned into the wood below its single window, sent Outside for three business suits, and sat back awaiting the visitation of fortune.

But it never came. At the end of six weeks he hadn't chopped out a nickel and the signals all pointed to more of the same in the future. Knowing what I do now, I can see a number of reasons for his failure. First, there were two practicing attorneys in Nome when he arrived. They already had what legal business existed, and that was precious little. This lack of opportunity stemmed in the main from the social and commercial structure of Nome itself.

Nome operated under the Common Consent form of government. The town was believed to have been the third American community to adopt this rule, the first being Cape Cod in 1620, and the second Sitka, Alaska. The phrase Common Consent government is very nearly self-explanatory. Briefly, the members of a community signed an agreement to obey by common consent all laws made and passed by their designated officials and to demand their observance from transients.

In Nome's case Common Consent rule was established in 1889, a year before the first big gold strike in the area at Anvil Creek, at a time when the camp was known as Anvil City. Improving on the archaic magistral system favored by the Pilgrim Fathers, Nome—like Sitka—dressed up its Common Consent structures by employing a mayor, chief of police, fire warden, municipal judges, a legislative council and health officer. However, the duties of these officials were extremely light. Since they had pledged their "consent" to the laws in force and were faced with disfavor or even boycott if they slipped, the ruling class of Nome generally made its word good. Therefore shady business practices or questionable ethics were held to a minimum. So much for Jack's chances in the fields of civil litigation.

On the criminal side, Nome was a far cry—regardless of what some historians say—from the Dodge City or Abilene, Kansas, of storied tale. Given a fast horse, a brace of small arms and a head start, a Western troublemaker could get a long way off before Johnny Law could have at him. But this fellow did not operate so dashingly and romantically in Alaska.

Regardless of the season, he was stuck with his mistake unless he chose to hide in the woods for the rest of his days. To get Outside in summer he must book passage on a ship for Seattle. But the authorities always had an eye on the dock and were on excellent terms with the shipowners and their captains and crews. In winter, of course, he was assured of no trouble with pursuit. If he could make it afoot across the ice packs of the Bering Sea to Seattle, it was felt that he deserved his freedom— whatever his transgression or crime. Students of Alaska will recall that surviving members of the Soapy Smith gang of thugs, fresh from the historic Chilkoot Trail rush, landed in Nome at one period or another. Somewhere along the way, however, they had taken a quick, moral bath. As a matter of fact a few of them became pretty good citizens. Perhaps someone had shown them a map of the Territory.

Criminal law offered no opportunities for Jack either. He was even denied the pennies that modern lawyers make from defending madams, gamblers, after-hours vendors of booze or perpetrators of simple assault.

The "consenters" felt that when miners came to town they were entitled to a little robust feminine companionship. Gambling kept money in circulation. There was no such thing as "after hours." So far as fist fighting was concerned, it was only another medium for blowing off steam.

It was Tex Rickard, I believe—one of the 1901 councilmen of Nome—who set the rules for polite fisticuffs. Tex decreed that all physical altercations in his Great Northern Saloon must be fought to a standstill or until the best man won. For this purpose the spectators must leave their tables and back up to the walls, leaving the gladiators room to punish each other properly. He would referee, and it made no difference which man won. The drinks would be on the house.

Tex's tactics gained widespread favor, not only among his commercial competitors, but in the ranks of the cantankerous and belligerent. Soon he found himself classed as both the instigator of a new social order and a fair referee. However, he eventually lost face. One night the foreman of a Salmon Creek mining crew took a dim view of the poker-playing technique favored by a member of the Goose Creek bunch, the two largest claims in the Nome area. Sticking to his ritual, Tex paired them off, hauled his watch to hand, called "time," and they went at it tooth and toenail.

The fight continued for a half hour, with each man going down a few times. Then one of them got a lovely break. When he fell, his hand jammed into a brass spittoon. Arising, he swung the trapped fist and caught his opponent under the nose, a contact that spelled finale. After some deliberation Tex awarded the fight to the boy with the spittoon. He claimed that the winner had shown "head." He hadn't asked the help of a spittoon or any other advantage. But when opportunity had come his way he had grabbed it. Despite the unpopularity of his decision in the days that followed, Tex stuck to his guns.

In any case Jack would have been wiser, from a career standpoint, to have established a welcome-mat brokerage in headhunter country, rather than try to pull a Clarence Darrow in Nome. A further stumbling block was his feud with Roberts. Jake had a finger in every pie. He was adviser to the city council, he was the creditor of every miner and mining company, and every whisper he uttered was heard—as I found even when I was listening in at my switchboard. Jack didn't have a chance to set up as a lawyer in Nome. As he considered gold-mining a demeaning occupation, it left little for him to do but find another town.

St. Michael was booming at that time, and he decided to take the packet that would be leaving in two weeks. Our marriage would have to wait; when he had established himself, he would send for me.

"What about my contract?" I asked.

"You'll break it," he said, his eyes flat with anger and his lips tight. "And you'll come to me when I send for you. Haven't you heard that a wife's place is with her husband?"

"But I'm not your wife," I said.

"You will be, as soon as I get rolling."

A week after this, he fell heir to one bit of luck. When he called on one of his competitors, Luswell Gaines, in a final attempt to ally himself in a legal partnership, he learned that Gaines was agent for the insurance company that had the Great Northern Steamship account. When Jack mentioned the loss of his cows and chickens, Gaines offered to settle on the spot, and Jack accepted a check for $2,200, which he promptly cashed at Chilberg's bank.

The windfall assuaged his bitterness and disappointment and for a few days it was like old times, with dinners at Thornton's, or cards and pleasant conversation with Al and Lucy. But then he fell into a black mood again, and this time I became really worried. By the time the packet arrived he was openly hostile to people in the streets, abusive to me and rude to Al and Lucy. The night before the packet was to sail, he got drunk in the Great Northern, passed out and had to be bedded down by Steep.

Dawn revealed a sad female, standing by Jack's side on the dock. His arm around my waist trembled from his hangover, his face was gray, his lips dry. But his eyes were kind, for a change, and his voice gentle.

"Chin high, little one. We'll make it yet. When we get to-gether again you'll be Mrs. John Bartlett." Then he was waving from the deck of the packet.

Back in the office, I was so shattered that Al had to take over the switchboard. Lucy finally put me to bed, where I could bawl in private.

It was Will, bless him, who saved the day for me once more, as he was to do so many times in future years. Indeed, I cannot recall how many times I went running to him with my troubles, real or imaginary. Two days after Jack had left, he came to the Boyd cabin and surprised me by creeping up behind me, yanking me off my stool, and setting me up on top of the switchboard.

"How's our little chee-chawker? How do you like us by now?" he said, laughing as I struggled to get my breath.

That was all I needed to unload on him my whole tale of woe. As usual, he listened sympathetically, asking no questions and offering no advice until I had finished. Then he cupped my chin in his hand and smiled.

"You're making a mountain out of a molehill," he said. "After all, this is frontier country; it's a lot different from an established society. It's easy enough to cut your cake in San Francisco or Seattle. But here you've got to be tough. Slug it out. It's like a prize fight. No matter how many times you're knocked down, you just get up and keep slugging. If you do that you can't lose. Sooner or later your opponent will wear out. Then you've got him."

"But why won't Jack go into mining or business, or something he can make a living at? At this rate it'll be years before we can be married."

"It's just as well he doesn't. He knows mining isn't every-thing, even if it's the lifeblood of the country right now. Sooner or later we'll need lawyers—and teachers, doctors, ministers and even politicians. As for getting married, you're better off to wait. Your marriage wouldn't be worth a plugged nickel if a headstrong, opinionated person like Jack had to support you with a job he disliked. You should realize that."

"But if he sends for me—what about my contract?"

"We wouldn't hold you to it if it affected your happiness. Now sit back and let events take their course."

Just then a call came and Will lifted me down to the board and waited while I completed the transfer. For the first time I noticed how tired he looked; he needed a shave and his clothes were rumpled and travel stained.

"When the Boyds come in," he said, "tell them I'll be around this evening. About seven. We'll do the town together, the four of us."

"Will! That would be wonderful!" I'd been so lonely that his invitation sounded like a trip to Paris. Then I recalled Jack's jealous rage when he had seen me in Will's arms two months before, and my spirits took a dive. "But on second thought I—"

"You don't need to explain any more," he said briskly. "I understand. I don't intend to compromise you, ridiculous as I think Bartlett's attitude is. When you're with me, Lucy and Al will act as chaperones. You can't spend the winter in a cave, like a bear. This is tough country. You ought to get out a bit and be amused. And I intend to spoil you as long as I'm here."

"How long? All winter?" I asked. I forgot my misgivings.

"No. I have another job to do in St. Michael before I go Outside. But two weeks, say, anyway. Meanwhile you're going to have some fun."

"Good. I can't wait. Jack will understand."

"You tell him," Will said dryly. "I'm not interested."

"You don't like him, do you?"

"I can't give you an honest answer, honey. He may be a champion, for all I know. But his temper needs a tuck or two taken in it. So does his opinion of the people hereabouts. Alaskans aren't pinheads. They won't put up with his arrogance and contempt. He'll have to change or go under."

"Do you think the Robertses have anything to do with people's attitude toward Jack?"

"Undoubtedly. He ran afoul of them in the worst way. But if it hadn't been them, it would have been somebody else. But Jack's not all wrong. Roberts is a louse, and his wife is a dreadnought. It'd be hard not to run afoul of them."

I was in a much higher state when Will left. And he didn't

disappoint me either. For the next two weeks, until he left for St. Michael, I had a wonderful time.

He showed up that night dressed in one of his smooth, black business get-ups, sheared, shaved, polished and smelling like two million dollars; and after a dinner at a restaurant called Al's Golden Pheasant we went to the weekly dance at the Northern Commercial Company's warehouse, one of the few buildings in Nome with a wooden floor that was large enough to accommodate a crowd. Several years earlier Will, recognizing the need for recreation during the long winter months, had put the place at the disposal of the local populace for dancing and other social occasions every Saturday night. The idea had caught fire, and other businessmen had adopted Will's policy and turned over their premises one night a week for social diversions. Tex Rickard closed his Great Northern Saloon to gambling, drinking and general horseplay on Wednesday nights, turned his bar into a glutton's paradise, gave his crew and girls the evening off, and welcomed—free of charge—the area's puritans and near puritans, who had previously been limited to cards and gab in the cabins of friends in their quest for relaxation. Tex's competitors were quick to see the value of such excellent public relations, and soon, by staggering the program, there was a dance going every night save Sundays. Squired by Will and policed by Al and Lucy, I began making them all, or almost all of them, and I suddenly found myself—strong boost to my ego—the center of attraction. I was the only girl kid in Nome at the moment, and I had a pretty fair figure in those days.

True, I was beset by qualms at times, innocent as my flirtations were. I wanted to respect Jack's rights as my betrothed and to fit my behavior to his ideas of how I should conduct myself. But it was not easy to resist a subconscious pirouette when I was ringed by such gallants as Louie Lane, an owner of the fabulous Goose Creek claim, brown-eyed and rich; Johnny Stonehouse, blocky, cocky, black-eyed and owner of the equally fantastic Salmon Creek property; Jim Hunt, Nome's most successful gambler and the last word in Mississippi river-boat elegance; Eugene Chilberg, the banker, whose scholarly face and precise grammar would have made him conspicuous in any crowd; or Rex Beach, whose feet, when dancing, seemed never to touch the floor.

Neither was I able to control an arched eyebrow and lilting laugh when Will, Al, Lucy and I played poker with such friends as "Biff" and Martha Slater, who worked a claim off Goose Creek; Mike and Fanny Nichols, who had made their money on the Outside but lived in Nome because they loved the town; and Bart and Emily Moss, who ran a successful assay office.

All in all, Will—true to his promise—did a thorough job of spoiling me, but at the same time he made me keep a balance. While he taught me to hold my whisky like a lady, he also decreed that we should attend church regularly; if he made me stay up dancing half the night, he was just as insistent on my being at the switchboard promptly each morning. While he encouraged me to spend money, he also showed me how to make more.

"Anyone can make an extra buck," he said one day as I was closing the board. "I'll show you what I mean. Put your boots on."

Down on the ocean front he pointed out a group of people near an Indian camp just back of the shore line. They were all making rocking motions, as if they were putting children to sleep with a lullaby. They were "cradling," Will explained to me, using wooden cradles with which they scooped up the silt on the beach which was laden with fine gold, and rocking the scoops until the sand washed out, leaving them the gold dust.

"With your thirst for lucre," Will said, "I thought it might interest you."

It did. I discovered that in Nome nearly everyone with a little extra time devoted it to cradling gold. Later I calculated that while I lived there I was able to put an extra forty dollars a week on the ledger in my spare time.

But Will characteristically kept a blance on the wheel. Pointing out the Indian camp, he said, "I want to show you something," and taking my hand, led me off to see it.

It was something to see. The Indians, with ragged clothing and open sores, sat stoically amid garbage and filth, resigned and apparently callously unaware of the condition of their children. The stink of the camp added to the squalor. They greeted us in dull silence.

"Will!" I cried. "Somebody ought to *do* something!"

"I was hoping you'd think so."

"What's the matter with the white people up here?"

"What's the matter with people anywhere?" he countered. "They don't care. That doesn't mean Lucy. She's doing all she can. Maybe you can help her and the few women in Nome who are interested in pulling these people out of it." He threw up his hands. "They have enough to eat. They simply need to be scrubbed and medicated."

"Well, I certainly can do that! But how about the money for medicine and the like?"

Will lifted his hand and motioned toward the ocean front. "Dig it out of here."

"Dig—you want me to cradle the money out of this—to help these Indians?" As always, the idea of working hard, getting money for it, then turning it to someone else's use, caused me to blow hot. "Why don't you squander a penny, if you're so interested?"

"I intend to. You start the wagon rolling. You and Lucy and the other ladies. Then I'll not only come up with some money, but I'll try to persuade some others in the same direction."

"But why us? Why don't the men of this town do something?"

"Because most men here are interested only in getting rich. So, okay for them. I've nothing against getting rich. But women are different. For the most part they are willing to leave it to men to get rich. And they like babies and children, even if they are Indians. I'll expect a report of your activities among these people within the week."

"Merciful heavens!" The wind, shifting a little, brought with it a strong smell of the camp and I felt as if I needed a bath. "We'll have to do something."

"Right. As I said, I'll expect a report. Within the week."

"You'll help?"

"I'll match every dollar that you spend—with two."

On the way back, mulling over our conversation, I had a disquieting thought and one which, once I'd voiced it, I wished had never been uttered. "Will, you've got money—much more than I have. Why don't you just foot the whole bill?"

"You silly girl," he said, his voice flavored with the acid that he invariably employed when I stubbed my toe. "Of course I have the money. That's not the point. My purpose is to educate you. Whenever you take a dollar out of this country you must feel obliged to put a quarter back. That's our way up here. Working with these Indians will give you the feel of what I mean. They're Alaskans too. And when an Alaskan needs help he gets it—from the first person that comes along. If you live by this code you may also ask for help. If you don't you can't expect to come crying to anyone."

I learned, during that week when I spent all my spare time with Will, a good deal about his philosophy. He was an avid reader of ancient history and an authority on the campaigns and the statesmanship of conquerors such as the Mongol Genghis Khan, the Macedonian Alexander the Great, the Mongol Tamerlane, and, more recently, Napoleon. He thought Genghis Khan the most effective of the ancients because he had been a colonizer. For that reason the Mongol empire outlasted his death more than 400 years, while Alexander's fell apart almost as soon as he drew his last breath. The others he held to be mere opportunists and soldiers of fortune, comparable to some of the people who were exploiting Alaska now, but sinking no roots there. I sat slack jawed and spellbound while he and Al talked of ancient history, modern Europe, and especially of Alaska—its geography and people, wildlife, and the heroism of its real settlers. They got far afield into such subjects as future statehood, federal subsidies, uniform political structures and a balanced economy.

Stung by Will's reproach and his hint that I was only interested in getting money out of the Territory, I determined to do my bit for the Indians by earning whatever extra money I could, and also by sinking some more roots.

Recalling Jack's settlement with Lawyer Gaines in the matter of his lost livestock, I determined to pay the gentleman a call too. At my noon break on the following day I left the board and succeeded in cornering the solicitor as he was leaving his

132

office for lunch. By employing some powerful gabbing in relation to my loss aboard the lighter, I came away with a check for $200.

This I promptly cashed with Gene Chilberg and proceeded to the Yukon Trading Company store where I managed to sweat out Andy Whipple's gabble long enough to buy some things for my cabin.

Since Will, during the afternoon, had got into one of his high-stake poker games at the Great Northern—one that lasted for forty-eight hours—I was given a chance to get at my hut, something that time and shortage of money had so far prohibited. Al, on a trouble call at one of their line camps, was not underfoot either, and as a consequence, Lucy and I had a lot of fun in petting and powdering the place.

In fact when Will finally walked in, we were putting the final punch to it—that of tacking oilcloth to my table top. Glancing around, he made an exaggerated leg and bowed low.

"Tell me, is one required to remove his shoes before entering?"

I was pretty pleased with the implied compliment, especially as nothing I'd done during our short friendship had exactly knocked him stiff with enthusiasm. I was beginning to think that I had my foot stuck in my mouth permanently.

"Some box," he said, looking over my cabin.

"One more remark like that," Lucy said, "and you'll be thrown out."

"All right. I apologize, Margaret, for calling your spacious home a box. To get to the point. The *Victoria* is due in from Seattle tomorrow and leaves Monday. Tex Rickard wants to be on board when she leaves. This is Wednesday. We're holding his going-away soiree tomorrow night. So get out the glad rags. Tex's got a big hand coming to him. He's done plenty for this country."

He told me that Tex, determined to invade New York City, had offered his Great Northern Saloon for sale some months previously and had named his friend and bartender Barney McCready as his favorite heir to the scepter. Never one to haggle unless it involved money, Tex had added only one rider to the offer. He wanted to leave Alaska before the freeze, and if

Barney wanted his squiff shop, then Barney would need to lay gold on the line on schedule.

Since Tex could have sold the Great Northern to any business-man in Nome, Barney had gone to work, and the first person who had got the shake was his pal Rex Beach. Rex, who had been trying to draw a bead on a hefty poke, also went to work. Between them they managed to get the money together on time. How they scraped it up, I don't recall. But they both had a lot of friends, despite the fact that Rex was pretty successful at his gambling and Barney was too—in his off hours as Tex's barkeep.

I put some spur and quirt into the crease of my skirt and the polish of my new shoes that night and during what leisure time I had from the board the next day. Al came home in the early afternoon and went to bed for a short nap, but by the time I had seen myself in the mirror for the tenth time he was up and talking to Lucy and Will over the cheery stuff in the Boyd cabin.

At the Great Northern that night we saw, the moment we opened the door, that the lid was off three times over. The center of the place, carefully scoured of sawdust, rumbled under the combined weight of the prancing citizenry, male and female. Conspiring in the dance were the cornettist and the harmonica artist that I've mentioned, aided by a toothless codger whose dead cigar, clamped between his lips, was at glaring odds with the bow of his violin.

Rex and Barney hadn't neglected the wishes of the hungry. A battery of butcher knives, forks and spoons at the far end of the long bar invited earnest onslaught on steaming caribou roasts, platters of thickly sliced smoked salmon, crocks of beans, tall tins of tomatoes and slabs of sourdough bread. Squat settle-ments of tin plates yawned here and there, waiting for anyone interested.

They had peeled an eye for the thirsty too. Both were tending bar that evening, having let the staff off, and both were put-ting their hearts into it. If anyone asked for a glass of cham-pagne, he got a bottle of it. Anyone who was brave enough to order a straight shot of hooch got one—enough to temporarily stun a fighting bull.

"Will!" I took one look at the scene and lost my heart to the Territory and its people more than ever. "I'm flabbergasted! What a wonderful country!"

Chuckling, he steered me toward the bar. "That's the stuff. You'll be a sourdough yet."

Today I wish that I had the energy to drink the champagne, eat as much and work up the enthusiasm on the dance floor, as I stood champion to that night. Moreover, I didn't suffer from a lack of beaus. At eighteen I was some twenty years younger than the average Alaska bravo there, and as I have noted, my form was nothing to sneer at. Consequently I got plenty of action on the dance floor. So far as Tex, the guest of honor, was concerned, he made me feel good, too, long before they cheered him to his quarters at the Golden Gate Hotel in the early morning.

"You ever come to New York," he invited, his lips as thin, pursed and cautious as those of a horse trader, "look me up. S'pose you heard I'm startin' somthin' there. Be called the Diamond Horseshoe." Reaching into a vest pocket, he excavated the beautiful gift that had been presented to him at midnight by Cherry Malotte—courtesy of his friends. Cherry had taken up a collection amounting to some $15,000 and sent it to a jeweler in Seattle along with a sketch of the stickpin she wanted made for Tex. It was in the shape of a large diamond horseshoe, its center a pigeon-blood ruby surrounded by half-carat diamonds.

"Gonna call my night club in New York after this stickpin. If you ever come to see me, you'll get fed."

(I later regretted accepting his invitation. But my trouble wasn't Tex's fault. It lay in my lifelong devotion to anything that's free. In 1915, I believe, Will and I checked into Tex's successful Diamond Horseshoe Club in New York City, and while they talked I went at a couple of lobster courses, washed down with champagne. The result was that I foundered, promptly became sick, and had to be lugged off to the Algonquin Hotel where Will and I were staying.)

But to get back on the trail—during Tex's farewell party I won my first good stake in a poker game. While bouncing around I was invited by a group of bearded sourdoughs to sit in at their table. Fattened by a loan of $50 from Will, I won nearly $400. Whether I triumphed fairly or was permitted to cabbage my winnings, I'll never know.

The party broke up at dawn. With barely two hours sleep under my belt, I thought the next day at the board never would end. I was more than willing to take it easy, save for my nightly trips to the baths, for the next week. But in the last essence these nightly sessions were the most enjoyable and rewarding of that period. Seated in the Boyd cabin drinking hot chocolate or coffee royals, I was a fat cat. I was in love for the first time; I was engaged to the man I loved; I had a good job and a bank account, and I was flattered by the attentions of warm and worldly people. What little greenhorn could have helped feeling tall in her stirrups?

At the beginning of the following week I determined to get busy with the Indian welfare project that Will had suggested. I bought a cradle, and Will showed me how to use it at the sand pits and instructed me in the religions, taboos, societies and politics of Indian tribes such as the Siwash, Tena and Ketchikan, Chilkoot and Athabasca. His word was more than good in the matter of helping foot the bill for medical supplies and equipment for the wretched people on the beach. For every bandage or bottle bought by Lucy or me or an occasional donation by other interested women in camp, he produced a half dozen, and when we pooled our resources and purchased a tent or blanket, the Yukon Trading Company supplemented it by a dozen or more. Although we were never successful in getting the Indians to bathe, we were soon rewarded for our efforts. Their sores and coughs began to disappear, and smiles greeted our arrival instead of their former dour surliness or stoic indifference.

Then one night Will abruptly announced that a mail packet was sailing the next morning for St. Michael and that he intended to be on it. When he made ready to leave, he shook hands with Lucy and Al and turned to me.

"Want to walk a way with me, Margaret?"

Depressed over his announcement, I nodded, went to my cabin, and pulled on my jacket. It suddenly seemed as if someone had tied both hands behind my back. At the corner of Main

Street he stopped and urged me into the doorway of a building, to avoid the crowd, and squared me off to face him.

"I won't be seeing you for about a year, I guess," he said, "and I wanted to tell you why."

"A year? But you said a couple of weeks ago that you'd be back this spring."

"I know I did," he replied. "But I've changed my plans. One thing, then I'm off. While you're safe with Al and Lucy, I want you to watch yourself with Bartlett. I think you know what I mean." Taking a cigar from his pocket, he bit off the plug end, spat out the fragment, and lit up.

"I suggest that you two marry as soon as possible. I'm sure he'll find nothing to his liking in St. Michael and he'll be back shortly. So I have instructed Al to offer him a job, at better than good wages, with us. That'll get you started. Meantime, he can find plenty of time to establish his law practice."

Sudden gratitude for his many unselfish kindnesses, his unwavering friendship and thoughtful counseling, made it tough for me to keep back the tears—particularly since he had just offered help to a man who had insulted and embarrassed him. Indeed, I was a bit over my head for the moment.

"I don't know what to say."

"I want you to have everything you require from life. Whatever I may do for you is reward in itself." Bending his head, he laid his lips against my forehead. "Good-bye, and good luck." He turned and began shouldering his way into the crowd. A few yards farther on he paused, stopped and faced me once more.

"You see, my dear, I love you too."

Chapter Eight

HALF drunk and in a brutal humor, Jack returned to Nome late in September, and he missed no bet in wrecking what little standing he had left among the respectable element and the easy-going fraternity alike. He was even more arrogant, rude and insulting than before, and he played no favorites in his apparent desire to become the most sincerely disliked man in town.

He started his campaign by lighting into me. Unshaven and disheveled, he entered my office just as I was closing the board for the night, and he couldn't have arrived at a more awkward moment. With the freeze approaching, the temperature had steadily dropped, and several nights previously I had carelessly and idiotically exposed myself. Blood hot and skin tingling from the blistering waters of the baths, I had carried rather than worn my parka home. Consequently I had gotten a bad cold and had planned to pound my ear early, hoping to ache and groan it off in bed.

"Ah," he drawled bitingly as he stepped inside, "my devoted slave. So busy she couldn't meet me at the dock."

"Jack!" I was so happy to see him again that I ignored his

deliberate sarcasm and my uncomfortable condition. Running to him, I threw my arms around his neck. "Darling!"

But he made no move to return my embrace, much less to kiss me. So I let go, and to conceal my surprise, hurt and embarrassment, I made a show of rearranging my hair.

"You're looking like life on Park Avenue," he continued in the same unpleasant tone, "simply rolling in clover. But why the airs? Have you been practicing the act before the local yokels?"

"Oh, Jack!" At that moment I would have given my right arm to have had whisky on hand. The symptoms of his past jealousy, economic maladjustment and bitter contempt for his surroundings, were all there and glaringly obvious. He had reached a stage where only a stupefying drunk, a fight or a unique adventure, could spike his vicious mood. "Please, dear, don't be mean. You're just tired."

"I'm not tired. And I'm not mean. Why didn't you meet me at the dock? Too busy yapping at your scabby friends on the telephone?"

"Darling, how could I meet you?" His attitude was so ridiculous that I almost forgot my determination to add no fuel to to his fire. "I didn't know you were coming. I haven't heard from you."

"Oh, let it ride," he rasped. "You're in a class by yourself. You're a star at shirking responsibility. Get your parka. We're going uptown. I need a drink, and I want to tell you something."

I understood him too well to argue, even though, considering my cold, I should have kept warm and stayed inside. I had learned that silent obedience made things easier for me when he was off on a tangent. Moreover, I must admit that I had become a little afraid of him, although he had inevitably treated my person with the last word in respect and even a kind of deference. So I dressed as ordered. But for the remainder of the evening I felt as if I were next door to a volcano and sitting on a couch of pins and needles. His program started the minute we reached Main Street.

My hand buried in his fist, he highballed it up the sidewalk toward Thornton's, his shoulders bumping and flinging people out of his way. He was looking for a fight and he nearly got a couple of them. While the Nome citizen of that day was used to the jostling of crowds—by reason of the narrow streets— he was quick to resent a bully. However, much as Jack thirsted for a brawl he was disappointed. The miners took a look at his size and face and slogged on, muttering angrily to themselves.

In Thornton's, Jack ordered a bottle of Old Crow and got into the second act of his play by filling a tin cup half full and pouring it down straight. The slug had barely hit bottom when he built an even larger one, and the eager desperation with which he handled the stuff recalled to my mind an admission that he had made during one of our conversations aboard the *Yucatan.* At that time and for a year or so previous he had been on the wagon because he considered himself a potential alco- holic. I decided to chance broaching the subject, hoping that refreshing his memory might serve as a kind of homemade psy- chiatry to head off what looked like the beginning of a monu- mental binge. But he had an eagle eye for the curve.

"You run your store, I'll run mine," he snarled, his eyes like bright blue stilettos. "As I said, I've got something to say. And don't interrupt."

Then it came out, somewhat incoherently of course, that he had been run out of St. Michael.

Finding even less opportunity for exploiting his trade in that town—a community that was only a ten-gallon gold camp— he had taken to gambling. By late July he had won several thou- sand dollars and was exploring the idea of rounding up a backer or two and sprouting his own house of cards. But things failed to work out in that direction. Sitting in a high-stake, six-man game in a sod tiger known as the Fang and Claw one night, he was challenged by a burly miner who owned a claim about four miles south of town.

The gentleman did not appreciate the manner in which Jack riffled the cards, and, while he hurled no charges of cheating, his inference was plain. Getting out of his chair, the miner pulled on his parka, announced that he couldn't lick a pro- fessional in any league and that he was going home. Jack's tem- per being what it was, he naturally unsheathed his talons. He immediately found himself faced with a thousand pounds of

human beef—representing the miner's friends at the table—
and, tough as he was, he was forced to climb off of his horse.
But the worst to come was yet in the hopper.

The following day around noon he was roused from a sound
sleep by a United States marshal, one Dan Rhone, a bony, soft-
spoken man whom I got to know well upon his retirement to
Fairbanks years later. Rhone held a unique record with the
service. While he packed a gun, according to regulations, in
his twenty years with the department he had never been required to use it in the performance of his duty in patroling
the St. Michael area. One gander at his periodic sessions in
target practice, and the lawless—by and large—decided that it
was better to be a live coward than a dead hero. He was also
as polite as he was courageous.

Rhone informed Jack that the man with whom he'd had
trouble the previous night at the Fang and Claw was Jim Berra,
a successful claimowner and one of the best-liked men in St.
Michael, and that not only Berra but all his friends considered
that Jack's handling of the cards was at least highly suspicious.
I had been in Alaska long enough to know that Alaskans considered a cardsharp only slightly lower than a dog stealer.

Admitting he had no grounds for running Jack out of St.
Michael, Rhone nevertheless advised him to leave of his own
accord. Once the word got around, Jack would find it very difficult to associate with anyone there, and Rhone didn't want
trouble.

Three days later Jack discovered how correctly Rhone had
called the turn. Silence and surliness met him at every step. An
attempt to sit in on a card game caused the players to rise of
one accord and leave the premises. At mealtimes, in either of
the camp's two restaurants, he was the last to be served and then
only indifferently and contemptuously. The crowning blow
came when the proprietor of the store from whom he had
rented his room asked him to vacate, under the pretext
that he needed the space for storage. Nerves raw, Jack cracked
at last. Picking the man up, Jack threw him into the mud of the
street, followed him, spent an hour cussing out every man who
passed by, and beat Rhone to the packet by ten minutes.

"The scum," Jack growled, his eyes moving glassily over the crowd in Thornton's. "If I'd had a gun I'd have killed that two-bit harness bull and then wiped out everyone in town. Guilty or not, they all had it in for me just because I was a floater."

For a moment, as usual, I took his part, and my temper was boiling as furiously as his own. I even forgot that he'd pushed me around a bit in the last half hour. Then a thought came to me that I couldn't quite shrug off, and I finally had to speak it. "Jack, you didn't cheat, did you?"

Fumbling with his tin cup, he got it to his lips and threw down another three fingers of whisky. "I know how to cheat," he said evasively. "If a game calls for it."

That was the last coherent remark he made that night. At midnight, he got up staggering, and I piloted him to the Golden Gate and handed him over to Rafferty, the tosspot room clerk. From that moment until Jack hit the hay, it was a case of the blind leading the blind, as Rafferty was carrying a jag equal to Jack's.

The next few weeks were so excessively unhappy and mortifying that even today the memory of them depresses me. Having alienated everyone in town but the Boyds, Jack managed to offend them too. One night Lucy invited him to dinner, and Al offered him a job as overseer in one of the line camps. The salary was good, the work would take only four months a year, and there would be time for Jack to build up his law practice.

Jack listened to Al with a half-plastered smile on his face, then leaned forward, his eyes narrowing. "Whose idea was this? Burke's?"

Al admitted that it was. Jack turned to me.

"And did you ask him to employ me, my solicitous, ever-loving bride-to-be? And if so, when have you been seeing him?"

Al answered for me. "Yes, she's seen him. Well chaperoned. And she didn't ask him to give you the job."

Jack stood up, flexed his arm muscles and buttoned the collar of his shirt. "Let's get this straight. I wouldn't work for that ribbon-clerk dictator if he was the last man on earth. That soul saver, preacher, patriotic imbecile—and swindler. The hypocrite! He doesn't believe in that holy American hogwash any more than I do, but he'll do anything for a buck. I know all about him. He's dearly loved because he throws a quarter back where he's stolen dollars——"

"That'll do, Bartlett!" Al interrupted. "Get out of my house!"

"All right. Come on, Margaret!"

"Margaret's not going."

"No? Al, I can lick you with one hand."

"While you're shooting buffalo, I'll get some rabbits."

Looking Al up and down, Jack suddenly grinned. "Al, you're my friend. I couldn't lift a finger against you."

Oddly, he didn't insist on my leaving with him, but asked me to meet him the next night at Thornton's for dinner. I agreed, and the reprieve allowed me one good night's sleep.

But he spent the next day querying all my friends and acquaintances about my dates with Will, and at Thornton's that night he pinned me to my chair for more than three hours while he railed and cursed, accused and abused, and let up only when his cup was empty. So it went, night after night.

During this time Lucy, God bless her, was a stone wall.

"Honey, your Mr. Bartlett is a bad boy. He isn't going to fit up here or anywhere else on earth, so far as I can see. But you want him. And that's good enough for us. Stick it out. Maybe he'll surprise all of us. Then you'll live happily ever afterward."

Lucy was correct in one sense. Jack and I did live happily—for a time. During the period that followed, no girl could have enjoyed a more exciting time while waiting to be led to the altar. This welcome change in our relations got its start with a rumor, then a rumble, in the restaurants, saloons and dance halls, that a big sports event was to be staged in Nome. Verification, represented by black headlines on the front page of the *Nugget,* came within the week and also clarified its athletic classification.

An accompanying story, written by a George Bohlman—an itinerant printer-reporter—announced in towering prose that on a date coincident with the first light frost the eyes of the entire universe would be focused on Nome. A marathon race would be held which would feature a number of internationally famous runners and be sponsored by the newly founded Sportsman's Club of Greater Nome and Alaska. This truly fine civic organization, the article continued, had been formed early in July, shortly after the arrival on the *Victoria* of a Mr. B. Alton Ridgell, a Mr. Carvell Bridges and a Mr. Lazo Wheatly. They were all former successful businessmen, now retired from the dull life of making fortunes in San Francisco as stockbrokers, and currently numbered among the live-wire boosters of this new and invigorating land.

Disclosure of the fraternal establishment had been kept a secret until a charter had been approved by the city council, and this authorization had come only two days before. Any man of good character was free to join. Membership would be $200 a year, the dues to be expended to finance the building of suitable quarters and to underwrite sports events. The first board of directors would be personally appointed by Mr. Ridgell, President; Mr. Wheatly, Vice-President and Treasurer; and Mr. Bridges, Secretary, because they were experienced clubmen and knew their parliamentary law. After that, popular elections would be held periodically. These, needless to caution, were to be conducted on a basis that ignored race, religious beliefs or political credos, and would demand that all candidates, without exception, be recognized publicly for their honesty, integrity and sense of fair play. Prospective members would be welcomed by the elegant and gentlemanly Mr. Ridgell, Mr. Wheatly and Mr. Bridges in the club's temporary headquarters on the second floor of the Golden Gate Hotel, where the organization's bylaws and deportmental requirements would also be explained.

As far as the club's choice for an initial extravaganza was concerned, the story went on, its founding officers had decided on a marathon race, because such a contest permitted a wider participation than, say, a prize fight, wrestling match or long-distance swim. In short, the local greats on the trail were not only invited to compete with the professionals for the $15,000 first prize that the club had in mind for the victor, but were urged to do so. The club, however, had its conditions in the latter respect. Sports events of such importance were bound to attract the attention of sharps and professional gamblers, and infiltration of that nature could sound the death knell for any

institution devoted to the purpose of clean, wholesome, unfettered athletics. Friendly betting under the auspices of the
club would be allowed, but all bets between members were to
be paid promptly and with good grace.

In relation to ground rules, the article concluded, the location of the race, workout arrangements, names of the athletes
and further progress of the club's plans, would be reported on
the *Nugget*'s next publishing date, same day, same time, next
week. The little sheet kept its promise. I still have the clipping,
although—like a great many of my old notes and diaries—it
makes pretty blurry reading these days.

The big combination steamship *Corwin* was due to arrive
from Seattle on the following week and numbered among its
more distinguished *voyageurs* would be an even half dozen of
the world's outstanding long-distance runners, according to
Mr. Ridgell, Mr. Bridges and Mr. Wheatly. At great expense
and by virtue of exhausting negotiations, the gentlemen had
at last been successful in signing for Nome's first major sports
event two Finnish champions, two Russians, a Norwegian and
a Japanese, all of whom were stars in the field. They were, respectively, Aarvo Riskoni and Pelvi Pelsinko; Ivan Petersgrad
and Georgei Muscovy; Thorwald Sinkstrom and Wado Suzi-
kawa. All of whom—considering their importance in the sports
world and their cooperation in lending their great talents to
the launching of Nome as a sports center—would be royally
welcomed, it was hoped. For the rest, the track would be laid
out according to the wishes of the athletes and their managers,
the training schedules would be worked out in the same manner, and the Sportsman's Club now boasted more than 500
members and was going strong.

Nome went wild with enthusiasm over the impending race.
Overnight the town burst into what the *Nugget* chose to call
"galvanic action" and the transition from gallop to belly run
was the more pronounced when the athletes hit the beach. The
Nugget gave this description: "Tall, clean-limbed, handsome
as gods and moving with the light, graceful, effortless ease of
stalking jaguars, these splendid athletes were welcomed by the
red-blooded sportsmen of Nome as only the strong and the virile
can welcome kindred spirits."

The *Nugget* omitted one detail. This involved Wado Suzi-kawa, or, as he became known more familiarly, Wado the Jap. Where the others were "tall, clean-limbed, handsome as gods and moving with the light, graceful, effortless ease of stalking jaguars," Wado was short, bandy legged, moon-faced, slightly gray-haired—and he waddled.

Wado was placed in residence at the raunchy Alaska House near the beach, but his colleagues enjoyed the finest that the Golden Gate had to offer. While the Finns, Russians and the Norwegian showed a fine appreciation for the free liquor and the attentions of dance-hall girls, Wado wasn't even invited to eat with the bears or to pinch a squaw. His companions retained managers to help out with their pigeon-toed English and ignorance of American customs; Wado spoke excellent New Yorkese but he didn't have shucks in the matter of professional counseling.

Garbed in a frayed turtle-neck sweater and blue jeans sawed off at the knees, moccasin clad and wearing a stocking cap, he was a poor-looking fish when stacked against the height, good looks and resplendent sports clothes of his colleagues. Moreover, one of his pitches caused many of the sportsmen to consider him largely insane. This conclusion came during a conference between the managers and Mr. Ridgell, Mr. Bridges and Mr. Wheatly as to the track rules.

Inasmuch as he lacked a manager, Wado personally appeared at the confab and insisted that the track be laid out in a circle one mile in circumference and that it be covered by each runner a total of 25 times, the winner to be the trackman who got the laps in first. Since the managers didn't care enough one way or another to haggle over a few miles and apparently were not frightened senseless by Wado's physical appearance, they concealed their smiles, politely mentioned that 15 miles was the accepted distance for marathons in most circles, then agreed to Wado's demands. The next week, in response to a ringing call from the *Nugget*, every man with sportsmanship in his veins and a few free minutes was out on the tundra north of town, hacking out a track in the area approved by the officials.

Then the workouts began, and these spectacles did not lack for spectators. By this time news of the coming event had reached inland, and only the old, infirm or financially harassed were left to work the claims. Business became the second order of the day in Nome, although some enterprises boomed despite the prevailing indifference to commerce. This was noticeably apparent in the mercantile line. There was an unprecedented demand for derby hats, razors and string ties, cologne water and celluloid collars. Stocks of scarfs, curling irons, and umbrellas—particularly those with surrey fringes—disappeared quickly, and one man was reported to have even asked a storekeeper for shoe polish.

Then the betting started. Every Nome sportsman had his champion on the track—indignantly so when challenged as to his athlete's prowess—and was willing to back his superior knowledge of the sport with pay dirt. Consequently the gold-dust pokes tossed about soon took on the aspect of a beanbag brawl among a horde of sixth-graders at recess.

Meanwhile, Wado's track performances added to the general opinion, current among the more sagacious and experienced of the sportsmen, that he was a has-been or never-was. Perhaps, as Mr. Ridgell, Mr. Bridges and Mr. Wheatly had suggested, the Jap had been good *once*. Maybe they needed, as they had said, an Oriental performer to round out the continental flavor of the race. They probably knew their stuff. But it seemed that, with a billion Orientals around, they could've got a younger runner. The Jap was sure past his peak.

"Poor little fellow," I said to Jack over dinner one night at Erickson's. "I feel sorry for him. He must be over forty."

"Uh huh," Jack said.

He was so preoccupied that I tried the gambit of changing the subject. "I'll be glad when it's winter. I'm dying to ride a dog sled, aren't you?"

"Yeah. If I can do that, my life will be complete."

I recognized his dark sarcastic mood and fell silent.

"Sorry, honey," he said, with one of his lightning changes. "I was thinking too hard, I guess. Listen. Can you keep a secret, even from Al and Lucy?"

"Yes, if you say so."

"How much money have you got? Ready cash?"

A touch, even from a loved one, has always caused me to look for high ground. So I must have shied away from Jack's question pretty handsomely. "About two hundred dollars. But why?"

He laid his hand across my lips none too gently. "*Shh!* Keep your voice down. I don't want it for myself. I want to bet it for you. On Wado."

"Wado?" He couldn't have surprised me more if he'd announced that he was taking holy orders. "Did you say *Wado?*"

"Precisely," he snapped. "Now, you mustn't breathe a word of this to anyone. Okay?" Looking intently about the interior again, he bent forward so that his lips touched my ear.

"This race stinks. I felt it at the start. But I couldn't put my finger on a reason until today, when I watched Wado's workout for perhaps the fifth time since he got here. Then I had it."

"Something like—something dishonest? Crooked?"

"You've guessed it. When that Japanese dwarf landed, his looks struck a bell. I knew I'd seen him somewhere. I like sports and I know a little about them. But I never heard of long-distance runners with names such as Aarvo Riskoni, Pelvi Pelsinko, Ivan Petersgrad and those other bums. They sounded like handles copied from the registry of a Kowloon flophouse or the enlistment papers of the French Foreign Legion. Also, I've known Finn and Russky sailors who spoke fair English. Their accents were nothing like the strangled gobbling these clowns are trying to put across."

A bird, to say nothing of a fly, could have found ample accommodations in my mouth. "Jack! You think—?"

"Shut up! Let me finish. Yesterday I got on the trail of Wado. A couple of hours ago I had it. I saw our sorry little Wado's picture about two years ago in a New York newspaper. He had won first money in the annual International Sportsmen's Club race, cross country from Paris to Geneva, Switzerland, and from a field of more than six hundred of the world's top runners. Naturally his win caused some speculation. He was short and the others were what the estimable *Nugget* calls 'splendid athletes.' He waddled while the rest loped, and he had some gray hair. But if I remember right, he was twenty-eight years old at that time. Finally, a columnist whose name I've forgotten suggested a simple answer to the question. It amounted to the fact that Wado never seemed to run out of wind."

"*Ahhh-h.*" To date I had been denied any part of a scandal smellier than snatches gleaned from unethically eavesdropping on conversations through a busy switchboard, and I began to sweat delightfully at the prospect of being personally hitched to one. "Then Wado's just pretending he's old?"

"Maybe he's gray." Jack grinned. "But he can't be more than thirty now. Yep, I fear that our wily Oriental has sold our august and aristocratic Sportsman's Club a bill of goods. To cinch it even tighter, he's also brought in a bunch of former dock-wallopers or college lads—probably on a daily-wage basis —and palmed them off as the real McCoy. They probably couldn't run far enough or fast enough to catch cold. So he's got it all buckled up before the fiasco starts."

"Then you think there is no risk?"

"There's always a risk," he said irritably, "when you place a bet. Anyway, I've got eight hundred dollars left. It's going down on Wado. Ought to get ten-to-one, maybe even better odds. You can come in with me or stay out. I don't care. That's what a man gets for trying to do someone a favor."

"Jack, please." It was apparent that I had put my nose out of joint again, and I decided to go along with him whether it went against the grain or not. Life had unexpectedly become comely, if not beautiful, and even two hundred lovely dollars was a small price to pay if it would stopper any trend toward a relapse. But I *had* to know something more, and this time I was smart enough to throw a little flattery into the question.

"Excuse me, dear. I'm lost where money matters are concerned. Of course I'll come in with you. I can't wait to see the faces of those other athletes when Wado walks off with the fifteen thousand dollars! It'll be a scream, won't it? But fifteen thousand dollars doesn't seem like much money. After wages are paid to the other crooks, and all. I'm wondering why a big star like Wado would be dishonest—for so little? But you would know, dear. I'm just curious. That's all."

"Fif—" Jack's eyes were blank as they traveled from my chin to my nose, to my forehead and back. Then his lips bent, his dimples came out of hiding, and for the first time in months he laughed like he enjoyed the effort. "There is such a transaction known as betting on one's self, little goose. I'm sure that Wado has not ignored *that* possibility to riches."

"For goodness sake! This *is* getting complicated! I wonder how he managed to fool Mr. Ridgell and those other gentlemen?"

"I don't know all the answers, honey. My guess is that Ridgell and company were great as stockbrokers, but a little short on the clubman side. Everyone who comes up here blows up his background and importance. So it could be with them. I believe they contacted an agent Outside who arranged for Wado's appearance here. It was probably understood that Wado would line up a troupe of cinder-burners, top performers preferred. Only catch is, they aren't. They're setups for Wado. He saw to that."

Pushing back his chair, Jack stood up, reached down and took my arm. "Come on, kitten. We've been jawing long enough. I've got work to do. I'll walk you home. And remember, not a word of this."

By early afternoon of the following day the betting fever had nearly everyone in town running a temperature and the transactions—in gold dust and nuggets—had reached such a state of confusion that the Sportsman's Club agreed to act, out of generosity, as a records-and-deposit bureau for bettors. An abandoned building was rented and equipped with long tables and gold-weighing scales, and three of the athletes' managers took their places to police the betting.

The place had barely opened when a line formed at the door, and within thirty-six hours it looked like open house at a free-lunch counter. The club's service expanded to include the coppering of bets. For instance, if a sport was sold on a favorite but could find no one to bet against him, the countinghouse would dig up someone. Bettors would, of course, be expected to observe a couple of minor statutes: no one would be permitted to recall a bet, and the bettors must accept the odds posted on the board. Aside from these trivialities, the sportsmen of Nome could regard the place as their own little bank.

I drew my savings from Chilberg's bank and handed them

over to Jack, who put them down, along with his own, on Wado at ten-to-one odds. Already he was regretting that he hadn't waited a little longer: the odds were soon twenty to one.

Then abruptly the *Nugget* blared that the race had been scheduled for two days hence. The *Corwin*, last ship to Nome before spring, must beat the ice pack, and the athletes would have to be on it when it sailed.

I did not see even the start of the affair when the great day dawned, much as I pouted and groused at Al for even a peek at it. All of the Nome Telephone Company's clients who had been forced to stay home wanted a description by rounds, and during the tendon-bending my switchboard became a diabolical thing. Foreseeing the threatened thirst for information, Al had appointed two of his varlets to observe and report to me. This they did, on the hour, for some thirty hours. In fact they so harassed me by their mongoloid incoherencies that I forgot my wager on Wado—that is, until they began to cool off and to mention his name more frequently. After that it was only a matter of time.

At the finish all of the splendid athletes were on track and doing their desperate best. But Wado, still waddling, had racked up a total of seven laps, if I remember right, on his nearest opposition. I recall answering the last "How's it goin?" at around seven o'clock in the evening of the second day, a few minutes after Wado had been declared the winner. Then Al took over for me. As I had been in thrall for the entire race, save for intermittent spellings by Al, I was allowed to sleep late the next day, and it was evening before I awoke again.

My feet had only touched the floor when the details of the contest returned to my mind. After wounding myself four times with a hatpin, neglecting to nest one of my hair rats, spilling a box of rice powder down my front and still clutching my comb, I finally got downtown. I ran Jack down at Erickson's. If he had undergone rapid changes before, he now was a completely different personality.

"Honey!" he roared. Picking me up, he pinwheeled me hand to hand around his middle, then set me on his shoulder. "We're rich!"

His enthusiasm, it became apparent at once, was not shared

by everyone in the restaurant. The smiles that greeted his proclamation were in the strict minority, compared with the expressions of silent suffering that were the current vogue. Over dinner I learned the reason for the differences in the general outlook. A lot of puzzling developments had come to light while I had been in hibernation.

A substantial chunk of money had been taken out of Nome as a result of the race. Eugene Chilberg, the banker, estimated it roughly at $250,000. Most of the local sportsmen had been happy to bet against Wado, and all of them had found takers among the other athletes' managers, who had shown a mystifying lack of confidence in their own runners. Records of the Sportsman's Club countinghouse showed that the athletes themselves had wagered on Wado. The unpleasant redolence that the affair was beginning to take on was increased by the fact that Messrs. Ridgell, Bridges and Wheatly and all the athletes and managers, were nowhere to be found; the *Corwin* had sailed by the time anyone thought to check.

"We won, then!" At that moment I fell in love with Wado. "That Wado. What a—I mean, he is a crook, isn't he?"

Jack pushed a chunk of steak into his mouth and chewed thoughtfully. "I'm not so sure. At first I had him pegged for the fix, but now I wonder. Anyway, let's not look a gift horse in the mouth. We're wallowing in money. Fourteen thousand dollars."

(Years later I got the low-down on what had really happened from an informative book called *John Bunco*, by one Percy Whelan, who—since the publishers condemned many of the incidents therein as improbable—issued it himself for his friends and acquaintances. One of the con men whom Will numbered among his friends gave it to him. There was a chapter on the Nome episode in which it was made clear that a Mr. Ridgell, a Mr. Bridges and a Mr. Wheatly had engineered the whole event, and that Wado had been hired to run against a field of which he knew nothing—largely members of a roving stateside baseball team who were after a fast buck in an off season.)

In any event, innocent or not, Wado's introduction to Nome opened a new door to me. When Jack handed over my winnings

I could have cleared the top of the Great Northern in a single leap, and by the time I had received my deposit slip from Gene Chilberg I'm convinced that I could have made it over Mt. McKinley by simply lifting my arms. Then came a headlong rush to the stores—where the clothes and cabin accessories that I bought would have caused my mother to believe me lost to idolatry—the adoption of a fresh set of social airs, and a determination to change my name to Bartlett before Jack could spend all his money.

However, he needed no restraint. Where I had expected an extended binge, he went on the wagon, salted his winnings, quit gambling for high stakes and began looking for something to do. Where, before, he had grown careless in his dress and indifferent to the bloat of his extended drinking, he now wore his well-tailored business suits and even embarked on a short diet, an operation that quickly returned the hard planes to his face and slimmed up his magnificent body. But to my delight these alterations of character amounted to only the beginning of his change of pace.

Heretofore he had been virtually impossible in his public relations; now he became courteous overnight—if not precisely friendly—and his first move was to apologize to Lucy and Al, who instantly accepted him again.

But perhaps the biggest boost toward our social reinstatement came as a result of Jack's sudden and surprising interest in the beach Indians. I had hesitated telling him about my work among them, or of Will's connection with it, for fear of his usual contempt for such charitable operations. But when he dropped in one afternoon as I was quitting the switchboard for my weekly visit to the beach, I told him of our missionary endeavors without mentioning Will.

His eyes reflected a genuine interest. "Honey, I'm proud of you. I never suspected such unselfishness in one so addicted to money-grabbing."

"You like Indians?" I asked hopefully.

"I'm not sure I like anything but you," he said. "But I can sympathize with any underdog. The aborigines are the sole element of honesty left in this world of war, famine, social execution and professional dog-eat-dog. They kill only for food, breed to beget young and dress only to fend off the cold. Their reward is social ostracism. So they must be helped. I'd like to see your copper-bellies. Mind if I come along?"

He took to descending on the Indians every Thursday. He was strong enough to move the sick Indians, and he could pitch and repair tents and tools along with the best; and moreover, one glance from him would make the most surly and uncooperative Indian reach for his peace pipe. He bought supplies with his own money, and always included some rock candy for the small fry. We were noisily laudatory of his work, and since news traveled fast, people began to warm up to him.

So we started on the merry round of dances, dinners, shooting matches, poker sessions, dog auctions, community sings, amateur wrestling and bare-knuckle fights, that marked the opening of Nome's winter social season.

Many of the people I met during these good days are now long dead. But old-timers will remember such figures as Alexander Pantages, a bartender for the Great Northern Saloon and later a stateside theatrical magnate; Key Pittman, a mining claims organizer and lawyer who later, in Nevada, rose to a brilliant political career and died as chairman of the United States Senate Foreign Relations Committee; Jack London, the author, who stopped briefly in Nome before revisiting his old haunts on the Yukon Trail; Scott Friselle, the defrocked priest whose wife Nobi was half Chinese and half Negro; the freighter-miner-businessmen, Scotty Allen and Leonard Dodge; and Judith and Lew Crouch, owners of a saloon called Punch And Judy's, a nag-crazy couple who dedicated most of their sober moments to the program of forming a riding club. For this purpose the Crouchs had imported on the *Corwin* two light saddle horses, both geldings, and soon their wild lurchings as they squired their knuckleheads over the tundra became familiar sights to the town.

To encourage interest in their project they offered complimentary joltings to anyone so disposed, and Jack and I, among others, put in a large slice of our spare time aboard their ponies.

For a welcome change I was living in a fur house and nobody was throwing moths. But the best was yet before me. I got another brass ring one bitterly cold night shortly after I had joined Jack for dinner in Thornton's.

I had been to church, and since he put organized religion in the classification of labor unions, Indian rain dances or Druid councils, I was always forced to attend services alone or with other friends. We began meeting for our Sunday evening meal quite late, unless the Reverend Gardner O. Lester of First Church ran out of brimstone early. Jack waved me to a chair, mockingly inquired if I felt reborn, and as usual, adopted a pained look when I yapped in defense of my religion. But his grin appeared at once, and although his humor obviously was genuine, I sensed a sly hook somewhere, and I was immediately on guard.

"You look like a cat that's swallowed the canary. What's got into you?"

"I'll tell you after dinner," he replied. Humming a tune, he continued to smile, and when a waiter approached he ordered only coffee. "Don't hurry it," he instructed.

Naturally this switch added to the puzzle. While he ate little or often nothing at morning or at noon, he had always stocked up, regardless of his whisky intake, sometime during the dark hours.

Suddenly Jack dropped his arm below the table top, fumbled for a moment, then came up with love, laughter and the pursuit of happiness in his palm. The base and circlet of the ring were of heavy gold and the center inset was a tiny cat's-eye stone. The oval-shaped lip of the set was scalloped and hand worked into a colony of tiny whorls, and the center ensemble was surrounded by a crust of chip diamonds.

At the moment I was so flabbergasted that I even neglected to appraise the ring from a standpoint of value. It's—what?"

"It's a ring." He laughed. "For engagement purposes. Hold out your hand."

I slid it across as requested. Then the circlet was on my left hand.

"I sent Outside for it a few days after we got here. That's why I was so broke for awhile. The *Corwin* brought it in. Like it?"

"It's just—" I couldn't get out another word. However, a

short time later, calmed by a drink, I got back to normal. "I'm sorry to be so silly, dear. But the ring—"

"I know, I know," he interrupted. "Let's forget the ring. I want to talk about something else. Let's get married right away. I'm satisfied that I've money enough to start us now. Leonard Dodge—you know him—has something in mind for me." He leaned over the table, pulled me close, and kissed me. "But first, let's get married."

"Well." I had discovered that I was ambidextrous. With the ring on my finger, I was able to wave at people and do many things with my left hand which had been practically useless before. "You set the date."

"All right, make it November the twelfth. Okay?"

The following two weeks were a delicious, lacy dream. When the news of our engagement got out, the *Nugget* sent over a photographer and reporter, took our pictures and shucked us of our personal history, and thereafter we couldn't sneeze that it wasn't reported in detail on the newspaper's front page. Since Nome's last formal wedding had come off, roughly, during the era that man invented the wheel, the announcement had the effect of a minor social revolution, and it became impossible for us to accept even a portion of our invitations.

People whom we had never met hailed us on the streets, mashed my knuckles, added more contusions to Jack's back, insisted that we come over for drinks and such, and assured us that they would be on hand for the knot, rain or shine. The only sour note in the crescendo arose from Jack's attitude toward the church and religion in general. But that didn't last long. At first he stubbornly refused to be married by a minister and even threatened to call off the splice if I insisted upon a church wedding. However, I was able to call up reserves in *that* battle. I had some persuasive women on my side, and we were soon able to turn his charge.

Piece by piece, the project took on pattern. Al was to give me away. Lucy would be matron of honor. Leonard Dodge— the bluff, wealthy freighter and Jack's first real friend in Nome —was to be best man. My wedding ensemble was a plaid skirt, white blouse and felt boots. Plans for our honeymoon posed no problem. After the ceremony we would leave for an extended trip to Thornton's or Erickson's.

We made it to the Reverend Lester's altar three times in practice sessions before the cow, for a second time, jumped over the moon. The last was on a Sunday night, precisely one week before the real thing. I got an inkling of events to come when Jack telephoned me at noon on Monday while I was at work. His voice quivered with excitement.

"Honey! I'm at Erickson's. Can you come down? Right away?"

"Why, dear—I suppose so. What for?"

"Don't ask questions! Hurry up!"

Fortunately Al was doing paperwork at home, so I was able to shake loose, and twenty minutes later Jack was helping me into a chair. If his voice had sounded agitated on the telephone, he had the looks to go with it.

"Margaret! You'll never believe it! We're practically bogged down with the yellow stuff!"

"Gold?"

"Gold! Gobs of it!" he yelled. "Listen to this!"

The city council, he told me, had felt some discomfort in the late matter involving the marathon race. Since the mysterious and unexplained disappearance of Mr. Ridgell, Mr. Bridges and Mr. Wheatly, many people had been hollering fix and swindle, and not a few accusing fingers had been pointed at the council. The more audible of these dissenters were members of the defunct Sportsman's Club. These people wanted to know how and when they were to get back their dues. Inasmuch as no dues had been found intact, the council had been confronted with a stickler in the matter of responsibility. Some of the more vocally outraged had demanded that the council refund the membership fees, return the founders for a sweating, admit publicly that the council had been hoodwinked, or reactivate the Sportsman's Club.

"The council decided to sponsor the club," Jack added with satisfaction, "as a civic program. Its activities will be financed by the city, and it will be headed by a single director. Now who do you suppose he could be?"

"Why, I have no idea. You, maybe?"

"Good Lord, no." He laughed. "I wouldn't have that job as a gift. Our boy is none other than Jake Roberts."

"Jake Roberts? That dirty old man who had you arrested?"

Jack nodded. "He's a bum, for sure. But he's got influence and drive. And he's come up with an idea that'll make us rich."

"Wonderful! Wonderful, dear!" I imagine that I must have looked at him, then, the way commoners look at kings. "Glory be! Scads of money—and married to a handsome man that I love! I just can't believe it!"

Then abruptly, rudely, his manner changed. He yanked the makings from his pocket, started to roll a cigarette, flung it all away and sat back down. "I knew you'd bring up that marriage business. Especially at a time like this."

"Oh, Jack— Please—"

"I'll need every cent I can rake and scrape to float this. Our marriage will have to wait. This is simply too big to disregard."

"But—I don't understand. You said we'd be rich. Don't you get paid—or something?"

"I do not. I have nothing to do with the Sportsman's Club. I'll make my money on bets. These lummoxes know about as much of professional sports as a hog knows politics. I'll need all the money I've got to bet with."

"But, dear, I've got a job. And the money I won on Wado. Getting married wouldn't hurt anything, would it?"

Jumping to his feet, he stabbed both fists deep into his pockets, gazed moodily at the doorway for a moment, then turned and crashed down into his seat.

"I told you before," he bit out, "that I don't want your support. When I marry I'll support my wife. Can you get that through your thick head?"

"All right, dear. Whatever you say." I didn't realize it then, and very probably neither did he, but his consistently erratic behavior was rapidly turning a girl into a woman. "What's next?"

"Merely sit back for a week or two. As I said, Roberts came up with an idea that'll put us on easy street, if the council approves it. And I'm sure the yaps will," he continued, talking more to himself than to me. "Then I'll buy this town, just for the pleasure of burning it down."

"Buy the town?"

"What? Oh, sorry, Margaret. I was so carried away by my plans to make hay that I forgot to tell you what Roberts has in mind—as a next step for the Sportsman's Club. It's a dog race. Team, sled and driver. For a prize of twenty-five thousand dollars. No second or third prizes. Winner take all." Scraping his chair around, he located a waiter and lifted a finger. "You're seeing history in the making, Margaret. Of a sort."

"Oh?"

"The first professional, competitive dog-sled race in the annals of sports! It could only happen in Alaska!"

Chapter Nine

THE *Nugget*, blessed, smudgy little wad, helped spike my yowls of anguish by running a nice face-saving lie on its front page to explain the postponement of our wedding.

"This outstanding young couple are to be congratulated for their awareness of their duties as citizens of Nome," the piece read, just below the black headlines announcing the dog race. "Miss Knudsen's efforts as the city's only experienced telephone operator will be indispensable. Communications must be kept open." And so on. Nome owed us a debt of gratitude for our public spirit.

I felt a good deal less like a woman scorned, and Jack was pleased with the story. He should have been; he had fed it to them.

That night at Thornton's, as we stared morosely at the bill of fare—beans, pancakes, sourdough bread, canned tomatoes—Bill Thornton approached and whispered, "I have a surprise for you. Come with me." We followed him to the back room, where he showed us four hefty steaks wrapped in waxed brown paper. "Been saving them for your wedding," Bill said, "but we might as well have 'em now. Leonard Dodge is coming over to join us. You know him, Jack."

"I certainly do. The first man to give me a break here—"

He was interrupted by the clump of boots outside, followed by a whoop and a hearty laugh. Then Dodge bounded into the room grinning out of his russet beard.

"Arise, chee-chawkers!" he yelled, first belting Jack, then Bill. "And greet your king!" Turning to me, he bent over and smashed a kiss against my cheek. "Cherub!"

I had met Dodge several times before and had been drawn to him mainly because of the pleasing paradox that was so much a part of his personality and way of life. He was a college graduate, he told me years later, and had been dedicated to agriculture and stock raising upon his escape from the ivy and the hall. A stubborn bachelor to the end of his days, he had homesteaded a piece of ground in North Dakota in 1894, hoping to round out his life in the combination role of gentleman farmer, cowboy, swineherd and gooseboy.

But between 1895 and 1897 he was hailed out three times, and his crops, upon which he had counted to fatten his livestock, had been stoned so roundly that they resisted all efforts at salvage, to say nothing of resurrection. Broke and discouraged, he sold off his animals and equipment and got rid of his land by simply walking away from it. His wandering eventually landed him in San Jose, California, some forty miles below San Francisco, where he took a job as straw boss of a bunch of field hands in thrall to the owner of a large truck farm. Here he managed to sequester a quarter or two, and when Alaska's gold rush of '98 became common knowledge, he was on his way north like thousands of others. And like thousands of others he failed to hit pay dirt in the Yukon.

But Dodge was made of the same stuff as Al Boyd and Will Burke. He loved Alaska, intended to stay, and at heart he was a builder. He took the route that Al was to take in a later day, looking for gold with a pick of a different shape and purpose. He visited a number of camps and towns such as Fort Yukon, Sitka, Fairbanks, St. Michael, Ketchikan and Seward, and even lingered for a week in a haphazard shock of sticks, mud and debris known as Anchorage. But he decided that the place was not for him; regardless of any opportunities that might exist, it was too far south to be true Alaska.

"In Nome," he was fond of saying, his body shaking with laughter, "I found what I wanted. A lot of dogs and Indians, and only a few smart white men."

He meant it as a joke, but there was a good deal of truth in it. In Nome's rawer days, the freighting business was the monopoly of a dozen or so white men who kept it intact and bred no competition among themselves. Most of the freight was delivered to inland camps by dog teams herded by Indians or hit-or-miss drunken whites. In summer the camps could be serviced from the ships, even if it meant dispatching crews on foot to bring the supplies piggy back from the Bering Sea beaches. But in winter, when the camps were isolated by freezing temperatures and hard-packed snow, regular and dependable contact with Nome was a necessity.

The monopolists serviced the camps by the rotation system, charging exorbitant rates, and paying small attention to the care of their dogs, harnesses, sledges, and other equipment. These conditions gave them pretexts for postponing or refusing to make a scheduled trip.

Leonard looked over the situation, came up with some new ideas, and started a program which later made him generally recognized as the father of successful dog-team freighting and dog-team training in Alaska. To start with, he dug into his poke and bought a team of five dogs and a sledge from Bill Gagnon, a successful freighter, who laughed up his sleeve at the deal. The dogs were past their prime, and the sledge was a regular One-Hoss Shay. Since Gagnon and his colleagues regarded Leonard's venture with amused contempt and felt no concern over his competition, he was quick to pick their brains. He learned the art of candling, an important operation in handling working dogs. After literally sleeping with the mutts for a while, he bought tiny shears and began clumsily clipping the hair between their toes, burning the stubble down with a candle flame, then treating their feet with oil to remove any substance on which ice or snow could clot and lame an animal. Then he bought the best walrushide dog shoes he could find, repaired his broken harness and sledge, and within a month was on the snow, headed for the inland camps. Three months later he had a new sledge, painted a bright barn red, another and younger dog team, and money in the bank. He combined showmanship with the simple element of getting freight delivered on time, and it paid off.

At this point Gagnon and the other members of the syndicate began to feel alarm when their biggest accounts, the Goose Creek claim and the Salmon Creek diggings, started patronizing the upstart Dodge. They decided it was time to bring the lamb into the fold. True, Dodge had proved his loyalty by keeping up the rates; but his zeal in meeting schedules would have to be toned down; there was no use spoiling the men in the camps. And he would have to get rid of that red sledge.

Gagnon called the meeting that would make the newcomer one of the lodge, and when Leonard arrived at the Anzac House, a sod-hut hotel that was growing moss by the time I arrived in Alaska, he found the freighters assembled on gunpowder kegs, passing around the whisky. Gagnon gave him the grip, told him he was in solid, and passed him the bottle. It tasted good, and Leonard got roaring drunk.

"I've always thought of the incident as a bad dream," Leonard recalled. "Someone seemed to have got off on the wrong foot. One moment I was happy and at peace with the world. Then someone nodded to someone else. Someone asked me if I wanted to be a good boy, a regular fellow. I said I would love to, but I wanted to make some money. Someone said that I lacked the right attitude. I agreed. Someone else said this bird should be taught a lesson. Then the room was full of fists."

Leonard dimly recalled stepping over Gagnon and his syndicate members where they had fallen. But he actually came alive when confronted by the syndicate's Indians. During the fracas they had run outside, and as he lunged through the door they came at him. He decided to treat them with consideration, since they were only savages. Instead of caving them in with his fists he knocked their heads together and left them unconscious in the snow. After that the word got around.

By the year 1901, Leonard had the freighting industry in Nome by the horns and was recognized as the best dog breeder and trainer in the Territory. Two years later, he had nineteen teams running. His men were paid top wages, got a percentage of the gross take, and were required to stay sober, refrain from pinching a neighbor's *klutch*, and meet a monthly tonnage. With Leonard's drive, talent, and horse sense, they were better off than they had ever been.

Leonard also established good kennels where he bred dogs for sale; he designed a new sledge to replace the clumsy old ones—a lighter, stronger, narrower and longer vehicle equipped with metal brackets to keep the runners aligned and pointing true—an innovation that decreased the dog team's work and made steering easier. He also made improvements in the harness field. All his ideas caught fire, and he soon set up a plant for manufacturing equipment, putting drivers and Indians to work making units during slack seasons. By 1903 he was well-fixed and in a position to expand his interests.

He began grubstaking and bankrolling likely miners and prospectors in the area, and a number of them paid off in a steady trickle of gold. Backed by this new wealth, he began a program of generosity and open-handedness that amounted to a splurge. By 1904 he hadn't an enemy in the town.

It was not merely his generosity that made him esteemed; another reason for his popularity lay in his delightfully contradictory personality. There wasn't a stuffy, selfish or conceited bone in his carcass, and he loved to disparage his own character and position and to strip any pretense from others.

Where he had courage to burn, he insisted that he was a coward. Although his body was iron hard, and as far as I know he never suffered from so much as a cold, he insisted that he throbbed and ached from every known ailment, including thin arteries, a corroded set of bellows and a faulty plumbing system. He boasted of exploiting his Indian labor and of swindling his fellow whites, yet they worshiped him and ran to his cabin when plagued by bad dreams or squaw trouble. No man in Nome was owed so much handout money, with the exception of Will Burke, and no one had ever complained of Leonard's business methods.

He drove himself relentlessly, but liked to say he was lazy and that every dollar he owned had rolled in by pure bull luck or crooked manipulation. He professed to be an atheist like Jack, but his contributions to our church were the largest of any donor in town. His voice was like that of a cannon overcharged and backfiring, but he was the gentlest man I have ever known. He also possessed a streak of what kids of today call "corn" or "ham," but in my sinful day was known as "just putting on."

"I'm going broke," he said as we sat down to Bill Thornton's smoking steaks, sourdough biscuits, canned tomatoes and black coffee. "I need you, Jack. You can save me from a pauper's grave. Give a lonely old man a chance to recoup his fortunes and die in peace."

"Uh." Jack's mouth was crammed with food at the moment; when he wasn't drinking he was a wizard with the knife and fork.

"I've got some good dogs," Leonard went on. "I'll sell you a team, give you a route; I take twenty-five percent, you take seventy-five. Pay me for the team out of your earnings. What say?"

Jack grinned, forked another wedge of meat, and chewed a long time. "I'm a lawyer, Leonard," he said finally.

"And I'm the only client you've got."

Then I learned that Dodge had given Jack his first break as a lawyer in Nome by putting him on the payroll as company attorney at $200 a month—a bald gratuity since the firm had no need of a lawyer.

"All right, you're a lawyer," Leonard said. "But what's wrong with panning gold from several streams? Get into the running now before it's too late."

"Thanks, Leonard, but I'll stick to my own guns. I don't fit otherwise. Except in gambling."

By this time I was exasperated by Jack's stubbornness in refusing help from Al Boyd, his disdain of mining, and now his lofty indifference to Leonard's outstretched hand. His manner was particularly galling since it stood between me and marriage and home and family. I mistrusted his ability and his professional capacity for the first time, and began to understand the doubt and dislike in which our friends held him. I began thinking along lines that were unbecoming in a 1904 bride-to-be, if not inexcusably seditious. I was uneasy about my reasoning; but one thing was certain: I must have him at any price. I would have broken rock, robbed, or sold myself into slavery for him. If we were to prosper, I would have to lead the charge. By the time we got around to our coffee royals, I had made up my mind.

"I'd like to buy that team, Leonard, if the price isn't too high."

Jack, who was rolling a cigarette, poised the paper halfway to his lips. Dodge stared at me, mouth half open. Bill turned with a tolerant smile on his face.

"When can I look at the dogs?" I said.

"You're not serious." Leonard threw Jack a puzzled glance. "You're the boss. What do you say?"

Jack looked partly amused, partly annoyed. "Margaret often forgets that. She has a mind of her own. She is also the most intelligent and talented girl in the world. You'd better be careful. Sell her those pups, and she'll run you out of business." Then his face became more pleasant and he laid his arm on my shoulder. "You're joking, kitten. What would you do with a team? You're not much bigger than one of those dogs."

"I'm not joking." I realized that I was wide open to ridicule: Alaskan women in that day did not go in for freighting. However, I was too far downstream to quit, so I gritted my teeth and went on. "I've my own money. I want to buy that outfit."

Leonard chuckled. "Honey, I love your git and go. But freighting's not for women. It takes muscle."

"I can get a driver," I said. "He could do the work and I'll furnish the equipment, a fifty-fifty deal."

"Well," Leonard stalled, with an embarrassed grin, "I'm being put in the middle. Maybe you and Jack should talk this over first."

"No!" Suddenly I was bawling mad. "My money's my own. I'm not Jack's wife!"

Jack's eyes turned a chill gray, and he looked at me as though I were an acute mental case. Then, as Leonard cleared his throat noncommittally, Jack threw back his head with a laugh of genuine amusement.

"Sell her the team, Leonard. It'll give her a better chance to get away from me when I start chasing her."

That weekend our deal hung in suspense while Nome was snowed in by a sixty-hour blizzard. On Monday morning it was surrounded as far as the eye could see by four feet of white, and the air was like shaved ice. The community was in a holiday mood, and as I made my way to Leonard's office I dodged snowballs, hearing snatches of music from the wide-open saloons.

"Welcome, sucker," Leonard said as I entered his office.

"Oh, Leonard," I gasped, "where are they—the dogs? I'm so excited!"

"Here, sit down." He pushed me into a chair. "Rub your face." I rubbed until the sting was gone and took a cup of hot coffee.

"We'll go to the kennels in a minute," Leonard said. "But first I want to ask you some questions and I want truthful answers."

Then for the next few minutes he read me a stern lecture on what I was getting into. The cost of the outfit would be one thousand dollars; in addition, I'd have to feed and kennel my dogs at my own expense, get my equipment in shape, find a trustworthy driver and pay him. I took it all in.

"I'll get by," I said.

"All right. Consider yourself in business. I like your sand. I'll kennel your dogs free till you get started, and teach you to mush and care for them. I have to be in town a couple of weeks anyhow, and I can't wait to see the faces of the local heroes. Who ever heard of a woman freighter!"

Then he led me outside, up a steep path to a narrow, one-story building. As we went in, the interior came alive with yaps, snaps, short barks and growls. Leonard leaned over the top rail of one of the pens that housed five dogs each, and whistled.

"Come here, you scoundrels, and meet your new boss."

They were so pretty it hurt to look at them. Ears pointed stiffly and bushy tails tightly curled on their backs, they were all half grown and as alike as peas in a pod. All had the slanted gray eyes of the wolf. They were heavy-coated, red-gold in color, and with one exception, almost the same size.

"That's Pinky," Leonard grinned and pointed out a dignified fellow lounging comfortably in a far corner. "The other chaps are his brothers. Pinky was the firstborn of the litter. That makes him the oldest. Since he's also the biggest, he figures he's the head of the family and should be the boss. I agree. He's your lead dog."

"Leonard— Oh! They're beautiful! Let me in the pen, Leonard. I could love them to death!"

"Whoa! Hold on, my girl. You're not looking at Nebraska mutts. These dogs are one-eighth wolf. Mean anything to you? If not, I'll explain. A wolf is a man's animal. He thinks it's sissified to be kissed. You monkey with these boys and you're liable to need some stitches."

"But, Leonard, I want to drive them. You said, yourself—"

"I know what I said. I told you I'd teach you, and I will. But this team is only about ninety percent broken. It needs more work. All right?"

"Well, of course, Leonard. I'm sorry. I guess I'm too anxious to get in the swing. Whatever you say."

"Good girl. Now we'll go on to the next step. That'll be your sledge. Incidentally, I'm throwing in your harness. No charge. The set I've been using on them has absorbed their scent. They're used to it. Let's go."

The trek this time took us to a fortlike warehouse where a high board fence corralled an area about ten yards square, partially protected by a patchwork roof of tar paper and slabwood. Kicking open the door, Leonard herded me into an enclosure that combined the features of a lumbermill, harness shop and tool-yard, complemented by the general disorderliness that is traditional with junk dealers the world over.

To the left it was barren except for some snow-covered mounds. Boards and sticks showed through the drifts and portions of harness peeked through. To the right, a workbench held an assortment of bandsaws, handsaws and other cutting tools; coils of wire, nails and odds and ends of mutilated leather and lumber. An anvil sat on a stump at one end. A lathe, powered by a donkey engine, was attached to the other. Leonard took in the picture with an impatient jerk of his head.

"They didn't cover up the tools," he rasped. "The fools! First snow out, they're off and running."

Fighting the drifts, he stopped before a white-draped lump at the far end, turned and motioned me into the trail that he had broken. Reaching down, he put his shoulder into a mighty wrench. The effort dislodged a slide of powdery snow and brought into relief part of a high-backed, narrow-gauge sled. Grabbing the "gee pole," the steering apparatus that was standard equipment on all early day Alaskan sledges, he broke the runners from the ice with a series of sawing yanks.

"Get behind," he panted, "and push."

Ten minutes later we were through the gate, sledge and all, and resting in the yard.

"One of the first rules I made," Leonard told me as we sank down, puffing and blowing, "was that my freighters maintain schedules. I haven't changed my policy. So, when you get started, I'll ask the same from you." His thumb, directed toward his office, described a quick, short uppercut. "I make 'em go in there and sign out. Put their names and the time they leave on a piece of paper."

"But how do you know they don't fib? They could be an hour late—maybe more. If you weren't here to watch—why couldn't they just sign and—"

"They've caught me hiding a time or two. They never know when I'll show up."

"Suppose you catch one cheating? What do you do then?"

"Cut him off from a trip. Costs him about two hundred dollars. And if he does it again, I throw him to the wolves. I strip him of his route until he decides to become a good lad." Leonard brought out a fat-looking black pipe and a tin of Prince Albert tobacco. "You wouldn't be considering harpooning me —somewhere along the way?"

"Leonard! You're joking!"

"Am I?"

"Leonard! Honestly! I don't understand!"

"Perhaps you don't. So I'll try to explain. I don't like women who go against their menfolk. Especially I don't like hard-headed, acquisitive women. Far as I'm concerned, a woman's place is in the home. But that's not the point. Those eyes of yours don't kid me. I've seen 'em too many times. They look at you out of something crouched in a tree, hungry. That's all right too. I'll give you a start, as I promised. But let's get one thing straight. Jump me, you wind up talking to yourself."

Getting to his feet, he glanced thoughtfully at the sledge, pulled a new cloud of smoke from his pipe, stretched and sat down.

"Over in that warehouse," he said, "I've got two sledges. One is a light racing sledge. The other is a freighter. I built a fair chunk of retirement fund out of them, with the help of my malamutes. I was able to do this because of my honesty. So we come back to one thing. I'll put you on a route—if you arrange for a driver—and pay you a minimum of two hundred dollars a trip. I'll teach you to punch a team. I'll help you in every way that I can. But I have conditions."

"Well, of course. I don't expect—"

"I want you to work for me honestly. No bamboozling to get a few dollars. No skulduggery to keep Jack going. I don't want my little kingdom threatened."

"Threatened?"

"Let's get off the flagpole," he said harshly. "You're the annointed of God so far as Will Burke's concerned."

"Leonard Dodge! You're downright insulting! If you think I'd stoop to anything crooked—"

"I don't *think* you would. I *know* you would. I'm a pretty fair judge of human nature. I've got *you* pegged. Behind that doll face there's a mind that's conniving and unscrupulous and determined. I don't intend any insult either. I admire you. You get things done. But black is black and white's white. So there's no use in our beating around the bush. As I told you, I want us to start on the level and keep it that way. I don't want to take on Will Burke now that I've got my snoot in the gravy at last."

"What's Will got to do with it? You're talking in circles!"

"Maybe. If so, I'll lay it on thicker. I like Jack Bartlett in spite of the fact that the boy's unpredictable, temperamental, bigoted, dishonest, insufferably arrogant and as fumble fingered as they come. I doubt he'll ever get to bat in the practice of law. He'll always do something to gum up the works. I watched your face that night in Thornton's back room, and it told me a lot. You were bound to have this outfit and get into business for one reason. To put it roughly, you're going to have to make the living and you suddenly realized it. But there's a hidden card in the deck. One you haven't counted on. When you get a few bucks, it's going to be increasingly easy for him to forget his aversion to taking your money. And you'll give it to him. That's for certain. Then, his appetite for easy money being what it is, he'll want more. You'll give him that, too, if you can get it. But it's not going to come from cheating me. No false trip reports. No added expenses. No peddling of side-line supplies when I'm not looking. No swindling your driver out of his rightful cut. Am I making myself clear?"

"Yes, you certainly are! It's plain you want to be mean as can be!"

"I regret this conversation, youngster," he went on. "I wouldn't deliberately hurt your feelings. I want to help you. But we must understand each other. Let me draw you a picture. Maybe that'll help you to understand my position. Let's say you begin taking advantage of me. I couldn't afford to let you get away with it. I have plenty of potential Ali Babas working for me. They wouldn't accept any partiality on my part, woman or not. So I'm left hanging to a ledge, with a strong wind blowing. If I permit you leeway, they'll demand the same. I'd be forced to bust you in the interests of harmony and business policy. You run to Will Burke and deny everything. Exit Dodge."

"Leonard, how can you say such things?" Despite all I could do in the direction of gnawing my lips and swallowing, I felt the tears of anger and humiliation welling forth. Leonard was doing a better job of skinning me, in one way, than Jack had ever heard of, even at his uncompromising best. "I'm not that kind of a girl! Will's not that kind of a person!"

"Evidently you don't know him as I do. His loyalty to his friends is a disease with him. I wouldn't be the first man in the Territory to feel his whip. Once he figures he's right, that's it. And he believes he's always right where his friends are concerned. I couldn't buy a dollar's worth of merchandise if he decided to close the door. Between his own firm, the Yukon Trading Company, and the Northern Commercial Company, he controls the importation and sale of every commodity in Alaska. My little jerkwater keeps alive by buying and selling supplies. But if you can't buy them, you can't sell them. Am I making any sense?"

"Yes—I mean—I think you're horrid!"

"Sure," Leonard agreed cheerfully, "no one likes to be read the riot act, especially if the shoe fits."

An uneasy feeling steadied my chin and stopped the threatened flow of tears. I squirmed as I recalled the past times that I *had* worked a few questionable angles to get what I wanted.

Chapter Ten

IF some trail-wise dogman such as Leonard Dodge, Scotty
Allen or a dozen others, had explained to me what a trial by
fire the freighting business in Alaska was like in that era of
sourdough and beans, I would have said fie to the deal and
gone after an easier graduation from burlap to mink. But I
was to learn.

Still smarting from the effect of Leonard's verbal fanning, I
arrived at his diggings shortly after quitting time the next day,
struck what I believed to be a dignified pose, and handed him
a draft on Gene Chilberg's bank for $1,000.

"This concludes our agreement I believe, Mr. Dodge." I was
proud of my icy tone and self-possessed air, for I had rehearsed
the act while flouncing home. "I'll take ownership of the outfit
at once, if you please."

"You know where the dogs are. Your sledge is where you left
it yesterday. Your harness is hanging from the off post of your
pen. Hook 'em up and off you go."

"Hook 'em up?"

"Sure. You wanted to take ownership at once, didn't you?

When you finish your jaunt, come back, unhook 'em and pen 'em again."

"But Leonard, I don't know how to do that! You said you'd show me!" All my grandiose plans for putting him in his place went to pot, and my pose took off through the window. He knew that I didn't know beans about hitching and driving dogs! "You said you'd show me! You're just a big liar!"

"Me? Not now. I told you I'd put you through the traces and I will. However, you've got me fogged up. I thought you'd changed your mind. Learned overnight to punch a dog team." I could have throttled him cheerfully. Then the twinkle in his eyes got through to me.

"I'm sorry, Leonard."

"All right. Let's get to work, honey."

Moving to a wall rack, he picked off a block of smooth, white stone about the size of a brick and motioned me to follow him outside. "We'll begin with your sledge."

Reaching the unit, he broke it loose from the ice, flipped it upside down, stakes to the ground, and handed me the holystone. "Start from either end of the runners, front of back," he ordered, "and work forward. Use the stone as a carpenter would handle a planing tool. Don't stop until each one is slicker than owl spit."

"What does that do?"

"Conditions your runners. Makes 'em slip the snow easier. Rasps off the tiny splinters and hardens the wood. They don't wear out so fast. You won't need to do it more than once every two months after the first time. The constant usage keeps 'em in fair shape. Always remember one thing. The better the condition of your runners, the easier the pull on your dogs. Fast sled runners mean the difference in the load your team can handle."

"Uh—Leonard—I thought we were going to drive the dogs."

"Sure are. In about a month, if you learn fast. But first you've got to grow into your britches. Your eyes aren't even open. You start from the ground up. Okay, let's see some broken fingernails."

"You mean we're not going to drive the dogs for a month? You're just kidding me!"

"Nope. You'll need to know a lot of things before you get be-hind a team. Incidentally, let's put you right on a couple of things. We don't 'drive' dogs up here. We 'mush' 'em, or 'work' 'em. A 'sledge' is the right term for the article unless you're in Alaska. Then it's a 'sled' and there's good reason for the prefer-ence. Ever try saying 'sledge' with a mouthful of tobacco juice? Now get to work."

If I should suffer a complete loss of memory before the Peo-ple Upstairs order me home, the last recollection to go will be of my tutelage under that good friend and pitiless trainer Leonard Dodge. He kept me at those runners for three days be-tween my hitches at the switchboard, and backed off then only because my hands looked as if I had been making barbed-wire nosegays in a dark room. After that I spent a week learning to pack a balanced sled load, using such improvised educational material as an old trunk, blocks of firewood, blankets, a box of sawdust, sacks of dry beans and an English riding saddle—an article that Leonard had taken in pawn to aid a financially em-barrassed British black sheep who had passed through the pre-vious year.

But my miseries and despairs were still in their infant stages. Next to pop from the Devil's handbook of tortures were the mysteries of lashing the freight—an exercise that required the proper and repetitious tying of knots in coarse, cold-stiffened rope, then untying them. For a rest period I was permitted the lighter task of treating my rawhide harness with axle grease. But I was scheduled for even more cramming in Leonard's caves of learning.

The sleds, frieghters of the racing variety, were about four feet wide and ranged in length from six to eighteen feet. In either case they were fitted with upright stakes or ribs to secure a load, or, as the case might be, a passenger. A two-by-four at-tached to the back, chest high in horizontal position, acted as a steering device. Another, stretched across the runners and pierced by a six-inch railroad spike, served as a brake. When a person wanted to stop a running team he simply brought his weight down on the lower bar and drove the spike into the ice or snow.

The spike on my sled added a certain touch to my apprenticeship. When Leonard announced that I was ready to absorb the rudiments of making dog shoes and candling the animals' feet, I let off a whoop, dropped the rope, and jumped on the brake as he had coached me earlier. There should have been less enthusiasm in class. My left foot went under the spike and my weight drove it into my boot, shaving off a strip of skin between my first and second toes.

Leonard dragged me, blithering, to Doctor Andy Sheffield, a taciturn old fellow and the nearest of Nome's two medicine men, who probed for broken bones, pronounced them absent, bandaged my foot, then poured a bottle of horse liniment over his handiwork. The mishap put me in storage for some time. The abrasion was complicated by a bad bruise, and the liniment produced large, painful blisters. Due also to Leonard's salt-mine tactics, I was behind in my duties to the beach heathen.

The winter was well into its third blizzard before I was able to brave his next offensive. However, by December, having served my sentence at candling, feeding and harnessing the dogs, I came into a share of the silver lining. I was working, *solo*, my own team. If I remember rightly, Leonard turned the twelve-foot, braided rawhide whip over to me on our third day out. After he had bucked the kinks from the team, he waved his hand toward the rolling white drifts in the distance.

"Take 'em in a half-mile circle and come back. Remember, 'gee' for left, and 'haw' for right. When you give the command, crack your whip on the off side. I mean, when you yell 'gee,' pop it on the 'haw' side—and vice versa. Don't ask me why. I don't know who invented the method. Probably some Indian with two left hands."

At the end of the third whirl he walked up to me and stripped the mitten from his right hand. I still find it nice to remember his smile and the surprise in his eyes. "You're a natural, sweetheart," he said, squeezing my fingers. "All you need now is practice." With that he turned and started walking back to town.

So I got another slice of Alaskan life and I loved every invigorating moment of it. My dogs were young, strong, healthy and well broken. My sled was smaller and lighter than the average freighter's, and since my stature was slight, I was able to ride the runners most of the time on my daily excursions.

Soon I was venturing into the interior, and it wasn't long before I was crossing trails with the regular freighters and stopping for chats with miners and other people who were traveling in or out of Nome. I must admit that my conceit wasn't punctured by the surprise and confusion they showed in seeing a young girl behind a dog team.

My ego and enthusiasm were not dampened, either, by the reception that I got from Jack and Lucy and Al Boyd. While all declined my numerous offers of a ride, they were unanimous in their approval and unstinting in their applause. I suddenly realized that they had been sitting back waiting to see if I was worthy of a curtain call. Loving him as I did, I found Jack's attitude a particular favor of fortune.

"I'm proud of you, honey. As Leonard says, you've got sand."

"Piffle." I treated my engagement ring to an appreciative glance. "There's money to be made around here. Wait until I get someone to work that team. No more worrying for us."

"Piffle."

"What?"

"Let's go. I've got some tough lobo poker ahead of me. I'll take you back to your executive offices first, though."

"But, dear, I want to talk. We haven't seen each other for a month of Sundays, it seems."

"Hurry up." He grinned. "Before you get *both* feet in your mouth."

But if I had made the grade among some societies, I soon learned that such could not be expected in others. From the start Leonard's freighters showed that they wanted no part of me and made no bones about it, except when he was near. I suppose it amounted to the old universal story. A woman's place, so many people like to believe, is in the home. Anyway, I had only to appear in Leonard's freighting corral preparatory to unhooking my team and penning it, when the freeze set in. First it amounted to pure silence and evasive glances, muffled chuckles and crude gestures. But as the month went by this campaign grew outright offensive, loaded with vulgar remarks just short of the obscene.

One giant black-bearded Canuck was particularly insulting. About thirty years old, but almost toothless, he had the sloping shoulders and long arms of an ape and about the same degree of intelligence. He worked a full-size short-haul freighter and mushed three teams of malamutes alternately. To the un-initiated this information can mean nothing. To his colleagues it meant that he was so money hungry that he ran his dogs mer-cilessly in order to grab every open route that Leonard had to offer, and constantly rode his sled to save his own strength.

His real name was Jean Beaujolais, born in Quebec, Canada, and illegally in Alaska for the past ten years; but I never heard him called anything other than Caw, probably because his voice was that of a crow with laryngitis.

Dodge's other freighters were frankly afraid of him, and I'm sure—looking back—that their rude treatment of me took the form of appeasement to him rather than actual dislike or dis-approval of my presence or actions. At any rate, he hated me and didn't falter in showing it when he saw the chance.

My arrival at the kennels when he was in town was sure to send him into a smirking burlesque of the cancan dance. When-ever possible he would spit on my dogs, and I could count upon arriving at the kennels to find my harness snarled, my lashings tightly knotted or my sled overturned.

Needless to point out, I was near tears a good deal of the time, as the situation seemed to lack a reasonable solution. I was forced to board my dogs at Leonard's kennels—there was no other place in the area to keep them. I could work them only when I was free of my switchboard, or specifically, in the late afternoon. This meant that my return to the kennels was bound to coincide with those of the freighters who had concluded their round trips to the camps, and these invariably included Caw. Ducking him was out of the question.

I thought of going to Leonard with the problem. But that idea always ended in the discard. Understanding his streak of loyalty as I did, I knew that he would fire Caw and maybe some of the others. He ran a business and a good one, and his chief asset was represented by manpower. Freighters were worth their weight in gold at that time. I also shrank from calling in Al or Jack. I was afraid of Caw, and I didn't want Al or Jack hurt, perhaps seriously. However, the unhappy state resolved itself about two weeks before Christmas and in a way that gave me an overdose of bad dreams.

Returning to the kennels on a Saturday afternoon, I saw that, except for a couple of men, the rest of Leonard's freighters had come and gone and Caw was not in sight. His absence caused no sadness to assail my spirits, and I was so relieved that I was momentarily tempted to speak a friendly word to two men who were talking near the kennel door.

But alas for my hopes. A second later Caw came from the pens, leading one of his dogs. Stopping at his sled, he took a pair of walrushide gloves from somewhere inside, pulled them on, and jerked a short piece of chain from his parka. Throwing the dog to the ground, he began to beat it.

I learned sometime later that the man was employing the prescribed treatment for dogs that have become intractable, lazy or mean. Since the rawhide whips were reserved for guiding the animals on trail, they were not used for disciplinary purposes. The freighters preferred a length of thin chain to change their dogs' bad habits, thus establishing a line between direction and correction.

I might say in fairness to Caw that this brand of punishment was frequently needed by Alaskan sled dogs. Without exception, they had wolf or fox blood and they resented the collar of domesticity—to say nothing of their aversion to labor—and they schemed twenty-four hours of the day to get out of both. An undisciplined dog, if permitted to pursue his independence, grew increasingly dangerous. For no reason he would grab a jawful of hand or leg at any time, and too much laxity with the chain could put a person in the teething-ring business.

But I didn't understand this as I watched Caw beat the dog into whimpering unconsciousness. I could think only of the hatred and loathing I had for him, mixed with contempt for the two men who stood by and watched. I ran up, grabbed his shoulder, and began yanking at him.

"Don't—you dirty beast. Let him alone! You hit that dog again and I'll kill you!"

"Y—y'weel?" Dropping the chain over his neck, Caw pushed the dog aside and dropped his arm across his knee. Still squatting, he looked up, let his eyes travel from my head to feet, then worked his mouth and spit a great stream of tobacco juice over my boots. "You ack like man, mebbe you batt' smell l'ak w'on."

That's all it took, and had I been able to foresee the consequences, I would have unhooked my team right then, put them to the salmon, gone home and tried to forget it. But I was so angry that I left my team in harness and ran off.

I was in Erickson's drinking a cup of coffee when Jack slid into an opposite chair. "How's the globe-girdling going, honey?"

"Oh fine."

"Hey, what brings you here at this time of day? We were to meet at Lucy's and Al's later."

"N—nothing. Just wanted some coffee, that's all."

"Sure?" His tone was kindly.

Then it all came out. I couldn't keep it back, not at that time and under the circumstances.

"Well," Jack murmured. "Let us, by all means, go see this fellow."

"Jack—please! He's so big and—and ugly! He might kill you! Let's just forget it? Please!" There was ice in my stomach. The taste of panic was bitter to my tongue, for Jack's face had taken on that look of cruel, hungry anticipation so familiar when he was spoiling for a fight, and I knew that nothing short of death or disablement could stop him. "Please—Jack!"

"Don't be stupid," he said harshly. "Come on."

Much as I wanted to avoid the showdown, I realized that wild horses could not have dragged me from his side. The anxiety of waiting off-stage for reports of the outcome would have been impossible. And I was beset by a dilemma that came at me from two directions. While I was quaking with fear for his safety, I was also afraid of what he might do to the Canuck and land in the hooks of the constabulary. So I followed him into the street.

"Leonard know about this?" he asked as we walked uptown toward the kennels.

"No. I've never said anything to anyone."

"That's not using your head very well. Why didn't you tell me, at least?"

"Jack—I didn't want trouble! Please! I still don't!"

As happenstance would have it we met Leonard as we passed the bathhouses. He had been soaking in the hot water at the bathhouse and was headed for his office. Seeing us, his teeth sparkled in his beard and he split the air with his habitual yell. Then his smile went away and he looked sharply at Jack.

"What's up, boy?"

"Nothing. Nothing to get excited over."

"Where you children bound?"

"Your place," Jack snarled. "I'm going to bust up one of your men."

"Bust?" Leonard stopped and his expression of surprise turned to understanding as he looked into Jack's eyes. "You mean fight?"

"That's the idea."

"Wait a minute! There'll be no battling on my spread!"

"Yes there will. When you learn why." Jack outlined the issues as I had given them to him and even laid it on a little. "What else can I do? She's to be my wife, Leonard."

"Sure, sure," Leonard admitted helplessly. "But I don't know why I wasn't told. I could have straightened it out without trouble." He turned to me, his eyes angry and disgusted, and shrugged his shoulders. His gesture suggested that I, too, needed a touch of the chain and that he was sorry I didn't walk on all fours. "Why didn't you come to me?"

"I didn't want you to fire anyone over me and ruin your business, Leonard!" My voice at that point rose to an operatic tremolo.

"Okay," Leonard muttered, "I suppose you did what you believed was right." He pointed ahead to where, a few yards inside the inclosure, the Canuck was poking on hands and knees at a twisted stack of harness. "There's your fathead, Jack. But I wish you'd can the idea."

Jack pushed past us and with three rapid strides approached Caw from behind. Reaching down, he yanked off the Canuck's cap and fastened both hands in the man's coarse, black hair. With a savage jerk, he flung him into a threshing, astonished heap.

"Get up." He smiled. "Let's get better acquainted."

Whatever else he lacked, Caw was no slouch at putting two

and two together. Bounding to his feet, he squinted mur-
derously at Jack, stabbed a look at me, then clenched his gorilla
fists, sounded a strangled croak and went to war.

He never had a chance.

Jack caught the poor fellow's first punch—a ponderous, over-
hand right swing—in the palm of his left hand, as a baseball
player fields a hit ball. Then he swayed to the right, flung down
the Canuck's fist, reversed his stance and brought his right
across in a short, arching hook. The blow crushed Caw's nose
and sent him down, choking and wheezing on his own blood.

Up once more, the Canuck charged again, pawing, croaking
and spraying Jack's face and torso with the red mist of his
breath. Feinting once, Jack drew him off balance and knocked
him down with a wallop that tore open his eyebrow and very
nearly broke his neck. The third time that Caw made his feet
Jack switched his attention to the man's body, and his methodical, unhurried blows, landing on the man's stomach and chest,
had the sound of someone pounding a hogtied horse with a club.

Suddenly I was sick, unashamedly. I had seen fist fights before, both in Nebraska and in Nome. Some had been bloody,
some bloodless. But none had shown such sadistic overtones.
Angry physical conflict, outside of a dance hall in Blair or blowing off resentment over a losing card streak in Nome, was one
thing. Butchery, whatever the reason, was another. Inexperienced as I was, I saw that Jack was deliberately avoiding any
damaging or decisive contact with Caw's vulnerable spots—such
as jaw and temple—the better to prolong the Canuck's suffering.
I could stand no more. Retching and shuddering, I started to
turn away, tears streaming and hands fumbling for a handkerchief. Then Leonard stopped it.

"That's it, Bartlett. He's had enough!"

Springing back from the helpless man, Jack looked at
Leonard with the bright, polished eyes of a preying wolf, and
his expression was more hideous for the fact that simultaneously he licked his lips.

"I said, enough!" Jumping between them, Leonard pushed
Caw into a moaning squat, ordered him to stay down, and
turned to face Jack. "You slug him once more, and I'll get my
gun and blow your head off!"

"You'll do what?" The smile disappeared from Jack's lips, and as he met Leonard's eyes he moved a little to one side. "I don't get it."

"Oh yes you do. What you did to this poor clown shouldn't happen to a dog. From now on you stay clear of my men. I've got two forty-five caliber revolvers and a rifle that's good enough for kodiak bear. You understand?"

"Perfectly," Jack murmured, his frown vanishing. He moved over and took my arm. "We're going downtown. Want me to send up a doctor?"

"Suit yourself. It might help your case if this fellow dies."

But Jack's good luck held, and there was not even an arrest. Old Doc Sheffield repaired the Canuck, who recovered in a week and disappeared without ever having made a complaint. Though refusing to comply with Alaskan customs regarding women had started the trouble, the experience helped my original purpose—to get in the money.

Fortunately Leonard was quick to forgive and forget, and he and Jack were soon on easy terms; there was no difficulty because of possible hard feelings between them. But the next step was much harder. I had to dig up a freighter for the route Leonard had promised me, and that proved, as I had been warned, almost impossible. For a time nothing worked, including notices pasted on the town's public bulletin boards, ads in the *Nugget*, personal buttonholding and wild promises of reward to anyone who could find such an excellent and worthwhile citizen.

Once I even sneaked feelers through my switchboard to some line camps, a daring and hazardous operation. Using the board for such business, according to Al Boyd's lights, was a felony ranking above that of protesting the amount charged for service or eavesdropping on telephone conversations. But eventually Lady Fortune smiled and in a way that could happen only in Alaska. It was the outgrowth of the one insult offered by a wife that no man can forgive—the question of his physical prowess after he is gray. So I got my freighter.

Millie and Walter Stapf were a homely lovable couple who ran a wood-carving and ivory-sculpting shop next door to the Yukon Trading Company. They had been in Nome for about ten years in the same location, which included their living quarters in back. I met them early in December of 1904 when Lucy caught me making out a Christmas list and suggested that I drop over there.

"You might be surprised," she added, "at the quality of some of their stuff—bowls, cribbage boards, figurines. Give it a look, papoose."

This I did, and since I've always been a sucker for the Christmas holidays, I browsed away a good block of time in their place. I got to know Millie, for she, unlike her husband, was quite willing to hold up her end at conversation. Walter had been a bull cook until his retirement from the Army Signal Corps in St. Michael. They had been married for thirty years and had no children. Walter, with nothing to distract him in his off hours, had taken up carving. He had got good at it, too, and when he had been pensioned they'd moved to Nome and set up shop.

"Nome's been good to us," Millie was fond of saying. "Right smart good."

Physically, Walter was a beardless, white-haired Abraham Lincoln, save that his bony nose had the dashing uplift of a sled runner, his eyes were much less suffering, and his shoulders were narrower and more stooped. I never saw him dressed in anything but checkered woolen shirt and bib overalls, at least when inside, and he smoked a pipe that performed like an over-turned Yukon wood stove.

Millie could have been his twin except that she patterned her coiffure along the lines preferred by Texas bangtails, and where Walter had a few teeth left she had none. But she was equally tall, stooped, bony, homely and great hearted, and where Walter wore overalls Millie wore olive-drill coveralls.

I was looking around in their shop one day when I felt the need to lament the misfortune of owning a freighting team without a freighter. Millie was tagging me through the zoo.

Walter, who had been gouging a walrus tusk into a civilized state, laid down his pipe with one hand and his cutting tool with the other and looked up. "You got some dogs?"

"Yes. Fine dogs. But I don't have a freighter to work them. Like I just said to Millie—"

"Sled? Fittin' fer freightin'?"

"Yes."

"Y'say Leondard Dodge give you a r-oot?"

"I only have to get a freighter."

"Mebbe I'll give you a hand." Walter carefully avoided Millie's suddenly belligerent attitude; but she wouldn't be barned or corralled.

"Walter! We got a nice business! You stay t'work!"

"Man gits tired bein' cooped up," Walter growled. "Likes to git out in the snow once in a while. You kin mind the shop. We got plenty of stock."

"You do this—you kitch yer death! Cain't you see you're an old man!"

That did it. Walter slammed down his pipe so hard it almost exploded. "I'll be ready tomorrer, Marg'ret," he said. "I'll show you a thing or two. Old!"

I left at once, to avoid Millie's wrath; but when I showed up the next day, she gave me a pat on the hand and a smile, although she was still clearly peeved at Walter.

"So long, old woman," he said as we left. "Be back t'night!"

"No fool lik an old fool," Millie said. "Ketch yer death. See if I keer." She banged the door after us.

So I got my freighter. Leonard, in deference to Walter's age, assigned us a short-haul route servicing the upper Salmon and Goose Creek sectors, about twelve miles from Nome. Walter, an old hand at working dogs, loved every minute of it, and suffered nothing more serious than chapped skin in the week that followed. I nearly fainted when on the seventh day after the formation of our partnership, Leonard handed me a draft on Chilberg's Bank for $300. After expenses this left $250 to be split between Walter and me, and I took my share and continued my Christmas shopping with the air of a woman to whom price is no object.

Several years ago, when visiting old friends of that era in Alaska, I discovered that some of them still had my gifts of that first Christmas. Certainly they were lasting, after the fashion of most construction in Alaska, utilitarian or not. There were sturdy chess sets and cribbage boards, cedar tobacco boxes, mufflers, socks and mittens for the men; pictures, figurines, wooden bowls, blouses and underwear for the women; and beads, yards of bright cloth, rock candy and blankets for the Indians.

For Jack I chose a gold watch with matching chain and fob from a stock offered by a Swiss jeweler who ran a shop in the Golden Gate Hotel. I also bought an ornate eight-day clock for Lucy and Al Boyd from the same store, and gave Barney Mc-Cready and Rex Beach, who lately had appointed themselves to our inner circle of friends, a buckhorn-handled hunting knife apiece, pipes, tobacco and cigars. Leonard Dodge's gift from me was a stickpin topped by a medium-sized but real pearl. I had not realized how many people I had come to know until I had totaled my shopping list, and before I finished I had dropped nearly $500. However, as I sowed, so did I reap.

Barney and Rex gave me a gold nugget that weighed out, as I recall, at about $700. Leonard dropped by and left a heart-shaped gold-and-cameo locket inscribed with my name. Lucy and Al each handed me a $100 bag of gold dust, and Jack gave me an amethyst dinner ring. For the rest, I could hardly find room in my cabin for the scarfs, liquor and knickknacks that suddenly showered down, and I was a very happy girl, I can tell you.

But perhaps the most staggering surprise of all came from some of the outlying camps. Shortly before Christmas Eve a series of $100 pokes of gold dust, delivered to my office by freighters, began to arrive. In every case I found a slip of paper inside, topped by a pencil-scrawled "Merry Xmas," or "Merry Christmas," and carrying the signatures of as many as fifteen miners.

"I don't understand it," I told Al when I began getting my breath back.

"There's no dark plot afoot." He smiled. "You have always gone further than is required in doing your work. On top of that, you're pleasant and cooperative. Those fellows appreciate it. So they're showing you how much."

"But I don't recognize half of these names."

"Makes no difference. They simply want you to know, as I said, that your efforts are appreciated. You don't *have* to run some bird down—through ten saloons—because he's being telephoned from one of those camps. I've never asked you to do it."

That much was true. Company policy only required that I put a call through to a certain number. After that, if no answer was forthcoming, the service obligation was ended. However, in the years that I worked an early-day Alaskan switchboard I never could let the matter end there. Part of it was stubbornness, I suppose. I've never been satisfied to let problems dangle. But there was another facet to the situation. By that time I had begun to recognize voices and identify them. I'm sure that I have never been particularly inconvenienced by lending a friend a little extra muscle, and so it was at that time.

"I just don't know what to say, Al! It's simply unbelievable!"

"Anywhere but up here. I consider it a compliment to our company too. Congratulations, honey."

So I was riding a golden dolphin, and pretty smug to boot over the way things had turned out for me in the past three months. And there were good things to come, too, for Nome's holiday season was a round of open houses and partying that left most of us wondering how we would get to work in the morning. For me the situation was even more taxing. Jack was holding his temper and refusing every drink offered. His popularity was increasing by leaps and bounds. He slept until noon every day while I was stomping grapes, and come nightfall he was ready to go again. I began to get red eyed and found myself envying people with chronic insomnia.

Several days after Christmas, Jim Sutter, the oldest jeweler in Nome, telephoned and asked to see me in his store. I went there late that afternoon. Rummaging in a drawer, he lifted out a crescent-shaped silver box, roughly the size of a slice of watermelon, and shoved it across the counter.

"Memory's getting bad, I guess," he explained, apologetic and obviously embarrassed. "Will Burke said to give it to you Christmas Eve. Sorry, Miss Knudsen."

Springing the lid, I looked down upon something that caused me to believe, momentarily, that my lack of sleep had affected my mind. A six-strand lavalier winked up at me, its platinum, interwoven mesh encrusted with rubies and sapphires. A diamond about the size of a goober peanut was its pendant. It looked so fantastically expensive that I almost smothered in my own breath. In lifting it from the box my hands trembled so that I dropped it on the floor, and in retrieving it I noticed that there was a tiny envelope attached to the clasp by a red silk tassel. There was a hand-written card inside. It read:

> Happiness to you on your first
> Christmas in Alaska, my dear.
> Always,
> WILL

I struggled with the swelling in my throat, torn between gratitude toward Will and apprehension lest Jack should discover that he'd given me a gift worth approximately $10,000. Then I became aware that Mr. Sutter was standing by me nervously twitching his hands.

"Miss Knudsen," he said. "This is the biggest order I've ever had. It was sent up from New York. The thing is—I was supposed to deliver before Christmas, but my memory is getting bad. I just hope Mr. Burke won't ever know."

"He won't," I said. "Nobody knows but us. Will you wrap it up, please?"

"Thanks, miss. Just you and me. Better days are coming for us here in Alaska. Merry Christmas!"

Chapter Eleven

ANYONE could have hailed me with that greeting for the next two months and still have been in season. The Christmas celebration that year continued full blast into March, because of the general excitement about what the *Nugget* called the Big Dog Race. After I got over my feverish preoccupation with the most prosperous Christmas I had ever known and had settled down from the shock of my unwonted affluence, I began to realize that I had fallen behind the civic developments in Nome.

The race, set for March 20, between Candle, a large camp to the east, and Nome, a distance of fifty miles, lured hordes of men from the outlying sectors, and as in the case of the recent marathon race, the mine owners complained bitterly over their inability to keep their varlets on the job. The streets were choked with shouting, laughing humanity, most of whom, because of the jammed hostelries, were forced to sleep with friends or in the back rooms of saloons, stores, and even on the freezing floors of warehouses.

The bawdy houses and booze emporiums held their doors open twenty-four hours a day. Steep, flanked by Mike Kemp and Jim Crail, his two burly assistants, was kept busy belaboring the wicked and consoling the bruised. There was no hour when private parties and public dances were not in full swing, and every official was soon down with laryngitis, the outgrowth of extended speeches and bouts with the mash.

The committee of ten that handled the details of the race could be heard a mile away from its headquarters in the old Sportsman's Club at the Golden Gate Hotel. The counting-house, as the betting counter was called, was besieged by eager bettors who tossed their pokes of gold dust around with the abandon of professional jugglers.

For my part, I couldn't cope with the plethora of telephone calls that came through the board. Early in March, Al added six hours to our service and handled the extra time himself. He split my shift so that I would have an opportunity to learn the ground rules of the event, the identities of the contestants, the scope of the betting and the continually changing odds. It was part of the service of the Nome Telephone Company to act as an information center, since the *Nugget* came out only once a week, and Al proudly insisted on maintaining our high standards.

In addition to being a telephone operator and a dog-team owner, I became a reporter, and with the official approval of the *Nugget*'s editor, Howell Beane, I was allowed to seek information in dance halls and saloons, hotels, restaurants, stores, offices and the racing headquarters at Leonard Dodge's freightyards. Old Beane, however, drew the line at letting me write up the material which I turned over to the paper. "The *Nugget* has a style of its own," he explained loftily, and it certainly did.

The news of the big event had reached the Outside, and, since the weather had locked us in tight, newspaper reporters from the States had to rely on us for information. The wire services hooked up with the Army Signal Corps at St. Michael and the corps turned over the whole job of disseminating information—mostly betting odds and the experts' predictions on the outcome—to the telephone company.

When the race was about two weeks away, the odds began to change almost hourly. The reason was Leonard Dodge's decision to enter the race. He had refused in the early stages, since he owned the best dogs in the area, was the most experienced handler and felt that he might be taking an unfair advantage. But his friends finally persuaded him to run the race, and he did so on a grand scale, mortgaging everything he owned to Eugene Chilberg and laying all his money on his own nose, a reckless gesture that surprised no one who knew him.

His entry accelerated the betting, and it spilled over out of the countinghouse into the streets. It seemed that everybody wanted to bet on Leonard.

"I'm glad I played it close," Jack told me, "until I found out Leonard was going in. So far I'm down on Scotty Allen for three thousand. Okay, so it's lost. That still leaves me about fifteen thousand, and I was lucky. I put it on Leonard at five to one before the odds changed. What are they now?"

I looked in my notebook and made out that they were about twelve to two. Jack was pleased and convinced that Dodge would walk off with the race. He offered to put down some money for me, and I wrote him a bank draft for $500.

"Quite a plunger, aren't you?" he said, the familiar barb of sarcasm in his voice.

Actually I was well fixed, after the diet of snowballs and hot air I'd lived on for a few months; my Christmas gifts, my salary, and the profits from my freighting business, gave me a nice feeling of security, and I shied away from losing any of it. "It's all I can afford right now," I told Jack. "I want to branch out with my business." It was a dim explanation and on the gray side of the truth, but I felt that Jack was warming up to give me a hard time and I was too tired to take it. But he didn't argue as he pocketed the draft. Instead he turned to discussing the trial runs.

These preliminary workouts had been approved by the Sportsman's Club as a barometer for determining the odds on the various principals in the race. The officials had sunk a ten-mile marker on the trail to Candle, stationed a sentinel there, and marked the hour and minute when a dog team pulled out, clocking its time when it returned. Entrants had been hitting the snow every thirty minutes of the day on a rotation basis, so numerous were the contestants. Until late in February it looked

as though anyone who could beg, borrow, or steal a dog team
was cutting up the snow in all directions. But now the whole
thing was beginning to take on a professional aspect. The race
had been conceived originally as a face-saving device for the
city council and a sop to the disgruntled members of the Sportsman's Club who had not forgotten the way Messrs. Ridgell,
Bridges and Wheatly had hoodwinked them. Now newspapers
on the Outside had horned in, and no bungling or amateurism
could be tolerated if Nome was not to become the laughingstock
of the sporting world.

The committee's first step was to cut out the ragtag-and-bob-
tail element and pare the field down to the real professionals. A
thousand-dollar entry fee was slapped on each contestant, which
partially cleared the decks, and when Leonard Dodge announced his entry, all but ten or twelve hopefuls bowed out.

So far Leonard had clocked the best time in the trial runs.
Next to him was Scotty Allen, a wiry, gray-eyed man who had a
habit of nervously swiveling his cap around and around on his
head, running, walking, talking or sitting. But what he lacked
in conversational accomplishment he made up by the perpetual
smile that sat on his lips. During my scrounging for news I got
little out of him save that he had been "around and about"
since his birth in Wisconsin some thirty-five years ago, and that
he had been in Alaska for about ten years, the last five of them
spent in the capacity of handy man for Jake Roberts, merchant,
enemy of Jack Bartlett and president of the revitalized Sportsman's Club. For the rest, he was recognized as one of the best
dog workers in the game, and he had proved himself worthy of
the tribute on more than one occasion while sledding Roberts'
orders to the camps. Even Leonard Dodge, a critic of the first
chop in this respect, appreciated Allen's proficiency, and the
fact that Scotty mushed another man's dogs and didn't abuse
them added to Leonard's appreciation of him.

Scotty had a helper to crutch him in his jack-of-all-trades
capacity with Jake Roberts. This fellow was called Happy Jack.
He was a half-breed Siwash with stringy, night-black hair,
scraggly brows, eyes like undersized California ripe olives, and
a wide and open smile. Below that he looked like something
that had been wrapped in discarded bandages.

194

Another entrant was Jim Frame, who had one eye. He had never liked me from the moment when, in my zeal to get the news, I asked him what happened to his other one. After his curt dismissal of me on two occasions, I finally got his drift and had to be satisfied to learn what there was to him from his friends and acquaintances. That turned out to be precious little. He was a native Alaskan, having been born of an alliance between an English-French river rat and a Chilkoot woman in Sitka some forty years before. One of the few independent freighters who had escaped Leonard Dodge's marauding business grabs, he had come to Nome at the turn of the century and lived with a Siwash squaw and eight children in a slab hovel on the town's fringe. He also worked a magnificent team of malamutes.

Four days before the event the three were the sole contestants left in the field, and the odds on Leonard were still climbing.

On March 17 Al informed me that I was to go to Candle to report the race from that end. He'd already spoken to Jack about it, assuring him that I'd have plenty of protection, and for once Jack had not kicked up a fuss. Lucy also approved when she learned that I'd be riding up with John Masterson, a good freighter and now one of Al's most trusted aides in the telephone company.

"You leave tomorrow morning. Now cock an ear, my girl."

Then he gave me the recipe for my operations during the next three days. In the interest of a light load I was to take my usual outer garments such as parka and boots, two changes of underwear and nothing else. Candle was fifty miles away, and most of the trail was no trail at all. It amounted to hillocks of snow and ice for the most part, and to conserve my strength I would ride the sled. I was to take orders, with no questions, from Masterson to and from Candle. He knew his dogs, trails and sleds, and he knew Alaskan weather and travel conditions. He had been given another duty to perform and he wouldn't need any impatience or complaints from me while he was at it. He was to inspect and repair the telephone lines as we went along.

"These wild men in town," Al continued, "would stretch my neck from the nearest rafter if there was a ballup on the wires.

This is one time that my very life depends on the Nome Telephone Company."

The remainder of his instructions called for me to put up at Swedish Kate's, a respectable tavern and recognized center of Candle. There I was to clock the racers' arrival time *correctly*, observe the condition of their teams, and report back to Nome. There was no switchboard at Candle, and only one telephone —at Swedish Kate's. Al would be on the Nome end of the line to receive my report.

"Honey, this situation has grown pretty touchy. You've got to get the time of arrival down to the minute. The way this is going and the amount of money involved, there could be a challenge over a second or two."

He ended his briefing with the warning not to fudge in the interest of my friendship with Leonard Dodge and not to get into any arguments.

Nome was hog wild that night. Before Jack, Al, Lucy and I crowded into Thornton's we went to the Golden Gate Hotel and took a look at the bulletin board nailed to the wall with the elegant Sportsman's Club banner above it. It read:

YOUR SPORTSMAN'S CLUB HAS DONE IT AGAIN!

There followed a list of the names of officers, the rules of the race: "Up to Candle and back—and who cares who wins, as long as it's the best man!"

From some dark recess Bill Thornton was able to bring forth some canned tomatoes for us, and this delicacy, washed down with champagne, made the sourdough and beans more palatable. Few people had slept much during the last weeks. We were surrounded with boisterous humanity loaded with enough scamper dew to keep the riot squads on the alert. I managed to stick out most of the evening before going asleep on Jack's shoulder, but after I had got into my bunk groups of revelers on their way to some other party would pass the cabin and shout so that it rocked with the sound; they played horns and harmonicas and managed to keep me awake most of the night. Finally I stumbled from my bunk and went to the Boyd cabin where I made coffee and sat drinking it until Al came in with the news that John Masterson and his team were waiting.

"Don't forget," Al repeated, "to get the exact times of the racers." Picking up my parka, he tossed it at me, grabbed my carpetbag, and nudged me outside while Lucy and Jack brought up the rear. "Do what Masterson tells you to do. And for the love of heaven, get those arrival times right."

The team was lolling in the lee of the Yukon Trading Company building, and a finer team you could never wish to see. The dogs were black mouthed, smoke colored and matched in stature, from the chunky leader named Horse to Buttsy, the wheel dog in the string of five. The sled was a narrow twelve-foot racer. Occupying the buckboard region was a large metal flask, a tin of biscuits and a canvas pack. The remainder was loaded with furs, and two pairs of snowshoes were lashed to the ribs, one pair to a side.

A tall, rawboned man with twinkling blue eyes in a clean-shaven horse face lounged against the wall of the building, puffing at a corncob pipe. As we came up he straightened, stripped a completely bald head of a wolfskin cap, and gave us a smile that unveiled about four uppers and two lowers. But for all of his homeliness there was an air of friendliness and quiet confidence in his demeanor. Indeed, I was to find it easy to love this man, whose name was Big John, as only one friend can love another beloved comrade and fellow in arms.

I never knew much of his personal history, but the range of his knowledge indicated that he had had a wide and varied career. He possessed a wealth of information, ranging from history and politics to the proper way to make melon balls, the care of a hamster, and the correct use of a cargo hook in a water-front fight. The way he talked of any event made you feel that he'd been on the spot and perhaps even instigated it; but the minute anyone tried to pin him down he could change the sub-ject so quickly and expertly that no one ever cornered him. As far as he was concerned his life had begun in Alaska.

He'd come as a godsend to Al, who, being a shrewd judge of men, had hired him a few days after the Nome Telephone Company had been founded. Big John was then working a team of dogs as a freighter. But he did not like the life: he was basically a mechanic and electrician, and he wanted to be a lineman. The company had no dog teams or kennels, nor the necessary camp accessories for maintaining lineworkers. Big John had them all and his own tools too. Al hired him, with his dogs, for $1,000 a month, and Big John worked for Will and Al almost to the day he died in a San Francisco hospital in June 1917. When they incorporated several companies, he was given a wedge of stock, and I am always a little misty eyed when I recall that he willed it to me at his death. It was not an empty, sentimental gesture either; his bequest was gilt edged and embroidered with dollar signs, thanks to the clever commercial operations of Burke and Boyd.

That morning Big John shambled up to Al, nodded to Lucy, and playfully punched Al in the stomach. Al introduced him to Jack and me, and he took our hands in turn, smiling.

"I'm honored," he said. "Are we ready?"

Jack grabbed me and gave me a kiss that smacked louder than the popper on a freighter's whip. "Have fun," he said. "Don't lose your shirt at poker. And be a good girl."

After he released me I threw a peck at Lucy and Al, and the next minute I was sitting beneath the furs of the sled, the team was swinging around and we were yelping our way out of town.

At first the trip was like champagne and strawberries, peaches and cream. The cold and frosty air had a clean, still bite to it, and the temperature, I should guess, was in the radius of ten degrees below zero. The snow was packed hard, and riding the drifts behind the yipping dogs brought delightful tickles to the pit of my stomach. Big John's hoarse bellowing at the dogs and the ear-shattering reports from his whip's lash made the adventure even more exciting. When I recalled my own part in the over-all program, I began to swell up like a poisoned pup. However, the inevitable puncture was lurking just around the corner.

Suddenly, inexplicably, I grew restless and uneasy. Puzzled by the emotion, since I had been so sleek and sassy the moment before, I tried to get rid of it; first by stretching my legs, changing my position to a straighter seat, then by lying back. But it was no use. My agitation soon became fright and I began to glance fearfully from right to left. Certainly nothing I saw represented a reassuring sight, unless an occasional telephone pole projecting about three feet above the two-foot layer of snow could be construed as comfort. The air had changed substance too. Unaffected by the heat of the town, it was colder and frostier, and it was impossible to see more than twenty yards ahead or on either side. The dogs had quieted down and Big John was offering few commands. Aside from an infrequent crack of his whip and the soft hissing of the runners, there was no sound. The stillness was like a silent, watching, unseen thing. Big John's face, when I glanced back at him, showed nothing to dissuade me from wanting to crawl under a bed and hide. Nothing showed through the wolf hackles of his parka hood except his eyes, narrowed to slits, the lashes pale with frost. Just when I was ready to yell for Mama, John bellowed at the team, cracked his whip on the nearside, and pulled the sled near a telephone pole. His weight on the spike stopped the dogs in their tracks. Tongues lolling and their pants whipping up clouds of steam, they sank in their traces while John, throwing back his hood, came around to face me. His smile was as comforting as his comment was startling.

"Cry, if you feel like it."

"Cry?" I felt like it, all right. But my surprise took the upper hand. "I—I don't understand."

"You will, in time." Scrounging a greasy poke from a pocket, he opened the drawstring and filled his corncob pipe.

"Crying is often the best way to get over it."

"Oh, I see."

"No, you don't, honey," he said, chuckling. "You don't even know what I'm talking about. But I admire that stiff little neck of yours." He found a wooden match somewhere in his clothing and lit his pipe. "What you've got is ice poison. That's what we call it up here. Everyone falls ill of it. Even sourdoughs came down with it." He leaned over the buffer board, took up the metal flask, and handed it to me. "Use the cap as a cup. I'll act as caterer in charge of food." Opening a tin of biscuits, he scooped out a couple for himself and offered the container to me. "Nothing but the best for royalty."

The flask proved to be filled with strong tea, and the biscuits were but chunks of sourdough, yet I've never been calmed down so fast by a meal. After the last crumb, I got off the sled, at Masterson's suggestion, and stretched my legs.

"Feel better, eh?"

"I surely do."

"Then we'll start pretty quickly. We've about thirty miles to go. Meantime I'll check this section of the wire. Last month I got just this far before our first blizzard turned me back."

He wasn't gone two seconds before my depression set in again. Climbing back into the sled, I glanced over the surrounding terrain, and despite the comfort of thick furs, hot drink and food, I felt as if I were in a lost world.

"John! Mister Masterson!"

"Huh?" Masterson, who was monkeying with the wire or the telephone pole, straightened up at my squawk, thrust a tool into his pocket and came running. "What's the matter?"

"I—I don't know!" This time I took his advice. I wailed, and if I remember correctly I did a loud job of it. "I'm scared! I'm so scared—there's nothing to see—no people to care what happens if we get lost—all we've got to eat is biscuits and tea—all this snow and ice and silence. Nobody'll ever know what's become of us—and—"

"Shut up!"

Plunging up to the sled and pushing me over, he sat down, stripped off one mitten and hurt my hand with his grip. Then, speaking calmly—almost in a monotone—he told me the reason why so many people caught in Alaska's vast reaches of snow and ice became as panicky as I had.

"The snow and ice and the wild animals and the primitive quiet of Alaska are not much different in their effect on people than the dust storms, lack of water and absence of animals in the Sahara Desert of Africa. It's all loneliness, any way you look at it. Snow on one side, and sand on the other. You can become frightened in a beautiful forest, as peaceful as it may be. You can fear a golden, waving wheat field; be frightened of a deep lazy river; or terrified by the patient immobility of mountains. But it's all, in essence, loneliness. Wherever you go, Margaret, or whatever you do in this life, remember that being scared is only another word for loneliness. Look around you. This is mag-

nificent country. But everyone gets the chills at first. That's because it's so big. Someday they'll push a highway through here.
Meanwhile we'll have to shift for ourselves. We'll need to recognize nature as a friend, not an enemy. We must blame ourselves
for our loneliness, not the terrain around us."

"Mister Masterson—"

"John, honey, if you don't mind."

"I feel so much better!"

"Ready to go?"

I fell asleep almost before the team was in motion. I vaguely
remember several stops where the blows of a hammer and the
snips of a wire cutter disrupted my luxurious slumber. Then
I awoke to the yapping of dogs, candlelight in the windows
of a log cabin and an order from John to "check in with Kate."

"Isn't there something I can do to help you?"

"Not a thing, honey. Just ask Kate to keep the food hot and
get you settled in your room." He pointed out a square, hazy
obstruction in the gloom, perhaps fifty yards farther on and a
little off the trail. "That's the Candle branch of the Yukon
Trading Company. The kennels are behind it. I'll feed the dogs
and quarter them. Back in twenty minutes."

The cabin door swung open and the largest woman I have
ever seen stood outlined there. Around six feet tall, she must
have tipped the beam at 400 pounds, and every pound was quivering with pleasure and excitement. Her hair, parted primly in
the middle, had been peeled back so tightly that her dancing
blue eyes had an Oriental slant to them, and two yellow braids
hung waist length down her front. She was dressed in a stiffly
starched calico dress that snapped and crackled at her slightest
move. A leather belt, six inches wide, helped to keep her stomach in. Her broad, flat feet were imprisoned by calf-length Indian moccasins, worked elaborately and lavishly with beads
and porcupine quills; from one of them protruded the bone
handle of a hunting knife.

"Yee Viss!" she squealed. "Come in, kiddie! Mister Boyd
telephoned you vas h'ar to coom!"

Snatching my bag with one hand, she curled an arm around
my shoulders, and an instant later I was sure that every bone in
my body had been broken. Then she smacked me with a kiss

that pushed my chin under one ear, knocked off my cap and pitched me bodily into the center of the room. The place was 1904 Alaska in the raw.

While the lobby—if that was what it was—had originally been built of sod, the back of it had been knocked out and four wings of rough lumber had been added to make a dozen cubbyholes. Their doors faced the lobby and a couple of them hung from a single leather hinge each. There was a splintery counter, fronted by a dozen pine-pole stools and a Yukon stove cluttered with steaming iron pots and kettles. The floor was hard-packed dirt. Six tallow candles, roughly the size of rolling pins, lighted the room.

Kate led the way to a little room off to the right and kicked the door open. Beyond a double-deck bunk layered with gaudy blankets, a chair, and a washstand with a tin water pitcher and basin, this room had no excess fat either. Tossing aside my bag, I tracked Kate back to the lobby. For all of her walloping welcome, I was homesick even for the sight of John Masterson. To disguise my discomfiture I decided to telephone Nome and fill Al Boyd in on our current status.

"Where is the telephone, missus, uh, Kate?"

"Ya! Ya, sure! Telephone! Yust minoot, kiddie dear!"

Charging from behind the counter where she had been whaling away at the pots and kettles, she grabbed the door which was still standing open and slammed it shut so hard that a short acre of ground was dislodged from the sod wall and cascaded to the floor. "Dey're! Zee?"

Detaching the receiver from an outdated, yellow-grained wooden unit bolted to the back of the door, I gave the crank a couple of brisk whirls and was answered by a conglomeration of explosions, moans, shrieks and sputterings that nearly punctured my eardrum and left my head ringing like a lumber-camp dinner bell for an hour afterward. Finally Al's voice cleaved the racket, and after he had fought the connection a bit, he came in reasonably clearly.

"Hello. Hello. This is Nome."

"Al. This is Margaret."

"Hello, honey. How was the trip?"

"Not bad. John is an awfully nice man. He's putting the dogs away."

"Now, kitten, to business. Jim Frame's dropped from the race. That leaves only Scotty Allen and Leonard Dodge."

Frame, Al explained, had run into dog trouble during the afternoon's practice workout, due to the chief hazard that confronts anyone pushing a hard-running Alaskan dog team. His lead dog—a brute called Bones—had become snarled in his traces on a downhill grade, lost his footing, and, before Frame could set his spike, the others were upon the animal. Reverting to type, the wolf or wolf dog instantly attacks anything helpless or in a vulnerable position. Frame managed to save the dog's life, but by that time Bones had suffered a fang cut on a hind-leg tendon. It would keep him inactive for several months. Frame could have borrowed or bought another leader, but working with a strange team, any lead dog—even one of the best—would require at least a month of training, and the race was scheduled to start the next day.

"They gave him back his entry fee though," Al added. "I'd never have expected it, with Roberts running things."

The race was to begin at ten o'clock the next morning. An official Sportsman's Club timekeeper would see each contestant off, and the instant of their departure would be logged, attested to by witnesses, and a written copy given to both the Sportsman's Club dignitaries and the *Nugget*.

They were to mush for Candle, handling their teams any way they saw fit and taking any route they wanted. In brief, they could kill off their dogs ten miles out of Nome, or take a year to get to Candle and back. The best round-trip time would determine the winner. I was to call in the *exact* second of their respective arrivals. They had drawn lots to decide who would be first out of town. Scotty had won and had elected to pull out ahead of Leonard.

"Got it, honey?" Al asked.

"Yes—of course."

"Okay. Good-bye, then."

"Al! It's so lonesome up here! Can I talk to Lucy for a second—I—"

"Ask Kate to pour you a drink and shovel some food into you." Al chuckled. "You'll be all right. Besides, Lucy's at the bathhouse. Good-bye, honey."

I was given no opportunity to answer, for the severed connection at Al's end of the wire invited the telephone's lightning and thunder again. As I hung up, John Masterson came into the lobby, heralded by a spray of wind and snow and followed by what looked like three kodiak bears trained to walk upright and wear clothes. Kate began squealing out greetings, laughing, pouring tin cups of whisky and gesturing toward the counter.

They were upcountry miners, I learned, and all friends of Kate's, whose husband had married her out of a maid's position with a Seattle family and had brought her to Candle seven years before. The result of their combined industry had been the tavern, and when he had died of pneumonia three years ago, Kate had established herself as a combination cook, confidante and mother to all in the gold-camp vicinity. More, she was not hurting from a business standpoint. She seldom had room to accommodate visitors, such was her popularity with her steady boarders, and she had taken in John Masterson and me only because of her friendship with Al Boyd. She didn't injure any feelings, either, when she called in a few minutes later.

"My goodness! Soch pur-ty, pur-ty girl! Don't be scared, kiddie. Dese fallers look like goats. Bot d'ey treat you like a lady. You see."

Her prediction proved right. I had a high old time from the moment I sat down to the meal of sourdough biscuits, beans, stewed tomatoes and hot tea, served by the sweet old girl, to the delicious, blood-warming coffee royal that I sipped in the early morning hours.

Like the denizens of Nome, my new friends had surrendered to the sporting virus, and well before midnight the place was swarming with miners. Some of these numbered themselves among Kate's steady trade, but the rest—unable to resist the tension at hand—had abandoned their claims and camps to watch Allen and Dodge strut their stuff on the first lap. Sleep was far from their minds, and that went for me too. I was the only young white girl these fellows had seen for many months —even years—and to the amusement of both Kate and John

Masterson, they had me feeling as if I wore a rose behind each ear.

Around ten o'clock Paul MacMurray, the manager of the Yukon Trading Company, and Dick Overton, his assistant, joined us. Overton owned a fiddle, and announced that—in view of Candle's growing female population—the first public dance in community history would be held. I was caught in the middle of a square dance that lasted for nearly four hours, an exercise that, despite my refreshing sleep on the trail, left me a subscriber to the doctrine that people *could* be killed by kindness. When the happy squall finally petered out, they entertained me with jokes, singing and tales of life in the wilds. It was the first time I had been out of Nome, which suddenly took on an air of high civilization, and I learned a great deal about the primitive side of Alaska.

For instance, I had always assumed that there was plenty of fuel, since we had it in Nome; but now I learned how hard it was to even keep a campfire going out on the tundra. Every stick and sliver of firewood was brought to Nome by ship from the States and was allocated to the various inland camps on order. A slight miscalculation could mean that a shack or mine shorings or a sled would go up in smoke before the weather permitted the owner to travel to the nearest neighbor's fire. Even if fuel was to be had, hauling it was a major problem. A freighting team on a single run could only handle enough of the frozen iron-hard cordwood to last a week, and a single load was all that the most sympathetic miner could spare a needy neighbor. A miner caught napping when the winter set in was better off to find a friend and hug his fire and resign himself to losing a season's take of gold.

I was appalled to learn that most of these men had not seen a doctor since the first gold rush of September 1898. There was generally enough simple medicine, since medication topped the list of supplies ordered from Outside. But in case surgery was required, the patient was in the hands of amateurs; the nearest doctor might be hundreds of miles away. One of my friends that evening—a grizzled veteran of '98—proudly displayed a peg leg, hand whittled from a stick of cordwood. While looking for gold around Dawson with a partner, he had sunk a pick into his foot, and a few days later it was obviously infected and had to come off. His partner had performed the operation with a hunting knife, a handsaw and a bottle of whisky.

The loneliness could be coped with in several ways. A man could go crazy. He could play solitaire, or if he had a partner, a two-handed game; or he could go to the nearest Indian village and take a woman to his hearth. As far as gold was concerned, who cared? The game was the thing. In the final analysis, who'd want to live anywhere else? Alaska was the last place left on earth where a man could get a good lungful of air and stretch his legs.

By this time I was beginning to feel the whisky and decided that a good lungful of air was what I needed. So while Kate was batting away at the stove with pots and pans and several poker games got going, I threw on my parka and went outside.

No one, young or old, witless or wise, has, I'm sure, ever clapped eyes on a more dismal scene. There was hardly any wind; it was so cold that the air itself was frost. Up the trail, in the ghostly, stinging gloom, the Yukon Trading Company squatted like a brooding monster, surrounded by the usual hovels of sticks, sod and tattered canvas that constituted the normal Indian suburb of an Alaskan community. Overhead a pale yellow thumbprint showed that the sun had paid Candle a lukewarm visit.

Dick Overton came up beside me, fiddle in hand, and showed me over the encampment. This post had been Will Burke's first personal commercial enterprise; inside, over the counter, a burned-wood sign bore its name and the legend YOUR CREDIT IS GOOD. WILL BURKE, PROP. The sight of Will's name brought a haunting pain to my chest—a puzzling reaction followed by an equally disturbing sense of guilt. While Dick put the place in order for the day's business I stood there trying to analyze my feelings, finally attributing them to fatigue. But now I think that it was at that moment that I fell in love with Will. To the day that the post at Candle burned to the ground in 1911, it remained my favorite among our properties.

Kate charged through the doorway, surrounded by a halo of frost particles, and squealed, "Kiddie! Mr. Poyd vants to talk!" She almost tucked me under one arm and bore me to the telephone.

"Honey," Al said, "you all right? Now listen." And he went over again the instructions for clocking the arrival of the dog teams. "And don't let 'em give you too much booze. Those birds can drink you under the table left-handed." The resident gallants were pressing around the phone, eager to hear news from Nome, and I was nearly smothered in cocked ears, scratchy beards and whisky fumes.

"Scotty will pull out first at ten o'clock. Leonard will leave an hour later. That's so the teams won't get tangled up and get in fights. Honey, check 'em carefully. A lot is riding on this race. Leonard had better win. The Sportsman's Club says there's more than three hundred thousand dollars down on him."

"Why, who'd bet against Leonard?" I gasped.

"Scotty Allen has his backers too. Like his boss, Jake Roberts. He's on him for every dollar he can beg, borrow or steal. This town's gone crazy! Wait a minute. Here's Jack."

After a pause Jack's voice came over the wire. It sounded thick and lazy and I knew he'd been drinking. It was a blow to me, because I'd hoped he had quit the stuff for good.

"Hello, sweetheart! Tomorrow we'll be rich!"

"Wonderful! I'm so proud of you, Jack."

"I admire the way you operate too, sweetheart."

"And Jack, don't be mad—but—please don't drink any more tonight."

Snarling, he hung up. By this time I should have learned not to antagonize him when he was drunk. For months I had carefully avoided ever mentioning his drinking, and after awhile he had stopped and straightened himself out. Now he had slipped, and my thoughtless remark would probably push him further off the plank. Mentally scourging myself for being a fool, I started to ring him back, but I felt tears coming on and squirmed through the crowd and went to my room. Fortunately I was so tired that I dropped off to sleep at once, and when I awoke, shortly before noon, I felt fine. In fact there was something in the air that no one, whatever his grief or anxiety, could have resisted.

Everyone appeared to be toting his own personal bottle of skullbuster, and some were even brandishing globes of champagne. The card games were still enthusiastically in the spotlight. Some of the participants, squatting on the floor in a circle, had not changed position since I had last seen them, and even the iron washers which they were using in lieu of poker chips seemed to have maintained the same order of distribution. Sourdough in one hand and fork in the other, a dozen men at the counter were doing a fine job of shoveling, while Kate, still stirring and banging at her pots, kettles and pans, urged them on. A ragged series of sharp reports from outside, laced by howls and yells, sounded as I came into the lobby, and a peek through the door disclosed a group of riflemen near the trail. They were shooting at a wooden box a couple of hundred yards away.

"Kiddie! Kiddie, dear! Y'an't eat nothing today! You coom eat!"

"Yes—I—right away."

Before I could get set at the counter, a number of the happy warriors remembered that I was alive and soon I had some champagne in hand whether I wanted it or not. A couple of quaffs of the stuff did me plenty of good too. My appetite became a thing to be reckoned with seriously, and in a moment I was laying in some creditable quantities of noonday fodder.

As I finished I suddenly remembered Al's orders and realized that I had no clock.

"Kate! Do you have a clock? Al wants the time officially recorded by your clock."

"Yust min't." She disappeared, then returned with a stemwinder of an alarm clock with numerals large enough and a face big and round enough to be an Aztec sundial.

After lunch I went outside again to watch the slow destruction of the wooden box under the increasingly erratic riflefire of the whooping crowd. Then Kate called me to the phone again.

"Honey? They're off, as scheduled. Scotty first, then Leonard at eleven o'clock. Without a load a team can make about eight miles an hour, so Scotty should be there around four if he takes it easy. Then look for Leonard between four and five. Got it?"

"Yes, I'll do it, Al."

"Margaret." His tone was suddenly serious. "I can hear a lot of bellowing up there. Remember what I told you. You stay sober."

"Yes, Al. I'm not a baby."

"Sorry, I don't mean to nag. But we're all about ready for the strait jacket down here."

After I had hung up and glanced at Kate's clock, which I'd set on the telephone box, I went outside where several wrestling matches were in progress. As I watched I felt a hand on my arm and looked up to see John Masterson.

"Having fun?" he asked.

"Well, I'm not sure. I've never seen anything like this."

"It's not for long. Tomorrow we'll be back in Nome. What time is it?"

"A little after two."

"Be over an hour before we can expect anyone to show up. Maybe longer."

But ten minutes later, while I was engrossed in the wheezes, grunts and struggles of the wrestlers, I heard the harsh, sniffling cough of a working dog from upwind. Startled, I turned and squinted toward the trail from Nome; but there was no sign of life for at least two hundred yards, which was as far as vision could penetrate the glittering wall of white air. Masterson apparently had heard nothing; he was enjoying the role of referee in a new match that had just begun. I was sure that my imagination was at fault, and returned to watching the wrestlers. Then unmistakably the muffled snarl came once more, and this time it was followed by the brittle crack of a whip. The wrestling ceased on the instant; a second later spectators and participants alike were staring down trail.

"Hey, you donkeys, one of 'em's here!" someone bawled and ran for the door of the tavern. Suddenly the snow-packed courtyard in front of Kate's door was milling with a crowd, and I was knocked down two or three times before Masterson got through the excited throng and hauled me up against the wall of the building.

"Stay here," he panted. "And don't be sore at them. They wouldn't hurt you. They're just all het up and in their cups."

At that moment I was as hot blooded as they were and totally unaware of any damage. Just then a hard-running dog team burst from the bleakness of the near distance and the crowd's greeting rose like the bawling of a moose herd in a forest fire. Popping his whip, a wiry little man rode the runners of the sled, and as he pulled up he swiveled his cap around his head.

"It's Scotty!"

At the first yell that hit the sky I remembered my instructions and ran inside, followed by Masterson, slipped the receiver from the telephone, and rang Nome.

Al answered. "Nome. This is Nome." Fortunately there was little interference on the line. I needed every advantage at that second. The day's mounting tension had bottled up my breath, and now I could only gasp.

"Al—this is me. Scotty—he's here." I looked at the clock; the hands pointed to exactly two twenty two. I gave Al the time, then tried to describe the scene that followed Scotty's arrival. But Al cut me short, his voice cold and rough.

"Margaret, what are you saying? Are you sure you haven't mistaken some wandering freighter for Scotty?"

"All I know Scotty. It's him."

"But it's impossible! Don't you realize that?"

"Well, I don't care, he's here!" I couldn't get out another word, and Masterson, bless him, took over, snatching the receiver from my hand and pushing me aside.

"Al. This is Masterson. What Margaret has told you is true. What? I haven't any idea. I haven't talked to him yet. Yes, I'll tell her. Certainly—good-bye."

Slamming home the receiver, Masterson turned to me, lips compressed, head shaking. Before he could speak, the crazy, laughing, shouting crowd shoved Scotty inside the place and made for the counter. Pulling me aside, Masterson waited until they had lined up bellowing for whisky before he gave me Al's latest orders.

"Lord! What a day! Al can hardly believe Scotty's time. Neither can I. Anyhow, he wants you to interview Scotty about his trip—the trail conditions, performances of the dogs, opinions of his chances on the return lap, how he managed to make such time, and so forth. Then call him back. The *Nugget*, to say nothing of the stateside newspaper, is driving him to drink. This thing *really* caught on."

The welcoming committee was standing ten deep at the counter, and in spite of the pleas, entreaties and threats of Masterson and myself, the gentlemen showed no inclination to let us near their hero. We could have been there yet had Scotty been less concerned about his official time. But apparently remembering the rules laid down by the Sportsman's Club, he knelt on his stool, where he had been holding court, picked me out and waved. At his gesture the defense gave way. Then I was at the counter and fending off a phalanx of tin cups, hard elbows and big feet.

"Hello, Margaret." Wearing his usual mechanical grin, he pinched my fingers quickly and awkwardly. Then his glance, reflecting his natural shyness, shifted from me to the floor. "I got a watch on me. But the club says I got to be told my official time before witnesses."

I told him and was a little surprised that he showed no pride in his performance. If anything, his attitude was one of indifference and detachment despite the great howl that went up at my recitation. Moreover he chose to answer all questions by nervously twirling his cap, shrugging and smiling, acting as if he could scarcely hear me and loudly ordering drinks for the house. The only information he gave was his departure time and a few inconsequential facts. In a few minutes, he said, he would feed his dogs lightly, allow fifteen minutes for their food to settle, then mush off. No, he did not intend to sleep, or eat while in Candle. Admittedly, he was tired. But naps dulled the wits and made a man physically logey. He had eaten on the trail and was not hungry.

The picture was obviously off center, even if Scotty's boosters —on the surface—appeared to see nothing out of kilter, including the freighter's apparent freshness. Recalling what I had heard and remembering my personal experience on the trail, I had some idea of the wearying ordeal that a 20-mile trip, much less a 50-miler, imposed upon both dog and man.

Yet here was a fellow, who, having come the whole way, was permitting himself and his team about 30 minutes rest before squaring off at the last lap of a 1-day, 100-mile jaunt! It didn't make sense. Unless Scotty and his team had learned to fly, there was no plausible explanation for his time and appearance. Then I got a look at John Masterson's face as I began fighting my way to the telephone. His narrowed eyes and the set of his jaw told me a lot. I rang Nome. Still at the board, Al answered and his voice reflected the beating he was taking. He was so hoarse I could barely understand him.

I outlined the results of my interview with Scotty, including the local color, the enthusiasm of the Allen apostles and other sidelights that he had rejected earlier.

"Is that all?" he croaked impatiently, when I had finished.

"Well, not exactly. Scotty won't talk much—and—and something seems funny."

"What do you mean? What seems funny?"

I started to voice my suspicions. But luckily, I caught myself in time. From his tone, he was not in the market for shots in the dark, straws in the wind or left-hand monkey wrenches. My ears were still burning from the effect of Al's last vigorous boxing.

"Nothing's funny, I guess. I must've been thinking of something else."

"Okay. Stand by for Scotty's return time. Then watch for Leonard. And for the love of everything that's holy, don't tell me he's come and gone while we were talking. Good-bye."

His last blast steered me into a new and more dismal train of thought. Up to now I had been preoccupied with the strange aspect of the situation; I suddenly realized the full impact as it applied to me and mine. Aside from my $500 bet, Leonard was a close friend. The way it looked, he was a cinch to lose the race, and I knew that he had bet heavily on himself. Worse, if he did lose, Jack would be wiped out, and I chose not to speculate on the outcome of such a setback. Miserably, I wandered around for a few minutes. Then, for want of something better to do, I went outside and approached Scotty's team. My eyes could have been knocked off with a feather.

Save for the wheel dog, they were all standing, even mincing about. Their tails were erect and curled stiffly, and their hackles were bristling. Their tongues, which in view of a 50-mile pull should have been out a foot, were being used as cleaning attachments. The leader, a blunt-nosed sergeant called Baldy, was utilizing his rest period in persecuting fleas, first with one hind foot, then the other. Some of them had gnawed off their shoes, as sled dogs will do on a stop of any length. On or off, however, none of them had seen 20 miles of wear. I ran back, located Masterson, who was hoisting a solitary drink in a corner of the lobby, and grabbed at him.

"John, I want to show you something!"

Outside, his eyes, after a casual glance, began stabbing. Then he turned and took me by the arm. Forcing me off to one side, he glanced at the door and shook his forefinger in my face.

"You're right. But don't pull the trigger until you've got a shell in the gun. Wait until Scotty pulls out. Then we'll call Al again. He's the boss. Let him decide whether we're nuts."

"But it's so plain! That team hasn't been worked hard! Their shoes—"

"Their shoes," Masterson interrupted, "do not mean a thing. He could have changed them a hundred times on the way. It's the appearance of Scotty and that team. They aren't tired! In all my life, this is the craziest—"

Masterson's words were only half out of his mouth when Scotty, still surrounded by his fans, burst out of Kate's. Giving us a friendly wink, he went to his sled, took out a canvas sack of dried fish, and fed each of his dogs a thin slab; then he examined their feet, mouths and eyes, before leading the crowd back inside.

My dismay was rapidly changing to anger. Among all those trail-hardened sourdoughs, apparently not one of them had observed how fresh Scotty's team was or made any comment on it. If even one of them had said something the word would have gone around and Masterson and I would have had some witnesses to our skepticism. Masterson was nearly forced to muzzle me, and I realized he was right. As official timekeeper and an employee of the Nome Telephone Company, I was in no position to make a serious charge against a contestant in the race without something tangible to peg it on. Scotty and his backers could have sued us for our last drop of blood on charges of character assassination.

Fifteen minutes later Scotty came out, fitted his dogs with fresh shoes, and with a shrill farewell was off to Nome. As his myopic disciples filed inside again I collared Masterson, who was silently watching Scotty and his team disappear into the haze.

"Did anyone notice anything, John?"

"No," he grunted. "Those yahoos were so soused they couldn't see their mugs in a mirror."

Soused or simply worn out, all but a handful of them collapsed on the floor, and before Scotty was out of sight their snores were shivering the timbers of the tavern. This was even more regrettable because Leonard Dodge, who arrived nearly two hours later, could have used a few healthy hurrahs of greeting.

There was no doubt about the honesty of Leonard's run. While Scotty had arrived at high speed, Leonard's team was moving at a methodical half trot. One of his dogs, evidently hurt, was riding on the sled, and as Leonard stopped in the courtyard the other four animals sank down, muzzles resting on paws and tongues flopping. I rang Al and told him Leonard's time, and he answered with a groan; then I ran outside again to greet Leonard.

"Hello youngster!" His ordinarily ruddy complexion, beneath the frost accumulation that clotted his beard, was dappled grayly from fatigue and he stumbled once or twice as he walked forward. Reaching out, he put an arm around my shoulders. "How's my girl?"

Inside, he curtly declined all offers of drinks, and as the offended miners drew off he sank into a chair and lay back for a second, his eyes closed. Then he yawned, stretched his legs before him, looked up at me and grinned.

"Crossed trails with Scotty a few minutes ago. Must have got here, turned right around and headed out again. That rate, he'll kill his dogs in an hour. Oh well, I should holler. Hope he uses all the bad judgment in the world. What's his time?"

I told him, and I had to fight hard against the urge to air my suspicions. But a violent shake of Masterson's head switched me off for the third time within the hour. I would have failed to get it over anyhow, for Leonard jumped from his chair and his roar woke half of the house.

"You're crazy!"

"No—no, Leonard! It's true!"

"It's impossible! No team can make that kind of time! Not on this trail and under these conditions!"

"Ask John, Leonard!"

Masterson's faint, yet decisive nod sent Leonard back to his chair, eyes wide and mouth gaping from the shock of his amazement. Then he ripped his cap from his head and hurled it across the room. "I can't believe it," he muttered. "I was satisfied with my own time. But this—this is incredible! Margaret, are you *sure* about Allen's time?"

"Yes, Leonard, I am. Al's got it logged too. And all these people are witnesses."

"Well that's that, I guess." Then he noticed Kate, who for the past ten minutes had been dividing her time between serving drinks at the counter and trying to get a welcoming squeal in edgewise. "Hello, Katie."

"Laynort Dotch! Coom eat!"

Crossing the room, Leonard rounded the counter, gave her an affectionate cuff and a forehead kiss, refused a plate of beans that she thrust at him, loaded his parka pockets from a stack of sourdough on the counter and returned, gnawing at a thick slab. Halfway through it he grimaced and shook his head.

"Still can't get it through my head. But if that's his time, that's his time. Maybe he's overworked his dogs or will run into trouble. Looks like that's my only chance. Anyway, I've got a fresh dog, or one that's nearly fresh. He might make the difference."

"Fresh dog?" Then I remembered the animal that had been riding the sled as Leonard had pulled in—one that I had assumed was a casualty. "What do you mean? Isn't the dog hurt?"

"Not by a durn sight, my wench." Warmed by the fire and strengthened by the sourdough and his short rest, Leonard's old air of bravado was returning. "That's a trick of your uncle's. Always keep a fresh dog in reserve, especially on the long haul. Then when the team flags, throw him in. It works wonders. The rest of the team, in their peanut-brained way, are ashamed of themselves. Also, the fresh dog makes up a lot of difference in the pull." Cramming the last of the sourdough into his mouth, Leonard swiped his hand across his lips, rubbed his palms on the front of his parka, and sank back into his chair. "How long did Scotty lay over?"

"About thirty minutes. Maybe a few minutes longer."

"Okay. I'll shave that to the bone too." Bounding to his feet, he went to his team, fed them, replaced their tattered shoes, put his fresh dog in trace and came back. "You can tell Al that I left in exactly ten minutes."

Beaten, squeezed out, he mushed off on the nose at four o'clock, as he had announced. I felt better, much better, as I saw him off. But Masterson, who had a talent for logic, threw a shoe at me.

"Dodge's sunk. He knows it. His dogs haven't the bone and the guts to make it. He's only hoping that Allen will run into trouble. Otherwise, he's lost. You feel up to starting back?"

Sobered by his serious attitude, I threw my things together, thanked Kate for her hospitality, and, bundled to the eyebrows, was waiting at the door, bag in hand, when Masterson whipped up in front. Then we were off.

We didn't get a whiff of Leonard during the entire trip. Ten miles out, Masterson's wheel dog sprung a limp due to a defective shoe and quit his traces. Deprived of 20 percent of its pulling power, the team slowed perceptibly. Five miles from Nome, John began resting them each hundred yards or so, and also ordered me out of the sled. I clung to his belt as we made our agonizing way forward through the icy dark, and the lights of Nome were a welcome sight when at last they showed.

When we reached the kennels I took a short breather, thanked Masterson, and started to my cabin. I rounded the building, which stood on a small rise in the ground, and looked down on the spectacle of a city on a rampage.

As it had been for weeks, the area was swarming with people, some of whom, waving torches, ran up and down the paths off Main Street, while other groups here and there struggled or fought for breathing space. One man, straddling the pitched roof of the Little Church of All Faiths, was bawling—

bottle in hand—a warning that God was watching and that the end of the world was near. Close to the bathhouse to my right a fist fight, ringed by cheering spectators, was in progress. Next door to the Federal courthouse—or more specifically in an open space between the majestic seat of the law and a bordello —a party of sports was sicking a couple of dogs on each other. Three high-coiffed women were having a finger-shaking argument on the porch of the Golden Gate Hotel. Before the winner could be determined, however, a champagne bottle sailed through the window above, showering them with glass and driving them to cover inside. Lights streamed from saloons, dance halls and cabins all over town, and at each end of Main Street huge bonfires, shooting flames twenty feet up, had created a layer of black smoke that was as heavy as a caribou-skin blanket and almost as smelly. Altogether, the noise of the shouting and the laughter, the harmonicas and horns, the yapping of dogs and the crackle of the frost, was overpowering. And nowhere could I find a sign of Scotty or Leonard or their outfits.

At the Nome Telephone Company office I learned why. It was a mob on the prowl. The front door was guarded by three of the firm's burly linemen. Forcibly they held back a score of men, all yelling for news of the time made by Scotty and Leonard and demanding to talk with Al Boyd.

"Whose leg you geeks tryin' to pull?"

"Boyd knows who won! You tell him we want t' know!"

"Git outa th' way! We're goin' in!"

"Cer'aintly are! C'arn, George!"

Ducking low, I pulled my parka hood closer, ran around the cabin, and before anyone could spot me I was hammering at the rear door. It was barred. A second later the scowling face of Barney McCready appeared through the slit of the curtains, and before I could have spit twice he had reached out, jerked me inside and shot home the bolt.

"Lord o' maircy," he panted, "shure an' it's a good thing they didn't see ya!" Shirt limp with sweat and open to the waist, exposing an unbelievably hairy chest, and armed with a stick of stove wood, he resembled nothing human, now or ever. "Thay're moinds uv lift thim!"

"Barney, what's the matter?"

"Mat'thure, mat'thure, she says!" Rolling his eyes upward, he lifted his hands in the manner of an exhorting Old Testament prophet. "Mither, moine—"

"Margaret!" Lucy's ordinarily carefully groomed hair was a mess. There were dark rings beneath her eyes, and her nose was shiny. Her housedress looked as if it had been stolen from a poorhouse grab bag and her usual high color was two shades lighter. "We didn't expect you until tomorrow. Come on, Al will want to see you right away."

Inside the office Al looked as if he'd been dragged through a knothole. There were three armed guards around him, one of them old Steep, the deputy marshal, with his forty-five on his hip.

"Margaret! Why in heaven's name did you have to get here tonight? Did anyone see you? Where's Masterson?"

I assured him I had crept in unobserved and that I had left Masterson at the kennels.

"Floyd," Al said to a hulking youngster whose straw-colored hair had recently been cut with a jackknife. "Run Masterson down. Tell him to hole up. After that—"

A string of shouts and oaths from outside, accompanied by blows on the door, cut him short. Then a block of wood crashed through a window of the Boyds' front room, pulverizing the glass and taking half of the casing with it. This last suggestion for audience was all that Steep could take, at least for one night. Drawing his Colt, he went to the ruptured pane, pulled a chair close, hopped upon it, and thrusting the gun ahead of him, he jammed head and shoulders through the opening.

"Thet's a'plenty," he said quietly. "Yew got two min'ts to git out. Arter thet, yew are all under arrest."

The racket stopped magically for about ten seconds. But, as kids today observe correctly, there's one in every crowd; this one yelled, "Har! Haw! Goin to shoot us, Marshal?"

He'll never know how close he came to springing a leak. An ominous metallic click announced that Steep's forty-five was now at cock.

"One more yip and I shoots the fur off'n yer years and runs the rest of yew in."

Someone else spoke up. "We've got money on this race. We got a right to know who won."

"Yew'll larn tomorrow like the rules says . . . Git!"

Steep could be convincing when he chose. His cold, unblinking blue eyes above the equally cold blue barrel of the gun gave his words an unmistakable air of sincerity. There was a nervous shuffling on the gritty hard packed snow outside and a scattering of footfalls. Then the crowd was gone.

Al dismissed the linemen who had been acting as guards, then turned to me. "It's a good thing they didn't see you, peaches."

"Al, what's the ruckus all about?"

The back door opened and John Masterson, followed by Barney and the pumpkin-jawed messengers, strode in.

"Need any help, boss?" Masterson said.

Al waved him to a chair, went to the switchboard and pulled all the plugs, and while Lucy poured coffee for all of us he told of what had happened in the past eight hours.

Nome's sporting element, he related, had put most or all of its ready cash on Leonard Dodge or Scotty Allen, with the former, of course, an odds-on favorite. Having been in a state of all-out celebration for nearly two months, tempers had naturally become uncertain, and after the contestants had pulled out that morning the lid had literally blown off the town.

The Sportsman's Club finally posted a notice telling everyone to go home, since the results would not be announced until noon the next day. I would be needed to swear to the time made by both contestants at Candle and would not arrive until the following morning, so there was no reason for hanging around. The subterfuge was swallowed by the malcontents, and they quieted down considerably. Some even keeled over for a nap. Of course when Scotty Allen, then Leonard Dodge, in turn, arrived in front of the Golden Gate Hotel, they snapped on the juice again. But these splurges were roses in the path of the heroes rather than knuckles in the chops of each other. Both Scotty and Leonard took a friendly beating from their admirers before they could be rescued while still in one piece. A wedge of their respective friends finally succeeded in carrying them off; and they were installed in separate rooms at the

Golden Gate Hotel. Since these friends also chose to stand guard around the establishment, there could be no interrogation involving their time, trials or tribulations during the race. Shortly thereafter the spirit of good wine, good food and good company reigned once more.

"This," Al continued, wearily, "has been the worst day of my life."

"Al, there's something you should know." Freed temporarily from my fright, I couldn't wait to tell him what John Masterson and I had seen at Candle. "Could you and Lucy and John go out to the kitchen with me?"

"I suppose so," he answered, still pecking at the lip of his coffee cup. Then his tired eyes took in my expression and he stood up. "Come along."

The door closed on Steep and Barney, and I spluttered out my misgivings about the appearance of Scotty Allen and his outfit in Candle.

"It's insane," Al muttered, "but it all fits." He hooked his fingers over his belt, yanked up his pants, stabbed a crooked thumb at the inner corners of his eyes and sighed. "Scotty beat Leonard's time to Candle and back by forty-seven minutes. It can't be done. But he did it." Al shook his head and turned to Masterson. "John, you see it the same way?"

"If anything," Masterson said, after a careful pause, "Margaret has been too conservative. In my ledger the thing stinks."

"I got that idea," Al said, "after Margaret gave me Scotty's time to Candle. First I didn't believe it. Then you backed her up. Now I'm certain that everyone's going soft in the head. Including me."

"Well, what are we going to do about it?"

"Going to do about it?" His eyes narrowed and his lips tightened. "Surely you can't be serious, Margaret."

"The race was crooked, Al."

"Look," he answered sharply, "we're going to do nothing about it, absolutely nothing. And I want the thing to die here —right in this room. Not one word is to be breathed by anyone here, now or in the future. Is that understood?"

"But Leonard was fooled—somehow! A lot of people like Jack and me lost money on him!"

"I don't care who lost money on whom," he croaked, his color rising and his hair fairly standing on end. "This sort of charge has the punch of a carload of dynamite. Don't you realize that? A lot of people will be broke tomorrow. Some of them'll be suffering from hangovers. Some'll start drinking again. One yap out of you and the fat's in the fire. Some of them will refuse to pay off. I hope I don't need to explain what the result of such a welsh could be. It could mean a minor revolution with bloodshed. Meantime you'd be asked to back up your charge. If you can, then I'll back up. Otherwise, we all keep quiet."

The rest was anticlimax. We tended the board in relays that night, parrying requests for race information; and the next morning, after a short nap, I got up to go down to the Sportsman's Club to be "sworn." Then I was to try to interview Scotty Allen, find out how much money had changed hands, and return to the office to take over the switchboard again.

Jake Roberts received me with unction, looking like a cat that had swallowed a whole cage of canaries. I affixed my signature to the official announcement of the time, then asked him how much money had been lost on Leonard Dodge.

Roberts pulled a folded sheet of paper from his pocket and showed me the last column of figures. "See. Four hundred and sixty-three thousand dollars!" He gloated.

I reeled, and, swallowing my gorge, asked where I could find Scotty Allen.

"Scotty's a shy fellow," Roberts said. "And he's pretty tired, naturally, after a run like that. So I've sent him off to one of my supply cabins to rest. He'll be back in a week or so. You can talk to him then."

Outside, the town was subdued. The news had got around now. The losers were silently vanishing; the winners—about 200 of them—were noisily being paid off at the countinghouse.

Dejectedly, I began to look for Jack. Since I was no longer a reporter, I did not have the freedom of the saloons, but I looked in the cafés and hotels. At the Golden Gate the clerk mumbled that he'd been in the night before, changed his clothes, and departed again. I decided to go back to report to Al and then find some friend to fish Jack out of whatever saloon he'd holed up in.

Back at the office I learned that Leonard had come and gone while I had been out on my rounds, and that he was in bad shape. For one thing, he was exhausted physically. He did not believe, moreover, that any man alive had the stuff to beat him on the trail, and the knowledge that Scotty had done so had damaged his morale seriously. And he had been almost wiped out financially. He had mortgaged everything he owned and bet it on himself—a matter of around $40,000. Al himself had dropped $7,000 on the race, while Barney McCready, Rex Beach, Bill Thornton and Erickson were all several thousands poorer.

In fact all the betting element of Nome save the Roberts-Allen crowd was either broke or short of cash. It was painful to me to watch the pedestrian miners and occasional dog teams from my office window as they dejectedly plodded out of town and disappeared in ragged formation into the frost bank to the east. There was no more music or laughter drifting up from the downtown area. I was saddened further to learn over the switchboard from Steep that old Judge Scott had died in his cabin of a heart attack.

But the worst was to come. I had had no word from Jack, nor any report of him, and as the afternoon dragged on the waiting and uncertainty were driving me frantic. His past responses to adversity had conditioned me to expect the worst. As I closed the switchboard I was praying that he would be merely drunk or abusive. That would be easy enough. But I had visions of him running amuck and killing a man, and I knew that when he was drinking he was capable of it. Finally I left the office and headed for the cabin. As I tiptoed to my room, Jack virtually tore the door from its hinges and stormed in. He didn't kiss me or offer any gesture of satisfaction at seeing me. His hair looked like a clump of buffalo grass after the caress of a cyclone. There were bags beneath his eyes. His cheeks were dirty with a coarse blond outcropping of beard, and his lips were wet. His chin was set like iron, and the right side of his parka was coated with snow—the outcome, apparently, of a recent fall.

"Well, here we are, again," he snarled as he flung himself into a chair, "great team, huh?"

"Jack—we haven't anything to worry about! I—we've got my freighting business and it's making money! I've my job—It's not your fault—"

"Shut up!" he grated. "I can see it coming— 'I'll take care of you—I've got a business—we can be married—let's buckle down—let's go to work—there's money to be made in this country' et cetera, et cetera. I've heard it all!"

"But—dear—I was only trying to say that—what's mine is yours. I didn't mean to hurt your feelings—I thought—"

"You only think of one thing," he roared, "getting married! Well, get yourself another prince consort. I don't intend to be a kept man! On top of that, you can have *this* country!"

Lurching up, he staggered to the door, and hanging to the crossbar, turned and spat on the floor. "Queenie! Rule over it without a prince consort! The two of you go together—you and this stupid hunk of country!" Ripping the bar from the casing, he went out and staggered up the path.

So it began all over again. Day after day I worked, and night after night I sat with him in Thornton's or Erickson's, trying to reason with him, hoping to strike a healing note, or, as a last resort, deliberately humiliating myself with the forlorn idea that his senseless fury would spend itself. However, my solicitude made things progressively worse. Concessions seemed only to enrage him further, and at last, as a mistaken medium of escape, I began to drink with him. But as I have never liked the taste of liquor and certainly have never been able, for all these years, to hold it creditably, I pulled shallow water there too. Perhaps its influence even caused me to become more argumentative. It is possible. At any rate, he began to slap me around. Not that he ever really injured me. But a flick of his hand could be painful.

He was also able to change his mind about taking money from me, as Leonard had predicted. In the months that followed he spent a lot of time gambling, mainly in the early morning hours. His luck was bad, and handing him a check each week became an established ritual. Where he had caused me to feel ridiculous in offering him help before, he now had his hand out most of the time.

In April the ice broke and the tundra began showing through the melting snow in dirty patches. At sight of the sun the town's mood rose a notch on the brighter side, and when the first ship came in, the steamer *Victoria*, we deserted our winter diet of sourdough and beans and gorged on fresh meat and other delicacies until we were bloated. For a time it seemed as if Nome had regained its old, carefree prosperous way of existence, and the race and all its consequences were forgotten for awhile.

Not that economic prosperity had returned. There had been a great exodus after the race, due to news of a gold rush at Fairbanks; few business houses were collecting on their outstanding bills, and they were feeling the pinch. As the bulk of Nome's circulating money was in the hands of a few and those fortunates were hanging onto it, the saloons and houses were setting up a howl, and the future of the community was viewed with some pessimism. When the council called upon various winners with the suggestion that they invest in business as a civic duty, the gentlemen were told bluntly not to be silly. Moreover, when the *Victoria* churned off for the States, she took with her Mr. and Mrs. Roberts, Judith and Lew Crouch, Scotty Allen and his dogs, and a number of other big-money winners. While their abrupt departure was not particularly remarked—such sudden leavetakings were common enough— the state in which they had left their affairs excited some comment.

Roberts had not even bothered to sell or lease his profitable hardware store. He had simply mortgaged it at the first short-term figure offered by Eugene Chilberg, then left it at default. The Crouches had locked up and vacated, leaving all of their business equipment and many of their personal effects at both saloon and cabin. As to Happy Jack, Allen's half-breed helper, he had vanished, too, and as a check of the Crouches' stable showed it to be empty of horses, it was assumed that the ubiquitous tavernkeepers had given the animals to Jack and he had taken them and moved on to some inland camp.

It was not until months later that I heard any more of the

principals involved in the big dog race, and then only when I was on the point of leaving Nome for Fairbanks, where Jack had already gone. The day before I left, during the rush of last-minute packing and arranging business affairs, I had a sandwich and a cup of coffee with Barney McCready at Thornton's, and he told me what had happened to the Crouches' horses. Throats cut, their carcasses had been washed ashore about a mile up the beach that morning. Beyond a stab of pity for the animals, I thought no more of the incident. It was common practice for the owners of horses and mules to destroy them each fall when a feed shortage inevitably occurred.

But in Fairbanks one cold evening I picked up a little more data concerning the destruction of the horses. It started when Happy Jack, erstwhile employee of the Roberts', came into my office as I was closing up and asked for a handout. I had not known that he was in town, and I was shocked at his gaunt, ragged state. In the course of our conversation the reason for his appearance became obvious. He was dying of tuberculosis. Too sick to work, he had been sleeping in deserted lean-tos and getting his food from panhandling and from garbage dumps.

"People don't like Indians much," he muttered. "Even if they're half white. You always was nice to me, Margaret. I sure could use a dollar."

For once he was in luck. Two weeks before, a friend of mine had quit Fairbanks for an extended visit to the States and had left me his cabin to use or rent. I helped Happy Jack into it, got some grub into him, and put him to bed. Three or four times a week thereafter I brought him food, and because of his insatiable thirst for liquor, I also managed—off and on—to get him a couple of bottles. When this happened he immediately proceeded to drink himself blind. But as he was incurably ill, I figured that he had the right to spend his remaining days whole hog. In any event I was leaving his cabin one blizzardy afternoon just before his death when he called me to his bedside and told me a curious story.

Ten miles out of Nome, he mumbled, there was a deserted shack. Twenty miles farther on and in a direct line there was another. Both had been built as roadhouses at the tail end of the Yukon gold-rush frenzy, when any trail between two centers of civilization was considered a good bet to make money from traffic. But it had failed to work out that way. When a number of strikes around Candle petered out, the camp, which had showed such metropolitan promise, became only a wide spot in the road. The owners had moved on, leaving the monuments of their imagination and enterprise to be utilized at anyone's discretion.

"Roberts told me," Happy Jack hacked, "to take the horses to them cabins. I was to put one of 'em in each cabin. I slung a bale o' hay on 'em and did what he said. That was a few days before the race. When Scotty come by, he put his dogs in the sled and hitched the horse to it. When he got to the next shack he put the horse up and mushed on to Candle. When he started back he done the same thing. His dogs only went about half the distance Dodge's went. They's fresh—compared. Roberts said to take the horses out on the ice and get rid of 'em. Cut their throats. You been awful good to me, Margaret. I ain't sorry for what I done. I got paid. Not as much as I wanted. They had something on me. I couldn't talk. They're crooks. I'm telling you something valuable. Make 'em pay. They got it coming."

By now all the world knows the story of Alaska's first dog race and there is scarcely a sportsman alive that doesn't recognize the name of Scotty Allen. Today in Alaska the contest is held each year and it is not only recognized as a national sports observance in that country, but it is hailed throughout the world as man's triumph over the lack of wheels up there.

Sometime later Scotty returned to Alaska a rich man. In the interim he and his team had headlined every major vaudeville circuit in the United States. His dogs had been petted by the crowned heads of Europe and been put to good use in their spare time. Their pups brought as much as $5,000 each.

I have no valid factual evidence to offer regarding a possible fix in the race. I'm only reporting what I saw and heard.

Chapter Twelve

ONE morning that spring the report of a new gold strike swept the town, and before noon it had taken on the proportions of an epidemic. Felix Pedro, a famous Alaskan prospector who had discovered a dozen rich claims in the past, had hit pay dirt again, this time on upper Cleary Creek out of Fairbanks. I no longer remember how the report got to Nome. Anyway, it turned out to be correct, and by nightfall much of Nome's floating population, some mining-claim employees and even a good number of small businessmen, were packing in preparation for the first run of mail packets that would take them to St. Michael, the first lap of the trip to Fairbanks. Jack was one of them.

"The place is booming," he told me. "From all I can get from people who've been there, it's got bottom to it. It's the coming city in Alaska, and there's enough there to really build on besides the gold—the lumber, shipping, and all that. A place like that should have room for another lawyer. When I get settled I'll send for you." He wiped whisky tears from his eyes with a soiled, rumpled handkerchief, then walked swaying to the window and looked out. "This scrubby little dump don't want me."

For once I had to agree with him unreservedly, although I didn't say so. There was nothing left for him in Nome, not even a friendly word, save from me and a handful of our friends. Even that circle of long-sufferers had been narrowing down of late. Only concern for me and their recollection of his charming side had held them in check so far. But because of his rudeness, his drinking and his refusal to turn his hand to anything constructive, the social freeze was setting in fast. Perhaps, I thought, we both needed a new start. Somehow I felt that I had failed him, and I was willing to try anything.

"I think you're right, dear," I said. "I hear it's wonderful country. I can get a job there too. Al Boyd'll help me."

"That's not what I'm thinking about!" His voice was angry, and hoarse from his hangover. "I don't send for you until I can support you. Then I'll marry you and you won't need a job. Or"—his lip curled—"can't you wait to see Will Burke again? I hear he's up there."

"Oh, Jack, I only meant—"

"You only meant! You make me sick." In the old familiar gesture he spread his legs, raised his arms above his head, crooked his elbows and brought them down, fists clenched, muscles flexed. "I'll see you at the boat—Miss Two-Bit!" Jaw outthrust, he left.

Two days later I helped him tote his few personal effects to the dock. He had booked reservations on the *Montclair*, the first mail packet to leave. Before he went aboard he took me in his arms, pulled me close, and kissed me. Surprisingly, he was sober, and his kiss reassured me, despite the emptiness I felt at our parting.

"It won't be long, darling," he whispered. "We're starting over again now, and it won't be long."

"No, of course not. But please get started fast. And write to me. Promise?"

But if I had thought I could settle down to the happy prospect of a peaceful life while I waited for Jack to make good and send for me, I'd reckoned without fate.

I was working on the switchboard one morning on a new shift that began at six o'clock. In deference to the customers' demands Al had extended the hours of service and put me on the morning trick, which was the busier one, while he took the afternoon shift, and was able to keep abreast of his office work during the lull. When he had to be out of town, Lucy and I split that shift between us. We now gave twelve hours service instead of eight, and an added charge was made for it. I considered this an administrative master stroke, especially because I got a raise out of it.

I had barely settled my headphone in place when the cabin shuddered and windows rattled from the effect of a thundering repercussion. At that moment a shower of sparks, followed by a spear of flame, shot up from the vicinity of the Great Northern Saloon. Al, hair flying and eyes rolling, came from his bedroom, parka in one hand, boots in the other and trying to frog hop into all three at once.

"What th—what was that?" he yelled.

"It's a fire!"

"Get on the board!" he bawled. "Call everybody, every number you know! Tell 'em to bring buckets and get downtown! Hurry!"

Four hours later the fire was under control. By noon it was out. It amuses me to recall that Rex Beach played a prominent if not precisely heroic part in the proceedings. Although a number of buildings had burned on the west side of Main Street, the blaze had started in the Great Northern Saloon instead of at the Golden Gate Hotel. How it started I never knew. At any rate, when I came to Rex's telephone number I called him and got no answer. Several rings later I still drew a blank. Meanwhile Lucy, her paper hair curlers a bit on the tattered side, came into my office.

"Lucy! I can't wake Rex! I'm sure he's in his cabin!"

"Go get him. I'll take the board."

It was only a skip and a jump to Rex's cabin from my office, and I made it in jigtime. I didn't wait to knock. He was at home all right. Stripped off, save for a suit of long underwear, he was stretched out sound asleep, and there was a powerful scent of *eau de booze* in the air.

"Rex! Your place's on fire!"

"Wha—oh, Marg—"

"Rex!" Grabbing his wrist, I yanked at him so hard that he fell out of the bunk. "Get up! The Great Northern's burning!"

"Grf—mm—'ell." Then he caught the smell of smoke, blinked, floundered to a corner, picked up a pair of rubber boots, drew them on and took flight. Halfway up the path the back door to his long underwear came free of its buttons and he was a thought-provoking sight in his union suit, fisherman's boots and bottom naked in the breeze.

The next day Rex sold his interest in the saloon to his partner, Barney McCready. He got a good shake from him too. The Great Northern had burned to the ground. But, Barney reasoned, it was a famous name in Alaska. Tex Rickard had made it so. Besides, Barney had faith in the Territory, and he couldn't have been more right all the way around. He rebuilt the Great Northern and died a millionaire.

Rex, I am happy to recall, was as correct in his direction toward a goal in life. He had always wanted to write. Backed by the $12,000 which Barney had given him for his part of the Great Northern, he caught the last ship leaving for Outside. In New York he got down to brass tacks. Several years later he was an internationally famous author.

I'll never forget the next time I saw him, nor will I ever fail to cherish my appreciation of the moment. Will and I chanced to be in New York coincident with the publication of Rex's book *The Silver Horde*. To introduce Rex to the press, a party was to be held at the Waldorf Hotel at two the next afternoon, his secretary told us, and would we be there? Mr. Beach's publisher was particularly interested in our attendance, she added, since we had known Mr. Beach when he was a nobody.

"I mean," she added, "an unknown."

At the girl's deferential remark in relation to Rex's literary stature I recalled his appearance the day of the fire. When we arrived and I saw him bowing from the hips, freshly barbered, dressed like Mrs. Astor's horse and sipping champagne, I let out a guffaw that caused half of the room to look up. Startled, he turned quickly, spotted us and his décor went out the window. Tabling his glass, he leaped into the air and let out a howl that would have matched a Siwash's alarm over sight of a bathtub.

"Don't say it! I know exactly what you're thinking!"

That evening, over the fine dinner that he had ordered for us, he was avid for news of his friends in Alaska and the general political and industrial condition of the Territory. He was interested specifically in the past and present in regard to Nome, for the town had been the main seat of his operations there. We gave it to him by the yard, and certainly I was able to describe the scene in the month that followed the fire.

Lacking the poorest piece of mechanical equipment, the fighters had formed a bucket brigade. But such inadequate means meant that they could hope only to contain the blaze in order to keep it from spreading across the street. They confined their efforts to soaking the buildings still intact, and permitted the others to go up the flue. The next day the west side of Main Street, with two or three exceptions, resembled the remains of a titan campfire, overhung by a thick bank of oily smoke, and relieved in its spectral desolation only by an isolated tongue of flame here and there. Rebuilding on the instant was out of the question, for there was no lumber in town and the wreckage would need to stand until the necessary construction materials could be brought in from Outside. Due to the plundering of Roberts *et al*, money was tighter than a drum, and business was terrible. Except for the larger claims companies, people were slow in paying their bills, if they paid them at all, and those who did so immediately plunged into debt again. In less than a month several of the smaller saloons and houses went broke and closed their doors, and in the more genteel circles, parties and other forms of gaiety almost ceased entirely.

This period of inactivity gave me time to evaluate, to take inventory of my past, present and future. Some of it, I discovered, could be entered on the credit side of the ledger. I had broken the shackles that had bound me to my parents in Nebraska. Aside from being momentarily run down, I was healthy and not hard to look at. I was popular with my friends and I was proud to recall that I had made many pleasant acquaintances. I had succeeded at a good job and I was respected and appreciated by my employers. I was owner of a growing business and I was engaged to marry a handsome man.

But there was also a bitter taste of ash in my self-analysis. I realized that I was stubborn, even bullheaded. I was so self-centered that I had not written my people in more than a year, and I was much too proud of my face and figure. I was hopelessly greedy where money was concerned, and last but not least, I was sure that some of these faults had contributed to the restlessness and unhappiness that plagued Jack's and my courtship.

Then one day I decided to join Jack in Fairbanks whether he liked it or not. If *he* needed a new start, so did I. And I would be happier at his side. That night Al Boyd listened until I had finished my story. Then he called Lucy in and laid it all out.

"I see no reason why she shouldn't go, Al," Lucy agreed. "A woman *should* be with her man. This town offers anyone mighty little right now, and Will's up there, in case she needs a spanking."

"All right," Al said, "I'll write and tell Will you're coming. He'll make a place for you in one of our offices. You can leave anytime you like. Lucy and I can handle the board until I can bring in another operator. Now let's see you smile for a change."

A week later I gave all my excess possessions to Lucy, and sold my sled and my dogs to Walter Stapf—all but Pinky. I couldn't swallow the idea of parting from the little monster, for he had cottoned to me from the first and I suppose that in a way he represented the start on the family that I intended to have in the future.

The next day I boarded the *Blinky*, a wood-burning packet with a gasoline auxiliary engine which the captain, a black-faced oil-spattered spider monkey, kept at full throttle because of the heavy seas. So while the craft went yawing, twisting and spinning like a leaf in a tub of boiling water for 150 miles across the Bering Sea to St. Michael, the twenty-five passengers were nearly suffocated with gas fumes blended with the aroma of hot tar and blistered oil. Unable to stay on deck, we huddled in the galley, heads down and lowing painfully; some became seasick, much to the disgust of the captain and his two-man crew. There were no private accommodations on the *Blinky*, and we stayed below until we reached St. Michael sixteen hours later. It was doubly embarrassing for me, as I was the only woman aboard, all the men were strangers to me and I had no Jack Bartlett, Al Boyd, or Will Burke to fend for me.

My emotional status was hardly more stable than my stomach. I had grown soul sick with the pall of gloom that hung over Nome. I had missed Jack more than I'd realized and I was tormented by self-reproach over my self-centered, blockheaded stubbornness in the interest of a home, marriage, occupation and fortune. Besides, I was already homesick for the friends who had seen me off at the dock—Barney McCready who made me cry with his declarations of fealty; Al and Lucy and an assortment of ladies patting and pecking me, and bearded men hugging me.

By the time the *Blinky* slopped up to the wharf at St. Michael, a broken-boned little camp of 2,000 people, I was unsound both in mind and body; and the chilling gusts of wind from the north, the lifeless stretches of tundra lying inland, the dirty haze of predawn, and the run-down patchwork of wooden buildings did nothing to cheer me.

Pinky, my dog, who had been tied to a standard in the *Blinky*'s wheelhouse during the trip, was giving me no aid and comfort either. Once shut of the stenchy little tub, I anchored his leash to my wrist, and since he had been cooped up too long and apparently was immune to seagoing stomach disorders, he was out to paint the town. He was used to pulling heavy loads, and he obviously considered me a challenge in the way of cargo.

I suddenly realized that I had prepared no itinerary for my trip from St. Michael to Fairbanks. I had no idea where I was to stay there, and in my desire to get out of Nome as quickly as possible I had bought no ticket to Fairbanks, had not arranged for the transfer of my luggage or inquired about hotel accommodations. Then I remembered a paper that Al had given me as I went aboard the *Blinky*. I took it from my bag and read:

MARGARET, HONEY:

There never was a woman born who can remember travel directions. In St. Michael I want you to contact Will Burke's factor; name's Steve Wheeler. He's in charge of the *Hannah* and the *Sarah* while they are in port. They ply up the Yukon to Fairbanks and are owned by the Northern Commercial Company. Wheeler will put you on the one you'll take to Fairbanks. Write us when you get settled.

Love,
A_L

I asked the captain what to do about my trunk, and he told me that Steve Wheeler would take charge of it. He also offered to keep Pinky for me in a shack at the wharf's edge. Hard as Pinky was to handle at the moment, I resisted the temptation. The little ruffian was the only child I had, and I wanted to be sure he didn't get into trouble. So after receiving directions to the Northern Commercial Company's office, I untied him, took hold of my bag, and made my way to the two-story block structure that stood on a rise overlooking the end of the wharf.

I was about to ring the bell at its door when Pinky, who had hunkered a little behind me, set up a frightful uproar and lunged against the leash. The next moment my bag went one way and I was head over heels on the path. Rolling dazedly to a flat position, stomach to earth, I clutched at the leash with both hands. Then my heart came to roost in my mouth. Standing upright, forepaws drooped against their chests, pink snouts wrinkling, were a couple of black bears. They were not three feet from the jaws of the straining dog. Since I had seen but one bear in my life and then only in dim outline on the ice of the Bering Sea out of Nome, I was quickly wracked by a desire to climb a tree. Pinky or no Pinky, they would have been looking for me yet had the leash not been tied to my wrist. A big man with bushy red hair and beard came out of the door. He was clothed from head to moccasin in Indian-worked buckskin, and he clutched a chunk of half-eaten sourdough in one hand. His eyes, a brilliant blue, took in the situation with concern, then with amusement. Descending on the bears, he turned them about and gave each a lusty slap on the rump.

"Beat it," he said, chuckling, "or I'll put you to bed without supper."

A couple of quick motions later he had Pinky under one arm and me beneath the other. Moments later he set us down in the main salon of the Northern Commercial Company of St. Michael.

Although Steve Wheeler worked for Will until his Indian wife died in 1913—a misfortune that caused him to lose interest in the Territory and take his children Outside—he never wearied of recounting the episode with embellishments wherever friends met and a glass was enjoyed. Steve Wheeler was a welcome sight that night for a bushel of reasons, and my appreciation of him began with his next suggestion.

"You're Margaret Knudsen? We've been expecting you, my lass. Al Boyd wrote that you were coming. Bet you've been mighty seasick too. Nothing like rest and tea gruel for that." Knotting Pinky to a post, he pointed to some rickety stairs in back, defined dimly through the smoke cast by a kerosene lamp that rested on a vinegar barrel near its platform. "I'll take care of your dog. Up you go."

Topside, my room was a little glimpse of frontier paradise. Headed by two enormous, goose-down pillows, a broad bunk supported a layer of blankets a foot thick. Several brightly collored rag rugs lay on the rough floor, and a broad chest of drawers held a porcelain washbasin and pitcher set, and a kerosene lamp with a huge wick, a globular chimney and a brass base.

"You get into bed," Steve ordered, dropping my bag on the bunk. "Anything you need?"

"No, unless it's a shotgun for those bears."

"You'll love 'em when you get to know 'em." Steve laughed. "They're really excellent fellows and very friendly. We raised them from cubs. Unfortunately, dogs and bears come from different tribes. That's where you had your trouble."

"I'm a little hungry, too, I think."

"Good. Shows you're pulling out of it. But you shouldn't eat now. My wife'll look in on you from time to time. When you've had some sleep she'll feed you some gruel. By tonight, when you've rested and had a hot bath, you'll be able to eat your way through a solid wall of steak."

The click of the lock as he passed through the door was the last thing I remembered until the sun was on the other side of the house and I looked up at one of the most beautiful women to ever grace this earth. Her hair was black, parted in the middle and worn in two fat, waist-length braids. Her face was a delicate brown and oval in contour, and her brows were gently arched. Her tawny eyes, protected by lashes of a thickness and length that turned me green with envy, had a slant that gave her an Oriental look. Red, full lips, white teeth, a small, straight nose with tiny nostrils, and the body of a pagan goddess completed the picture.

"I'm Martha Wheeler. I've brought some gruel for you."

She handed me a wooden bowl and a long-handled tin spoon. The wispy steam that spiraled from the gruel had a salty, sweet smell to it, and as I got cross-legged beneath the blankets and prepared to have at it I was suddenly as hungry as a skid-row inhabitant on Thanksgiving.

"Thank you, Martha. I think I'm starved. I thought after that trip that I'd never be able to eat again."

"That's what everyone thinks when they are seasick." She laughed. "But they always can, after the sickness passes and they sleep. This will settle your stomach. Then you will feel much better. Later we will have a nice dinner and you will enjoy it."

"What is it?" The mess in the bowl looked for all the world like wet concrete. But it was delicious. It wasn't hard to chew but it had the adhesiveness of taffy candy. "It's sweet, and yet it's sour."

"It is mashed sourdough, strong tea and champagne."

"Champagne? You're not serious?"

"I am serious." She smiled. "I don't know where the cure came from. Steve says it's old as Grandfather McKinley Mountain. But it works. The sourdough strengthens; the tea provides the heat; the alcohol in the champagne tones up the stomach."

"Th'n y'r c'n eat a b'g dinner, hnh?"

Martha chuckled. "When you come downstairs I'll show you to your bath. We have a tin tub. And I always keep water hot. It takes a lot of it. Four children can accumulate much dirt."

"Four children?" The heaped spoon stopped halfway to my mouth. She looked no older than myself and I couldn't imagine anyone at my age with that many kids. "You're spoofing."

"No. I was married to Steve at fourteen. Well, I must go. Come down when you feel like it."

236

After she had vanished I licked the platter clean, then sank back into the luxury of the soft, clean bed. Presently I drifted off again, and when I awoke this time, as Martha had predicted, I felt much better. Throwing on my clothes, I poured water into the basin and sloshed my hands and face, made a feint at my hair, and went downstairs.

There were several customers in the store and Steve was hard at the business of making a profit. It must have been twenty minutes before he got rid of them and locked the door of the place for the night. Since I did not want to interfere, I sat on a box near the stairs and pacified my growing hunger by sucking at a nail and speculating on how it felt to fall heir to a restaurant. As he shot home the door bolt and turned about he saw me and grinned.

"Well, if it isn't the terror of the Spanish Main. You're looking much healthier, lassie."

"I'm feeling much healthier. You can bet on that, Mr. Wheeler. And—"

"Let's go home," he interrupted. "It isn't far. We've got our house nailed to the store."

Taking my arm, he guided me to a wooden partition to the rear of the long counter. As we passed behind it I saw a cavern just beyond an open door. But what a door! It was, at a conservative guess, six feet wide and ten feet high, and its girth and height revealed a room that complimented its stature. There were five or six bullhide chairs, two horsehide couches, a homemade highchair for infant feeding, enough kitchen stools to seat the year's immigration quota, a table that must have been at one time a part of the St. Michael dock, and several throw rugs, each as large as a blanket.

"Dad!"

Suddenly the children were all around us. The polite curtsies of the little girls and the friendly handshakes of the boys added to my early and lifelong appreciation of people of scant years. Martha's appearance was a bonus, too, as she started for the table, arms cradling tin plates, forks and spoons. Behind her a Yukon stove huffed and puffed, and the blast of heat would have caused the sun to sit up and take notice. But no hair was out of place, and no moisture showed on her brow.

"There," she said, dropping her cargo on the table. "You have slept well, Margaret? Are you hungry? Or would you like to bathe first? You have time."

A private tub in Alaska in those days was something only to be dreamed of—particularly one filled with hot water. I soaped and slithered, squirmed and collapsed in that tub until I felt like a withered prune, and I gave up only when the two Wheeler girls announced that dinner was on the table.

I'll never forget that feed or the warmth and love that ringed that table. I never saw them again, and I am always a bit sad when I recall that Steve disappeared after Martha died, taking their children with him. I don't even know what she died of. On a later date Will tried to find them, but he didn't succeed, and he was a master at policing his employees or former employees. They simply disappeared.

Anyway, there were no heavy spirits that night, and I was willing to go at the groceries without delay. A juicy roast of caribou meat sent up a delicious aroma from the center of the table. Smaller containers held hot canned tomatoes, tinned fruit and a brown, thick gravy, while a stack of sourdough bread teetered at one end of the board and a pot of coffee stuttered and hissed at the other.

After the petition for heavenly grace, offered by Steve and respectfully observed by the bowed, red-black crowns to left and right, we dug in. During the meal I learned some of their family history and the major reason for Steve's good job with the Northern Commercial Company.

Will, always on the lookout for an Alaska booster, had run into Steve in the Fifth Avenue Hotel, and over a drink he'd discovered that Steve was not only in favor of schools and churches but also intended to stay in the country. Will had hired him, on the spot, and put him in charge of one of Northern Commercial's best money bets—the Northern Commercial Post in St. Michael.

"Trouble is," Steve said, "Mr. Burke's ideas are too far advanced. Alaska is not ready for the niceties of civilization. People come up here for quick money. They are not interested in building a country. They want to get in, grab, and get out. Even the old-timers resent a collar—Federal anyway. So far as high-

ways, schools, legal marriages and the like are concerned, I'm
for it all the way. But the time's just not ripe."

"I guess you're right." At that point I could hardly keep my
eyes open, for the hot food and the relaxed, comfortable atmosphere had hit me like a double-edged sedative. A witch
doctor could have taken out my appendix with a stone ax and
I wouldn't have known it. "Everyone seems to agree."

Martha glanced at me, laughed softly, and went to the kitchen
to return with a tin cup of brandy.

"Take a long drink," she suggested, "then up to bed you go."

"Can I help with the dishes?"

"I should say not. Our girls are very good at such tasks."

Taking a pull at the stuff, I rolled it around in my mouth,
and the harsh, yet pleasant, sting provided a fitting climax to
an excessively delightful dinner. Then, obeying orders like a
good child, I got up, bade them good night and made ready to
head for the stall.

I put in a full day on my first visit to St. Michael. It began at
the St. Regis, where the cobwebs of my dreamless sleep of the
night vanished before the onslaught of a robust coffee royal.
The town, a replica of Nome in contour, architecture and general muddiness, supplied no sight-seeing thrills. Also, being a
veteran of Nome's recent insanity, I was not affected, adversely
or otherwise, by St. Michael's bellowing crowds, slouching Indians or hordes of dogs, the jangle of its honky-tonks or the gray
of its weather.

There were three or four little stores—all of the town's
crooked, narrow, main thoroughfare—and these carried a variety of merchandise that most trading posts had little call for.

For Martha and Steve I bought a hand-painted sugar-and-
cream set. For the boys and girls I found whistles and rag dolls.
I didn't neglect the bears either. In one place I stumbled on an
ancient jar of sorghum-and-rock-candy syrup, and at the post
that evening I bellyached them until they quit pawing me,
rolled on their backs, and begged for mercy. In this operation
I had some argument, of course, with Pinky. When I went to
feed him that evening he snuffled my boots, hackles lifting,
then retired behind the tether post where his disdainful sneez-

ing and low growls emphasized his opinion of anyone who would associate with such creatures.

At dinner Steve had suggested that it would be wise to begin picking up some loose ends. The next day was Friday and the Yukon River steamer, the *Sarah*, was scheduled to leave for Fairbanks at noon Saturday. In the morning we should get my luggage aboard, meet the captain, and learn with whom I was to share quarters.

Early on the following day Martha was pounding on my door. While I was eating a breakfast of sourdough flapjacks and washing them below with hot coffee, Steve directed two of his knaves to transport my trunk to the ship, ordered another to police the fort and boss the kids. Then we were on our way to the dock.

Although the *Sarah* was a two-decker and was smaller than the *Yucatan*, she was more comfortably proportioned and much prettier. Polished brass gleamed from many points, and the decks were holystoned to a fine surface. All rope was coiled primly and precisely, and there was a strong smell of antiseptic over all. The stewards, hurrying about, wore white jackets, blue jeans and black marine caps.

Captain Vernon McBride, whom we located in his office beneath the wheelhouse, could have passed as a twin of the late Napoleon Bonaparte, save that his uniform was not so resplendent. Fellow employees of the Northern Commerical Company, he and Steve had known each other for many years.

He gallantly squired us from stem to stern, and I could see that this was a happy ship. For one thing, at the rear was a raised deck furnished with observation chairs of real cane and floored with hard wood, suitable for dancing. There was also a comfortably equipped lounge or social room adjacent to the cabin areas below. There were two dining rooms. The cabins provided another nice surprise. Considerably larger than those of the *Yucatan*, they had walls of glistening dark mahogany, lamps of heavy brass, and two chairs each, the legs of which were nailed to the floors. The bunks, saints preserve us, had sheets, and if that were not sufficient to astonish the Alaskan voyager of 1904, each had its personal washstand.

"Ordinarily," McBride went on, "we are able to provide a

single cabin for husband and wife. However, the scene has changed. Everyone's going to Fairbanks or some other northern point. We're like a farmer caught in a locust stampede. We've had to split them up. By the way," he added, turning to me, "let me see your ticket. Perhaps you'd like to see your own quarters." I got it out of my bag and handed it to him. After a quick glance, he returned it and smiled. "This is a coincidence. You'll bunk with Mrs. Helfrich. Carol's her first name. She's the wife of Bernard Helfrich, a mining engineer. Dear friends of mine. They live in San Francisco, but they have mining interests up here and come in once a year. Let's see if she's in."

Mrs. Helfrich was not at home as we entered the second to the last cabin of the row on the far side of the deck. But evidence of her occupancy was plain. A half-filled steamer trunk, lid cocked and mouth yawning, was banked against a far wall. Clothes, shoes, stockings, hair rats, plumed and feathered hats, gloves and jewelry, had been hurled all over the place with reckless indifference. A heart-shaped, gold-embossed comb-and-brush case, large as a small suit case, had been upended on one bunk, its purple satin upholstery salted by streaks of rice powder. A note, pinned to a bunk pillow and scrawled in pencil, read: "Honey, I'm going uptown. Be back in a couple of hours. I want to buy a pet wolverine."

McBride read the message, then turned to Martha, Steve and me, shook his head and chuckled like a man who has found a fifty-dollar gold piece.

"That's Carol. She's crazy. Hope she never changes. You know them, Steve?"

"No. Not that I can recall."

"You missed something. Especially Carol. Say, Margaret, Carol's already here. Why don't you check in right now? Save you the fight with the crowd tomorrow."

So far, Steve and Martha had run my show in St. Michael, and although the idea was appealing—particularly in light of the long walk back—I didn't want to take over the reins high-handedly. "Doesn't everyone have to board at the regular time tomorrow?"

"This is a corrupt age." McBride grinned. "People in high places and favoritism and such."

"What do you think, Steve?"

"I think it's a good suggestion. I'll have one of my men bring your dog on ship. Your trunk is already here. You might as well stay put."

So I kissed Steve and Martha good-bye, admonished them to take good care of the children, and settled down to the task of tidying up the cabin. McBride left as one of his men dragged in the remainder of my duffle. His retreating shadow was still on the doorsill when the most outrageously raucous voice that I've ever heard sounded at my back.

"Get your claws off my clothes, you little thief!"

Carol Helfrich was near my size. But her tone and her muscular action had a certain similarity to the sound and fury of a Bering Sea ice purge in spring. Sheathed in red taffeta from shoulder hollow to instep and crowned by a garden-party hat, she came through the door as if she'd been shot from a cannon. Her eyes were wide, black and snapping. The nostrils of her thin nose were white with anger, and her lips were an ugly red slash.

I jumped as though I'd been shot, for she had nailed me from behind and by surprise, and I felt an instantaneous and powerful urge to flight. Then she did a thing that enabled me to forget my confusion and to look down *her* throat for a change. Jerking a dress from my hands, she gave me a push. I staggered back, and when I caught my balance again, I was ready for a busy scrap.

"I was only trying to help, you—you—!"

"Help?"

"Yes, help! I'm to share this cabin with you. I was putting away your stuff, just to do you a favor!"

"Oh." Her demeanor changed at once. Her smile became white and nice, and her eyes twinkled. "That's different. But you can't blame me. I've been robbed so many times. What's your name?"

"Margaret. Margaret Knudsen."

"Swede, eh?"

"No. Danish."

"There's a difference? I thought all of you Svenskas were frozen in the same mold." Snatching up an armful of clothes, she hurled them on the opposite bunk, kicked several pairs of shoes into a corner, threw off her hat, shook out her hair and offered her hand. "No hard feelings, I hope. These treks are bad enough without any hair-pulling and fingernail exercises."

"No, I can see your side of it." I was willing to let bygones be bygones, for I was beginning to like her and no one realized better than I the discomfort involved in an uneasy traveling relationship. "I'd like to be friends."

"Then we shall, we shall be, my sparrow." Going to her trunk, she reached in and dragged forth a fat box of real big-city, hand-dipped chocolates. "Help yourself," she invited.

Since I had eaten nothing more toothsomely sweet than horehound rock candy and molasses on sourdough flapjacks for more than a year, I was soon at work on the first layer. As I stuffed myself we traded a good deal of information. For her part, she had some first-hand, heavyweight Alaskan history of which to boast.

Her husband had been one of the successfuls of the 1896 Klondike stampede. By 1900 he was the head of his own multi-million-dollar mining concern, the success of which had arrived, in the main, by reason of his personal prospecting. By 1902 this restlessness had led him into the investigation of nearly every gold strike, large and small, in northern and northwestern Alaska.

So it was that he found himself, on the eve of Felix Pedro's discovery of the rich Tanana Mines, in old Circle City, below Fort Yukon and the camp of Forty Mile. News of the find emptied all three communities of human and animal life, including Helfrich, and when he had got his crack at the new diggings he returned to Circle City, soon to be renamed Fairbanks. There at one of the newer dance halls he met Carol Prentiss, an entertainer who divided her talents between hustling the miners for drinks and singing to the accompaniment of an old player piano. That was on a Monday night in late June. By Wednesday they were aboard a packet bound for Valdez, and thence to Skagway and the States. They were married in Skagway. Neither, according to Carol, had seen anything unusual in such romantic haste. Helfrich had been looking, he told her, for a wife who had been around and could handle herself when the going got tough. He had the money and she had the looks. It seemed to him like a good swap, since he intended to live and work in Alaska, save for business trips Outside, and would need a woman who could take the cold and other physical discomforts. He was prepared, moreover, to pay for the privilege.

After mulling over his proposition for an hour, Carol decided to let him do so. Life for her was not tedious, but it had become —at thirty years of age—a little hackneyed and more than a little uncertain financially. Everyone, it appeared, wanted something for nothing, and it had all started when she was a child of eight. Her father, a New York fireman, had died of too many doses of Old Shatterskull. Subsequently her mother had skipped town, and in the ensuing six years Carol had been passed from one relative to another, all of whom were perpetually in a hurry to give her away again. While visiting one set of kin in St. Louis, Missouri, she had wearied of her role of the tribe's chief squatter and had disappeared. By the time she was twenty she had served in succession in the vocational capacities of waitress, tramp, garment worker, cancan kicker in burlesque and honky-tonk canary. One night in Chicago, in 1901, in her room above the Michigan Avenue bistro where she was singing, she picked up a copy of the *Saturday Evening Post*. One story, specifically, electrified her. It had to do with the untold and undiscovered riches of Alaska, and it urged—if not in actual phrasing then in siren inference—going there and getting fat. At the time she owned $200. A few months later she was throating it at the Fairbanks dance hall and listening to Helfrich's logical approach to the seeking of a soul mate.

"I didn't expect much from him," she confided with overpowering frankness, "but he's a candy-coated apple. He's built like a sack of wheat with a string tied around the middle. He could root up trees with his nose. But I love the big boob."

Her good fortune didn't end with marrying Helfrich, she went on to say. In San Francisco, when Helfrich took her to see his father Hank—a grocer well to do in his own right—she had received a surprise. Her background being more colorful than respectable, she naturally entered the old man's big house on California Street with doubt and trepidation, for Helfrich had insisted on telling Hank the truth all the way around. Helfrich *pere*, her new husband explained, had been a commercial fisherman, sailor and cowboy prior to his grocery tycoonery, and was a down-to-earth character. Among his traits was an inability to appreciate a lie.

They found Hank seated before a crackling fireplace, in socks and undershirt, whisky bottle at his side, and bellowing obscenities at a labor-union paper. After the death of his mother, Bernard had explained on the way up, Hank had closed up most of the house, and was served solely by an elderly housekeeper. However, even her godly sense of orderliness and cleanliness could not prevent him from his daily program of moving familiar articles of furniture and knickknacks from other parts of the house into his room. Carol was not to be shocked by the clutter.

"It was a pigpen," Carol whooped, "if you've ever seen one. We had to climb over a million chairs and stools. Pictures were stacked all around, waiting to be hung. There were two big beds in the middle of the room. You couldn't move without stepping on a cigar butt, and there were enough empty bottles around to start a distillery. Funny part was, the old boy fitted the place like a skullcap. He looked just like a great big old tusker—a black one—grunting and puffing in his sty."

But in the next breath the room, despite its dirt and disorder, became the first real home that she had known. After a round of affectionate pounding between father and son, they accepted the lord of the castle's invitation to a drink, and the talk finally got around to the subject that she had been dreading. Her past. She could have saved herself the worry. Hank gulped a straight shot of whisky, then jabbed a finger at his son.

"A chip off th' old block! I'm tickled pink! While back, I's afraid you was gonna marry one o' them mush-mouth pasty-faces out at that college you went to. C'mere, Daughter! Gimme a kiss!"

Carol's brand of humor, I soon discovered, would have driven a slave dealer to drink, and her tongue was the sandiest instrument ever fitted to a voice box. When referring to her husband in general conversation, for instance, he became My Eagle.

Helfrich's stiff, wiry, black hair, clumps of eyebrows, fleshy, upturned nose, big teeth, dumpy body and laconic grunts, resembled the features of that majestic bird as much as a penguin
looks and sounds like a kodiak bear. On the same note of reverse connotation, Captain McBride was pointed out in her
dialogues as Admiral McBum, and following my inroads on her
candy I was pegged as Dainty Fingers. The sailors aboard the
Sarah were McBum's Elite Lancers, and the stewards were the
Disciples of Bounty-laden Hebe. All other voyagers were identified as Alaska's Future Leaders, and the trim ship itself was
McBum's Barnacle Preserve.

Whether she had enjoyed much formal education I don't
know, but evidently she had read a good deal, for she possessed
a bulky complement of knowledge and a few ideas of her own
to go with it. This became apparent at dinner in the small dining room that night, and as a matter of fact she wasn't unwilling
to air her views at any stage of the trip. She had a captive audience, for the wind—despite the approach of summer—was bitter and gusty, and save for a few hours of sun each day, we found
it more comfortable to ignore the deck and spend our time in
our cabin, the lounge or the dining room. She had no trouble in
snaffling a listener wherever she turned.

In any case, she was the first woman to rupture my faith in
the infallibility of conventional early American standards and
to stagger my devotion to blind and sacred cows. I never saw
her or her husband again after I left them at the mouth of the
Tanana River. I was bound for Fairbanks on a packet and they
intended to inspect Helfrich properties at this junction of the
Tanana and Yukon rivers, then return to San Francisco.

But I have been grateful to them, particularly to Carol. Her
militant rebelliousness caused me to think and to doubt. I am
certain that my narrow little mind was broadened appreciably
and that my manners and personality were also improved by
that courageous, uninhibited, early day female revolutionary.
Anyhow, I felt freer and happier from her first lesson, when she
stabbed a contemptuous finger into each of my hair rats and
ordered them into the discard.

"You have beautiful hair," she snapped. "Why make a crow's

nest of it? Here. Sit down in that chair. I'll show you something."

Unearthing a curling iron and a tiny, alcohol-burning heater from her trunk, she went to work on a new coiffure for me. When she was satisfied she wiped my face clean, and opening a box of fine powder, dusted my face and neck. After that she touched up my cheeks and lips with rouge and handed me a mirror. I liked what I saw so much that she had to take the mirror away from me by force.

Instead of being severely divided at the middle with an overhanging loaf on each side, the part in my hair was now set rakishly a couple of inches above my right ear. Since the growth was thick and naturally curly, a series of deep depressions broke the symmetry of the sweeping roach that Carol had built on top, and a fat biscuit twist at the nape of my neck rounded out the nobby effect.

This new styling altered my appearance from the shoulders up. My face and head reflected an older look and had taken on the contour of an oval, rather than a wedge shape. My eyes also appeared larger and set farther apart. The dainty dusting of fine powder on my skin, rather than my habitual troweling with ground rice, and the delicate touch of the rouge as a substitute for lip biting and cheek pinching, were innovations to quicken the pulse of any greenie's vanity.

"Why, Carol, I—I just can't believe it! I'm not the same person!"

"Right," she returned, "and you never will be again. Not if I can help it. It's time the women of this fool country woke up." Then she lifted me to speechless veneration by throwing me a couple of her evening gowns and inviting me to select the necessary shoes and stockings to match.

"We'll want you at our table," she said. "You're about my size, and I don't want to sit next to something out of Plymouth Rock by Macbeth. Those duds of yours should be in a museum. And you can keep the gowns and accessories."

"Oh, I couldn't!" But the more I considered the gowns the more I drooled, cooed and gasped. One of them was an aquamarine blue and the other a brazen hussy red. Both were hour-glass slinkers, backed by stiff, arching bustles, and were made of real silk. The hems swept the floor, and while the red darling was naked of sequins or other sparklers, it was no less "immodest" or "forward" as Blair, Nebraska, considered such clothing than if it had sagged with them. "They must have cost a fortune! I—I'd like to take them, Carol! But I couldn't!"

"Don't be a ninny," she interrupted impatiently. "I have all the clothes I need and all the money I want to buy more. And I'll hand you some good advice. When someone offers you something free, take it. Never argue. If you can't use it, throw it away. But always take it. That way the percentage is always working for you. Now get into one of those and spare me any more gabble."

She didn't need to slap my hands twice. However, I had one moment of indecision as I finished pulling on the stockings, stepping into the shoes, and squirming into the red gown. The dress was cut so low in front that my mother wouldn't have gone to bed in it, and as far as the back was concerned, I could have felt a draft on an ocean floor.

"Carol—I don't know—I've never even worn rouge before, and this—this—"

"Hush." Moving to the door, she opened it, glanced up and down the deck, crossed to her bed and sat down. Then, reaching into a pocket, she drew out the burned stub of a cigarette, fired it and fogged up. "Helfrich doesn't like me to smoke," she mumbled as the smoke purled from her lips. "Have to grab it on the sly."

"Oh, that's all right. I mean it's all right with me. But, Carol, about this dress and all—do you think it's—it's—"

"You mean do I think it's all right for a woman to look well groomed, feminine and exciting to men? Do I think it's reasonable for a female to have a mind of her own; be allowed a certain amount of human freedom and treated as people, rather than as chattels? If that's what you're referring to, I do!" Standing upright, she dropped the stub on the floor, then ground it beneath her foot. "Someday women will wear rouge and gowns like these as a matter of course. No gown such as you're wearing ever made a tramp of any woman. Neither did rouge. It's the mind inside and the deportment in company that does the trick, either way. For my part, I'd much rather be admired for my coiffure and my clothes, my jewelry and my independence, than for my modesty in taking a bath in the dark. Besides, a little shoulder, back and ankle in view are a vast improvement in the health department. I wouldn't wear a corset if Helfrich gave me one with gold stays."

The hours, days and months rolled back in an instant, and I was dancing with Will Burke once more at the Westminister Hotel in Los Angeles, heady with champagne and living each note of the music and fragment of the moment gloriously, and wishing that the night would never end. "Why, that's what Will said. He said a girl didn't need to be bad to have fun and even to drink a little—and dance—and wear modern clothes. Will said—"

"Who?"

"Will. Will Burke. He's a friend. I'm going to work for him."

"I've heard of him. He's a smart cob. You'd do well to remember his advice. Now look here. You're a nice kid, and I'm going to give you another lift. I don't know why, except that you might be worth something to the female rebellion that's on its way, if you've got the spirit to go with your looks. Anyway, you've got an impediment in your speech."

With that she presented me with a gift that money could never have bought. I had been plagued since childhood with a stoppage just short of a stutter. This handicap was particularly evident when I came under emotional stress of one kind or another, and at nineteen it had become distressing, for it had been getting worse.

"Before you answer a question," Carol continued, "go into a little act. Take a short, jerky breath, hold it a second, and let it go. Then swallow twice. Get into the habit and see if it doesn't work. No one ever will suspect your purpose. They'll put it down as a charming and individual characteristic."

I put her prescription to work, and a year later the impediment left me, never to return.

We were in rehearsal of the "act" when her husband showed up, accompanied by two companions. I liked the calm, good-natured, ugly man instantly.

"Hello, girlie," he grunted pleasantly, at Carol's introduction. Turning to a craggy-faced man whose curling, silver hair hid his neck and collar in back, he identified him as Humbert Smathers, a Federal official whom he had met downtown. "Mr. Smathers is an investigator for the Interior Department," Helfrich explained. "He's making the rounds up here. Annual inspection trip, y'know. And this is his—"

"Oh, goodie!" Carol interrupted. "Everywhere we go these days we meet up with high-muck-a-mucks. My husband is so smart! Makes a trip so much more fun, if you're associating with your own kind. This riffraff! You don't mind if I call you Bert— or maybe Bertie, do you, Mr. Splatter? It seems so much more homey."

"Smathers—Smathers, my dear," Mr. Smathers prompted, bowing over her hand.

"Oh, I'm so sorry. My husband can never get names right."

"And you may call me—uh—Bert, if you like, little lady," Smathers conceded gallantly. "Or even—"

"His secretary," Helfrich oinked, one heavy hand concealing his tusks. "Mr. Lyman Jones, the third," he added, addressing himself to a balding, bespectacled little fellow of about thirty who was dressed in a rumpled black suit and carried an umbrella. "These gentlemen are our guests at dinner tonight."

"Killer!" Carol cried. "He's a dead ringer for my cousin Killer Jones, the wrestler!" Flinging her arms wide, she embraced both men, kissed them soundly, then took the sting from her behavior by directing everyone into the dining room for champagne and dinner. However, both probably wished that they had gone to live in darkest Africa at an early age, for during the meal her harangues were interminable and her peeves inexhaustible. These diatribes were the more uncomfortably punchy since we sat at the captain's table, located in the center of the room and vulnerable to eyes and ears from all directions. Why Captain McBride or Carol's husband did not try to shut off her wind is a question that must remain unanswered. Perhaps, as their expressions indicated, they were too much amused by the spectacle. If so they were isolated cases, for she had the rest of the table—and possibly most of the room—virtually foaming at the mouth from her first word.

There was nothing right with the republic, as she saw it, and the heart of the trouble lay in the democratic form of government as interpreted, at least, by the masses and their leaders. All politicians were dishonest, she held, and were a species, rather than a product of environment. These animals should be painlessly exterminated and a new start made toward honest and intelligent government. The cleansing process could begin with the refusal of the people, en masse, to vote. Lacking such a "job-holding device," the politicians would be out on their respective ears, necessitating the declaration of martial law. And before a new set of lawmakers could be swept in, the voting public would be required to pass a written test.

Basically this would involve a cursory understanding of city, county, state and Federal law, a solid grounding in the articles of our Constitution and a creditable familiarity with the personal records and accomplishments of the candidates for office. Failure to measure up would automatically prohibit any citizen from exercising his right to vote. On the subject of citizenship, she felt that the native born, as well as the foreigner, should be constrained to qualify for his place in the American sun. She cited the statutes of ancient Rome, where citizenship was held in such esteem that it often was purchased at appalling monetary sacrifice by the plebs, and the loss of which had caused aristocrats to belt the hemlock.

"But in this country," she snarled, "any idiot can vote. He can even vote for another idiot, if both are born to the land. Well, nine out of ten Americans are idiots. If you don't believe me, ask the next hundred men you meet to rattle off the weight, reach, height, complexion, financial position, knockout record, future prospects and home life of any popular prize fighter. Ninety-nine of them can give you the answers on all counts. Ask the same herd to name the fourth American President and see how many correct answers you get."

The "tyranny" of the tax structure on a national level, she contended, was a prime example of "Democracy at the polls, refereed by the vampire bats in Washington." Marriage was even being used as a means of gouging the people, and worst of all, the innocents were swallowing the hook without a thought in the opposite direction.

"Little by little they're making it impossible for a man to support his family with his own sweat. That's because they can't get enough loose money to graft, waste or give away in forming their empire. Soon the wife will have to work to make ends meet. When that happens they'll be hog fat. They can tax two people in every family instead of one. It's getting impossible for a man to go into business and succeed. Business is a threat to their swindle. It ruins their tax structure. The businessman, large or small, can write off, by law, too many reasonable expenses. That simply must not happen. A rash of new businesses across the nation would plug the leaks, even though it meant economic progress. So the more people in the salt mines, the better."

Pursuing the subject of marriage, she believed that if level-headed people could not live harmoniously and profitably together without the legal influence or a marital contract, then they should not have tried to climb conventional trees. Aside from the documentary proof needed to establish the legal ancestry of offspring and the right to property claim, there was no reason to legitimate marriage. In fact the practice was a "job-holding device of the clergy," outmoded as the Sioux travois, spiritually, physically and morally, and kept alive only for its worth as a medium of extra revenue to the churches. Only Christians, Moslems, Buddhists, devotees of Baal and Moloch and tree worshipers, were so intellectually retarded as to dispute her contention, and she could prove it by history—see?

She professed to believe that the answer to good government was a monarchy over a "sick, slob democracy, where every man is convalescent, created equal, and mad at his superior," and while she referred to George Washington as a "possibly great man," she saw Abraham Lincoln as a "pants presser."

"Washington was a British peer when the Revolutionary War broke. He was also a millionaire. He had family and fortune and prestige in his adopted land. He threw it all over because he liked this country and wanted to see it hit out for itself. For this, Johnny Bull put a price on his head. But that didn't stop him. He went right ahead. He wound up broke and look what he got out of it. I'm not going to tell you. Check a history book. He could have been great. Except for what he had to work with—this country and its people."

She chilled me by referring to President Lincoln as a "Civil War bellhop" who had the political faculty of "making toothpicks look like split rails."

"I want someone to tell me if slavery was the real question before him," she prodded. "Was the South getting too strong with England? Was the South bidding for the seat of Federal government through its growing industrial strength? Were England and France paying too much attention to Jefferson Davis and Atlanta, and not enough to Washington? Was Lincoln, the bellhop, between floors? Gentlemen, your Abraham Lincoln was a maker of toothpicks rather than a hewer of rails."

Happily, the inmates of the dining room were to be given a respite from her bullyragging, although I was the unwilling means of contributing to their peace of mind. The next day I came down with another of my recently persistent colds and was directed by Carol to get to bed and stay there. Along toward evening a fever hit me, and Carol herded in the ship's doctor, a grizzled little man with mutton-chop whiskers, brown-flecked lips and a walloping odor of sen-sen on his breath. I don't recall his name, but he had powerful convictions about the proper way to treat the ailment. Throwing two more heavy blankets over me, he spooned some liquid into my mouth, the taste of which nearly blew my head off, and left a box of pills, each as large as a horse bean. Carol was to choke one down my throat every two hours, see that I didn't get up for two days, and not call him unless I developed pneumonia.

"More than one body sick on this thing," he rasped. "All with colds. Don't see why somebody don't find a cure for it."

In any event, the stuff did its work. Three days later I was on deck, and the sight that met my eyes would have given a jolt of good cheer to any convalescent. Even Carol, who had spent most of the time loading me with medicine, bringing in hot soup, and talking darkly of overthrowing the government, was silent for once.

We had left the dismal gloom of the Bering Sea and entered the roaring, white-capped Yukon River, at that point about twelve miles wide. White-shawled purple mountains towered in a horseshoe circle ahead, and groves and forests of tall pine, gigantic fir, quaking aspen, pungent cedar, silver birch and countless other breeds and brands of lumber on the hoof, stretched for incalculable miles.

As we plowed along, a bull moose and his harem would appear at the forest's edge; deer, fox, an old sow bear and her cubs, and wildcats. Once a pair of huge timber wolves burst from the thickets, probably on the trail of some small animal, stiffened their forelegs to a sliding stop at sight of the ship, erected their long pointed ears, sniffed, stared with unblinking green eyes, then slunk back into the gloom of the shadows.

On the sixth day out, the ship rounded a bend in the river and swung inshore toward a jagged, natural harbor aproned by a makeshift dock and populated by what looked like a small war party of Indians. Stacks of cordwood flanked the wharf on each side for a distance of perhaps fifty yards, interlaced by what appeared to be numerous clotheslines, and several fires were having a fine time with the wood.

"What's that?"

"It's a wood depot." Carol, who had been trying to sneak in a cigarette the entire day, glanced around the deck, and seeing no evidence of her husband, scooped a butt from her pocket, lit up, hogged it and stamped it out. "This basket's a wood burner. Out of St. Michael they carry enough to get us into the Yukon. From there on in they have to pick it up as they go along. They pay the Indians to get it. That's what that is." Flipping back a stray curl, she grasped my arm, took another snort of the sharp air and turned. "Ready?"

"For what?"

"We'll go ashore. Everybody does it. When we get to a wood depot. Those reddys have the best dried salmon in the world."

Whatever else she might have lacked in the way of good judgment, Carol was an authority on dried salmon. Wherever we stopped to take on fuel from that point to the mouth of the Tanana River we found the Indians' "clotheslines" loaded with the chewy, succulent food, and as it was a sort of free-lunch concession to their main source of profit—woodcutting—I gave them a run for their money.

254

"Part of the trip," McBride explained. "We consider that in our time schedule. We couldn't get along without our north-country troops. Magnificent people, aren't they?"

They were, to be sure. They were nothing like the scabby, quarreling, helpless Indians of Nome. These people, while of much the same stature, had dignity, spirit and independence, and were dressed in good buckskin, stiffly worked with stained porcupine quills. Best of all, they seemed happy and prosperous. The braves carried new rifles and a brace of bowie knives. Their tents showed no tears nor patches.

They were Tenas, Carol explained, cousins of the Arizona Apaches, excellent hunters and fishermen. They had salmon wheels in every river and stream in their territory hereabouts, and made a hefty side penny by supplying the Yukon and Tanana boats with fresh meat—moose, caribou and such.

There had been some speculation, she conceded, about the quality of their eyesight, and this had led to suspicion of the origin of the game that they had for sale. Mules, brought in by the mining camps, had been found dead minus their hindquarters and loins, and upon questioning of the myopic aborigines, it was admitted that they had a point. In the gloom of the forests long ears *did* resemble horns at first sight.

"You won't have to wet nurse these babies in Fairbanks," she added, referring to my experiences with the Indians of Nome. "They don't like towns and they don't like to be coddled by white people. They can take care of themselves."

At the moment I couldn't have been less impressed with the likes, dislikes, love, lives, history or hatreds of the noble redmen of Alaska, or any other element remaining between me and Jack Bartlett in Fairbanks. Despite my cold, I felt stronger than I had for months, and this beautiful country held me in slavery. I had that indefinable feeling that comes to every wanderer at some time in his life, that I was going *home*—even if I had never before seen it—and no medium of speed was fast enough to get me there. I recall with regret that I went aboard the packet *Chinook* at Fort Gibbon with a bare, mumbled acknowledgment to the Helfrichs for their many kindnesses and considerations. My only interest was to get to Fairbanks as soon as possible.

Chapter Thirteen

THERE is no city, town or major Alaskan camp that hasn't owned a piece of me, at some fork in the road—Nome, Fairbanks, Sitka, Juneau, Ketchikan, Seward, Anchorage, the Koyukuk, Fort Yukon, Yellow Knife, Devil's Bend, Tanana and the Klondike—to name a few areas at random.

When I go home up there for a visit I try, inevitably and futilely, to take in as many of my old community loves as possible. But I am no strong finisher any more, and when it's time to leave I am always caught with a passel of extensive travel plans, all of which are impossible to firm up. Which is to say that the northern freeze overhauls me and forces my weatherbeaten bones to call for a clime suitable to baking in the sun. However, I have never as yet missed Fairbanks on any of my excursions.

It is, of course, a delight for any old head of vintage 1900 to visit the Fairbanks of 1962, take on a glass and a good dinner, and just before sleep compare the rich, polished, self-assured sophisticate of today with the roaring, slab-sided, dirty-foot brat to which Senator Charles H. Fairbanks of Indiana had loaned his name in 1902.

But then, as now, she was a queen. Fairbanks, in my book of

quality people and places, is the only community left on earth where love, life and the pursuit of happiness is honestly considered law rather than lip. I like to think that my husband Will Burke helped to make that premise in our Constitution stick with the early birds in Fairbanks also. True, he was capable of showing a blue nose at times, as I had reason to recognize later. However, his insistence on lawful regulation of the city's social, political and industrial structure had its points. A man owed a certain percentage of himself to his country and his community, and it had to be paid, even if it hurt. In this opinion he never changed to the day of his death, God love him, and as I have said, I am sorry that he didn't live to see the forty-ninth star in our flag.

I flounced off the boat at the rambling wharf that lipped the outskirts of the Tanana River, a stone's throw from Fairbanks' bright lights, dry mouthed for a sight of Jack Bartlett. Half an hour later I realized that I had not written that I was coming, and as I criss-crossed the crowd for a third or fourth time the idea sank home that even Will Burke had not known the precise hour of my arrival. Al Boyd had written only that I was en route, and to date I had heard nothing from Jack. The passenger-boat schedules on any Alaskan waterway at the turn of the century were generously elastic. The *voyageur* could expect to arrive at a given destination a week early or a month late, depending upon the temper of the captain, the sobriety of the crew, or the condition of the rivers and the weather. It would have been virtually impossible for either Jack or Will to have anticipated and prepared for the exact moment that I would set foot in Fairbanks. However, it developed that Will had adopted the next best course of action.

As I started up the path leading toward town I heard a hoarse bawl.

"Miss! Uh, miss!"

I turned, and a stumpy, bandy-legged hobgoblin waddled up. Shod with knee-length rubber boots and dressed in long-handled underwear, the top half of which showed above ragged blue jeans, he could have jumped out of the pages of a Haloween scare tale. His eyes were pale blue, watery and red

258

rimmed. He had no teeth. His jutting chin and the thin, hooked beak that served as his nose, almost met in the center of his red face, and a network of scars on his bald head showed his familiarity with certain types of brickbats and their effectiveness.

"Ain't you Miss Knudsen?" he asked, jamming his wolfskin cap back on and reaching for my bag. "Y'are, ain't you?"

"Why, yes."

"Thought so. Mr. Burke said you had red hair and was skinny. Said you might have one of them checkered skirts and a straw hat to boot. Jist like you do," he added.

I wasn't exactly glowing over Will's description of me. "Who are you?"

"Name's Bill Bugle," he wheezed. "Know it sounds silly. But that's m' name. God's truth." Tearing the bag from my hands, he tucked it under his arm and shouldered me up the path. "Thank the good Lord. Thought you'd never git here. I work fer Mr. Burke and Northern Commercial. He's been in Fort Yukon. Be home tonight, mebbe tomorrow. Meantime he says fer me to camp on this here dock an' watch fer you. That's what I been doin' fer two weeks. Tired out, that's what I am. Sometimes Mr. Burke's sot in 'is ways. Good man, though. Pays well. I'm a swamper, reg'lar job. Now I kin git back to it. Got to take you to Sheila's first, though."

"Sheila's?"

"Sheila Wilson's. Sheila's one o' Mr. Burke's pencil pushers. Lives in a little cabin near the store. Nice girl. He wants you should stay with her. How's your trip? Bad, I'd say. Boats is a pore way to travel."

At the moment I was in no mood to hear his views on sea travel, much less to be taken away from my immediate preoccupation of finding Jack. I told him that first I must find a friend to whom I had to deliver an urgent message, and asked him where the chief hotels were located. He pointed them out to me —the Pioneer and the Great Divide—on one side of the street. And off to the right a third and smaller hostelry, lacking a porch or a second story, admitted to second class. It was the Regus.

Every other building was a saloon or dance hall, and the big ones—as distinguished from their smaller competitors by reason of their newel posts and second stories—claimed they were the Horseshoe, the Senate, the California, the Star of Alaska, the Ice Worm, the Polar Club and so on.

Mingling with the sights and sounds was the clean, sharp odor of newly cut lumber, a welcome relief from the musty, dead-earth fragrance of Nome.

Telling Mr. Bugle that I would meet him later, I entered the Pioneer, nearest of the hotels, and asked for Mr. Bartlett. The peppermint-shirted clerk had never heard of him. The Great Divide didn't have Jack, either. But the Regus did.

"Sure thing," the clerk told me. "Great feller. Gone hunting and won't be back f'r a couple months. Lives here all the time."

In a way, Jack's absence was a relief. Knowing his temper, I had been girding myself for combat. He had told me to stay put until he sent for me, and he wouldn't forgive me easily for flouting the authority that he felt was his right to exercise. I registered for a room at the Regus. I guess I loved him so much I wanted only to be near where he had slept. I can give no other reason for staying that night at a skid-row hotel when I had the money to go first cabin.

Around four in the morning I awoke, wild-eyed and ready for bear. I didn't recognize my excitement at the moment. But at breakfast in the Regus' restaurant it came home to me. Among other exciting things I was sitting in the middle of a gold rush.

After breakfast I went to the rambling Northern Commercial Company building on the south bank of the Tanana River. As I entered I saw Will sitting at a table, talking to some other men. He leaped from his seat and threw open his arms.

"Honey!"

I was so happy to see him that I forgot my new-found sense of maturity and dignity, my betrothed state or even that anyone else was in the post. As usual when we had been separated for some time, the sight of him was like a shelter in a storm. Flying at him, I laid my head on his chest.

"Hey!" He laughed, touching his lips to my cheek. "You're breaking every bone in my body!" He stood me off at arm's length and looked me up and down, crosswise and sidewise.

"What've you done to your hair?"

"Well, I got tired of that old—"

"And you're thinner, much thinner."

"I've been working pretty hard. And I caught a lot of colds. Also—"

"But you're looking wonderful, my dear. Wonderful."

He could have taken prizes for masculine beauty himself. Save for a darker hue to the natural swarthiness of his face, the powerful column of his neck and the backs of his fine hands—a gift, no doubt, of the Fairbanks sun—he had not changed a particle in the past year. There were no new wrinkles. The silver at his temples had not expanded. His crooked smile held its well-remembered infectiousness, and his coal-black eyes were as alive and snapping as ever.

"Oh, Will—Will, I'm so glad to see you!"

"*You're* glad to see *me?* Seeing you takes ten years off my age." Recalling the presence of his two unshaven companions, he turned and nodded to each. "See you later, boys. I've got some important things to do. Excuse me?"

Grasping my arm, Will pushed me before him and began steering me through the lines of milling customers and the stacks, bales and crates of merchandise around and behind the clutter of tales and counters. "We'll go to my office for the time being. After that, we'll get you settled. Meanwhile, I've a million questions, and I'll bet you do too."

Under the broad, worn stairs and a little to one side of a packing table, he opened a door and we were in an airy room lighted by real electricity and furnished with three desks, numerous wooden filing cabinets, an array of document-loaded clipboards on the walls and a brace of bearhide rugs on the pine floor. The animate occupants were a blond, blue-eyed woman about thirty with a flat form, thin nose, thinner lips and a mountain of hair piled grotesquely on top of her head. She wore a starched white blouse topped by a choker collar, and by a long, heavy black skirt. The appearances of the other two brought me smartly to attention. They were men of about the same age as the woman, and with their red kinky hair, light brown eyes, snub noses, freckles, identical height and girth, similar clothing and green eye shades, they were as alike as two peas.

"George and Jim Frazier, Miss Margaret Knudsen." Will

smiled. "George and Jim," he explained, "keep our books and are believed to be the only white twins in Alaska. They came up here four years ago, looking for gold. When they couldn't find it in the ground they settled for digging it out of me. Actually, they're another reason why the Northern Commercial does everything twice as well as our competitors." He dropped an affectionate palm on the bony shoulder of the woman. "This lady is Miss Sheila Wilson. Be nice to her. She makes out our pay checks."

Sheila Wilson closed a drawer of the desk, painfully cracked open a smile, leaned forward as if the effort was one to sap her strength, and extended her hand. In view of her other patterns of attitude, her grip was surprisingly cordial.

"How can you be alive after that trip up the Tanana?" she asked. "I'll never forget mine. Even after seven years."

Her remark reminded me that since I had slipped Bill Bugle's manacles the night before I had neglected to inquire of my trunk and my dog. Not that my clothes particularly concerned me. They could be replaced. But Pinky was another matter. Had he been a boy human instead of a boy dog, he would have been a candidate for what in those days was known, in whispers, as a reform school. But Will told me that Pinky was all right and so was my trunk.

"At present," Will said, grinning, "Pinky's in our kennels. Your trunk is at Sheila's cabin where you were supposed to stay last night. And, if you are interested, Bill Bugle is not speaking to you. I didn't get in from Fort Yukon until midnight. When I arrived Bill was waiting for me, trunk in one hand and dog in the other. I can tell you, with no exaggeration, that he was provoked. Looking for a wraith, with a heavy load on one's back and trying to handle a rambunctious dog in the bargain, was a job he didn't want 'no more.' I got on the telephone and learned that you were at the Regus. Since Fred Watterson, who runs the place, is a friend of mine, I knew you were safe and sound. I hit the shucks too. But Bill's still in a sputtering swivet. He has renounced women in general and you in particular." Dipping into a shirt pocket, he produced one of the slender, green-speckled cigars that he invariably fired up when he was relaxed and enjoying himself. "Now if you people will excuse us, we'll leave you for a little while. Margaret's going to work with us, and we've a lot of things to talk over."

Stepping to a partly opened door at his left, he swung it wider and motioned me inside. Then I was comfortably seated in an upholstered leather chair before a hand-carved black-walnut desk. A good water color of Mount McKinley and another of a Yukon River scene hung from the walls, and machine-tufted rugs of red and blue were spread fatly before two smaller leather chairs in opposite corners. A nickel-and-iron wood stove, a polished maple hat tree, cedar wall cabinet and three tiers of books—Dickens, Scott, Shakespeare, Spinoza, Goethe, Twain and assorted historical volumes—took up most of the wall behind me.

"I figure that if I must work eighteen hours a day to make a living, I'm entitled to some comfort and pleasant surroundings," Will said. "At least when I'm in town. I had a letter from Al Boyd. He said some gratifying things about you, my dear. I want you to know I'm proud of you, both for your efficiency and loyalty to us, and for the all-around, admirable person you've proved yourself to be. You're an asset to our organization and a credit to yourself."

"Oh, I—didn't do anything. And Lucy and Al were so nice to me. I just love them, Will."

"Everyone does." Getting up, he went to the cabinet, took a key from his pocket, sprung a tiny padlock on its double doors and swung them open. The shelves were crowded with expensive imported liquors and a row of genuine rock-crystal tumblers.

I declined his offer of a drink, and he poured himself four fingers of White Horse Scotch and sat down agin.

"Let's get down to business before we move on to more edifying things. Al says you want to settle in Fairbanks and he wants me to give you a job. That's easy enough. Unless, of course, you thought of replacing me."

I was never able to resist his charming good humor, even in my darkest moods, and this was one of those times. Suddenly it seemed as though there had been no months of heartbreak, loneliness and ill health in Nome; and I was ready again for a round of good dinners, coffee royals, cards or dancing all night.

"You know the kind of job I want."

"Telephone switchboard, eh? If that's the case, you've got one. It will be just like Nome, with a few minor exceptions. You'll be working for the Northern Commercial Company, not for Al and me—we can't get a franchise up here. The NC's got it sewed up. But the work will be easier. We don't service many of the outlying camps, and the board's a new electric one. How about two hundred a month, ten in the morning to eight at night, on a three-year contract? There's a fairly large cabin that goes with the deal."

I signed two copies of the contract, and each of us kept one. "Now you'd better have a drink," he said. "This is Tuesday. Take the rest of the week off and get settled. After awhile we'll go uptown and see the sights and meet a few people. Then you can start getting supplies and furnishings for your cabin—on the Northern Commercial Company. There are six men, incidentally, who are going to worship you. The mechanics and lineman who've been running the switchboard. How they hate it."

I sat down, and for an hour he listened to me as I told him about the marathon race, my work with the Indians and my career as a freighter. He was particularly proud of me for that; Al had written him all about it.

But, like Al, he refused to back my contention that the dog race had been fixed, sorry as he was for Leonard Dodge, and repeated Al's advice to keep my suspicions to myself.

"I don't see how Leonard could have risked so much. He's smart, courageous and efficient, and I don't see how such a man could deliberately gut himself, regardless of the odds in his favor. I don't want anything like that to happen up here—and this one-horse post is ripe for it."

Fairbanks, he went on to explain, was tossing with the delirium of its second gold rush. The first sprouted root in June of 1900, when Felix Pedro and his friends, Dan Costa and Ed Quinn, found black sand in the foothills of the Alaskan Range, followed their noses down the Tanana Valley, and in July of 1902 located a Midas hoard on Cleary Creek, Gold Stream, Fish

Creek, Dome Creek and Pedro Creek, the richest of the lot, named for its discoverer.

At one time it was estimated that there were 15,000 people living and working in and around a village originally designed to house, clothe, feed, entertain and regiment less than 2,000. The shady gentry had an easy harvest on the first lap, and they made a good thing of fortune's current good humor. Claim jumping, drunk rolling, card sharpery, blue-sky transactions, and other illegal passes at the pigeon, finally became so easy that the sharks frequently became bored and blew smoke at each other.

Naturally this condition of affairs was bound to alert Washington, D. C., sooner or later, and the Honorable James Wickersham was dispatched to the territory with the title of United States District Judge, to sympathize with the close-cropped, harry the transgressor, and remind all that the United States Senate had been responsible for this heavenly intervention.

Within six months he and his marshals had wrought law and order. Then the strike played out and reports of new ones at Hope Creek, Faith Creek and Charity Creek gutted the town. Wickersham closed his bench and moved on in pursuit of the godless.

"This means," Will said, "that we're back where we started. We've thirty-eight saloons, seven dance halls, and a dozen other places of—er—entertainment. To balance this contribution to civilization, we've no school, no preachers and no court of law. We've no city governing body, much less police—that is, with the exception of Phil North and Charlie De Belvois. They're regular United States marshals and supposed to keep peace in an area that embraces about two thousand square miles. They manage to get here once a year. By that time a prisoner could have died of old age. No one guilty of any crime or misdemeanor is held for trial. If you can't bring him to justice at a reasonable time, he's denied his constitutional rights. Even the most vicious must be protected there. Anyway, the situation promises to get out of hand again. We mean to do something about it before it does."

Recently, he said, he had headed up the Citizens Committee for Civic Improvement. This group was drawn from the platoons of community sinew, long-standing long-suffering and willing to serve.

"A month ago we asked Washington to give us a judge. Sheila tells me that a week after I left Fort Yukon the Army Signal Corps at St. Michael wired us—we've a Morse code here—that one was on his way. Name's Benjamin Moseley Britain. While he's on the bench I want to get some other things straightened out too. A lot of our senior citizens have Indian wives, but in name only. They've never bothered to marry, even though they have kids. They've got to be convinced that it's time to subscribe to civilization. One day this place'll be a big and important city.

"At the moment we have an opera house and a community hall where the genteel can dance, play cards, declaim for civic virtue and such. But we've no singers or players in the opera house, and no orchestra in the community hall. So our entertainment is limited. Drinking water is hauled from the Tanana by mule team and sled and it'll cost you a dollar a bucket. We've enough bathhouses to serve one person in fifty, and a bath is five dollars a throw. My outfit owns a two-bit electric generator. What juice is left over from company use has gone to the highest bidder. Consequently there are seven saloons and dance halls in town with electric lights. Everything else's lit with kerosene lamps or candles. On the credit side, you'll enjoy most of the people—the old guard. You can't beat them anywhere in the world. You won't need to worry about food. Unlike Nome, we manage to keep ahead of the demand for flour, dried fruits, tinned vegetables and other staples. The Tanana River is alive with fish, and you can shoot fresh meat, caribou or moose, practically from your back door. Well, shall we go? I want you to meet some people. Then we'll look over your office and cabin and have a good lunch."

Our first stop was at Will's cabin when I met his housekeeper, who maintained her quarters in back. I felt a little glow when I stepped inside of this home in Fairbanks. Here Lucy and Al Boyd had known many a happy hour in the early days of the Burke-Boyd partnership, or more specifically, in the interim bridging the formation of their Fairbanks lumbermill and the establishment of the Nome Telephone Company. Loving the experience as she did, Lucy had been nostalgically eloquent in her descriptions of the town, the accommodations of Will's cabin, the bedrock temperament of its citizenry, and the beauty of the surrounding acreage. She had been particularly swayed in this direction when a Nome lean-to's spindly uprights collapsed and it crashed, throwing the boundaries of Main Street out of kilter for a month; when her stove started smoking; when quiet evenings and serene days must give way to sports lunacies; and particularly when she compared the respective countrysides.

Will's cabin, half log, half finished lumber, sat in a cluster of smaller buildings in a fairly isolated semicircle, and I was willing to admit that Lucy had a good eye for appraisal. Located about four blocks east of the Northern Commercial Company, it sported three stair steps to a porch with a real roof, and there were flowers growing out of a thick slab of sod on top.

"Restricted district." Will chuckled as we walked up the chocolate-colored path, drenched in sunshine, savoring the stinging smell of pitchy lumber, and drinking in the colors, perfume and majesty of the fantastic mountains, forests and flowers beyond. "By common consent no one may build here unless he has paid twenty dollars for his estate and can prove that it took a week to build. First snobbery known in Alaska."

The interior of the place was another testimonial to Lucy's homemaking talents. There were furry rugs, leather chairs, a horsehair davenport, a cubicle of a kitchen dominated by a rangy Yukon stove and a heavenly smell of cooking food.

"That's why," Will explained, pointing to a fat kettle steaming on the back of the stove. "Up here everyone keeps a pot boiling—ptarmigan, moose, bear—all the time, summer and winter. We've only six months of light. So far as cold is concerned, Fairbanks makes Nome look like the difference between—well—summer and winter. But you never know when a snow-blind man'll stumble in. If you're not home, he may stumble in anyway. So it's better to have some grub ready. Just a minute." Stepping around me, he opened the back door and yelled.

Mrs. Elsie McKay, Will's housekeeper, was a buxom, apple-cheeked old grandmother with a gorgeous treasure of naturally curly hair, white as the cap on Mount McKinley and twice as unruly.

"Land sakes, child," she squeaked, when Will introduced us. "What're you doing in this Godforsaken place?"

"Oh—Mrs. McKay—I love it. I'm going to work here."

"Silly. Plain silly. Pretty as you are. What's the matter with the States these days?"

"Mother—" Will tried to interrupt. "She—"

"You be quiet, Will." She poked a chubby finger at his stomach. "He don't eat right. Give him trouble, one of these days. Runs around like a chicken with its head cut off."

Waddling to the stove, she rustled a kettle or two, then came back and started where she had left off. "We'll have the food on in a minute. Sit down, child, sit down!"

"Mother—"

"You be quiet, Will! I want to talk to this child!"

"Mother—"

"I ain't had a chance to talk to an Outsider for years! You leave us alone!"

"Honey, you'll have plenty of chance," Will stuttered. "Right now I've got to get her settled. We haven't time to eat. Later, eh?" Getting my eye, he gestured hastily toward the door. "I hope that you'll help her get bedded down and in harness."

Outside, he rushed me up the path and within a few minutes we were in the city proper.

"She's always mad at me," Will said. "She disapproves of everything I do. What a tyrant!"

He told me that her husband Donald McKay, now deceased, had been, prior to the sunset of the nineteenth century, the franchised favorite of one of the largest fur-trading concessions in Alaska and Canada. But he had made one bad mistake. He had thought of himself as a financier late in life and had begun investing indiscriminately in mining claims, some of which proved to be nonexistent. When he died at the start of the gold rush of 1902, he had left his wife practically nothing, and Will, who had been friends of both, built her a cabin at the rear of his own, put her on his payroll, and laid himself open to a brand of kindly tyranny that lasted for years.

As we passed a sign that read ALASKAN FIRST NATIONAL BANK, I thought of the draft for $6,000 that I was carrying in my purse, and asked Will if this was a reliable bank.

"I've always thought so. Anyway, it's the only one. Come on."

Inside he nodded to the tellers, then took me to an office in the back.

The man behind the desk of the sparsely furnished cubbyhole had brown curly hair, lusterless blue eyes, a baby nose, a gold tooth; when he rose and held out his hand, he displayed a stout, short body soberly draped in black. Later I learned that he was thirty-two years old, unmarried and on his way to becoming a banking wizard. He couldn't have missed, for he had a bloodhound's nose for a loose dollar, a remarkable memory for a nickle owed him, and a fanatical purpose in collecting *with* interest. He had been a Chicago bank clerk five years previously, and had founded the Alaskan First National Bank two years before on an investment of $5,000 borrowed from Fairbanks gamblers, of all people. Now he was on his way to becoming a multimillionaire.

His name was James G. Granning, and when he said more than a few words in a day he was suspected of being drunk. His every move was clumsy and dull, and he even blinked his eyes with calculation. But the secret of his financial success was no mystery to me. He was a piggy-bank watchman. Years later, after Will's death, when I was mired in a mare's nest of property claims, probate legalities, and the responsibility of handling a cash fortune of more than $1,000,000, he straightened me out within six months. For this service he charged me $2,000 when $10,000 would have been more like it. On the other hand, at lunch with me in San Francisco one day, he called for separate checks.

"Good morning to you, Jim," Will said as he took Granning's hand. "This is Miss Margaret Knudsen, our new telephone operator. She wants to make a deposit, and I wanted her to meet the head of the local moneychangers."

"P'lsd," murmured Granning.

My introduction to Granning marked the beginning of a fine day and a lasting memory, and the flavor of my delight was toned up by the fact that Will was an excellent guide. Soon I understood, and with a growing thrill, why Fairbanks had become one of the celebrated frontier towns of the world.

"Couple of years ago," Will pointed out as we made the street once more, "this little camp was pretty miserable to live in. But now people are making homes."

Presently we came to the opera house, proud boast of Fairbanks' contribution to culture and refinement in 1903, with a seating capacity of 300 and a raised stage, 20 balcony boxes and 3 dressing rooms. It was a haunting reminder of the town's former glory. Now it was a dejected, cobwebby hulk in the center of a weedy abandoned field. So it was also with the courthouse and the jail. Ungainly as a porcupine and less handsome, the clink was built of scarred logs and shakes, and its foundations gripped a patch of utterly barren ground, as if it had grown there from a discarded pine cone. Two iron-barred windows and an open door stared broodingly at the town and disclosed several moldy heaps of blankets and a couple of its private suites. One sign, burned into a slab above the door, announced in severe, stilted lettering that here was the ALASKAN TERRITORIAL FEDERAL PRISON. Another, just below it, read: PRISONERS MUST RETURN BY NINE EVERY NIGHT. OTHERWISE, THEY'LL BE LOCKED OUT.

"Soon as our judge gets here," Will remarked, "we'll scrounge it out and get ready for business. People are coming in thick and fast, and we learned a lot from the last rush. Hey, lassie, how about some lunch?"

As we headed for a restaurant Will steered me through a scene on Main Street that would have made the frenzied migrations of a caribou herd look purposeful. Everywhere broken lines of men were outbound, faces set, sober, ignoring the blare of the honky-tonks and abstaining every courtesy of sidewalk and street. Some hunched under heavy packs. Others pulled their picks, shovels, gold pans, and food on travois—the Indian method of transportation that involves the lashing of supplies to a couple of loosely bound poles and dragging the load, drafthorse style—and the rest simply ran out of town like kids on an Easter-egg hunt.

I was puzzled. Crowds in Nome had never acted like this, even in their more serious moments. "Those people act like they had pains."

"Sports fever is one thing." Will chuckled, drawing me into a doorway as a segment of the herd thundered by. "Gold fever is another."

He whisked me around the corner and dropped me in front
of a brockle-faced building that was belching mechanical piano
music. It was the Arizona. There were four people standing in
front of it. Three of them were nice-looking girls dressed in
pants and shirts. The fourth, a man, sported a reddish-brown
mustache topped by a big nose, brushy eyebrows and a black
derby. He had a gold chain across his middle and obviously
had bought his suit from an undertaker.

"Tex Coker," Will said, "an honest operator. Owns the
Arizona. These ladies are the Oregon Mare, the Utah Filly and
French Camille—Miss Knudsen."

"Pleas'd to—"

"Hello, honey."

"I'm very—"

"Don't you have any place else to go, honey?"

"Oh yes—but French—French Cam—"

"You got me wrong. I'm Utah."

"Oh, I'm sorry, Utah—I'm—"

"This is Oregon. The Oregon Mare."

"Oh—I'm sorry! But I don't want to go any other place—
Miss—Miss Mare—I—"

"Haven't you got a home, honey?"

"Yes—but—"

"Then what're you doing up here?"

"Well, Miss Camille—it's this way—"

"Utah, please."

"Miss Utah—"

Will decided that we should go, and the girls let us loose,
their smiles friendly and amused.

"Know who those girls are?" Will asked as we hit Main
Street again. "They're celebrated Alaskan beauties."

"Beauties? With those clothes?" They had treated me like a
child, and I was miffed.

"Wearing pants up here is no yardstick to measure a lady's
character," Will answered. "In the matter of fashions the first
thought is given to warmth and comfort. Besides, at night they
turn into birds of paradise. They're fine women, too, even if
dance-hall entertainers are frowned upon by some people. Each
of them has been on my books for a thousand dollars or more.

Most of the money was spent to grubstake out-of-pocket miners. They're the first to contribute to a worthy charity, and they've been known to leave their cabins and travel by dog sled fifty cold, miserable miles to nurse a sick man."

There had been an outbreak of scurvy in several of the camps on Dome Creek the previous winter, brought on by the miners' unbalanced diet of sourdough, bacon and beans, and the current ignorance of the dietetic importance of citrus and other acidulous fruits. However, a French-Canadian doctor, Moise Deslauriers, knew his stuff on the subject, and when word of the suffering struck Fairbanks he ordered a broth to be made of dried prunes, peaches and apricots, and called for nursing volunteers. Utah, the Mare and French Camille—as well as some colleagues from other dance halls—were the first to come in. Moreover, they paid for the fruits out of their own pockets, made gallons of the broth and took turns nursing at the camps for the remainder of the season. Sometimes they were rewarded, or at least paid back for their generosity, Will said, but more often they were left holding the bag. It never seemed to bother them.

The café that Will took me to, Art Williams' Restaurant, was a disorder of checked tablecloths, milling people and galloping waiters. A high counter at the far end stretched from wall to wall and blocked off four roaring, smoking stoves, each staffed by its own male cook. A brace of Indian kids, naked to their waists, kept busy filling the woodboxes that sandwiched the units. The air was filled with gabble concerning new strikes, the price of gold, business opportunities, the thievery of the Indians, the high cost of living and the ruinous wage demands made by good-for-nothings.

Before we had finished with a succulent caribou steak dinner a number of the Fairbanks citizenry stopped by our table and spoke to Will, who introduced them to me. Some of them were to become associates and friends until they reached the ends of their respective ropes. One of them was Art Williams himself, a pert, quick-moving whippet whose tufted topknot of red hair, multicolored vest and bright, eager eyes reminded me of a foraging robin; Bob Ryan, owner of the local bottling works, whose neatly pressed sober black suit, starched linen, string tie and pale aristocratic face complemented the position that he enjoyed—that of a city father; and those squatty, waddling knots of muscle and wonderful illiterates, Pat and Joe O'Connors, the village smiths.

"Some contrast, eh?" Will said. "But that's what makes Alaska great—contrasts." Noting my scraped plate and empty coffee cup, he gestured in the direction of the stoves. "Something more?"

I lacked the breath, thanks to the fiddle-sized steak, to do more than shake my head. Inside, however, I was crowing. The excitement of his company, the comeliness of the town and country, the rich food and the welcome of my new friends made me feel this *was* home, and at once I loved everyone and everything in it and around it and knew that it always would be so.

After lunch Will took me to a tiny cabin behind dance-hall row on the upper half of Main Street, and I entered upon a scene that remains one of my fondest memories. In one corner there was a desk littered with paper and supporting a kerosene lamp, a half-eaten bowl of oatmeal and a gnawed wedge of sourdough. A chair with a broken leg languished dejectedly in another. A felt boot lay on the floor between a new switchboard and the door, and obviously the place had never been swept entirely clean. As we stepped over the sill a nail-chewing snore ripped up from behind the board, and as it fluttered out to a mush-boiling sigh Will winked at me and yelled.

"Mooney!"

His voice ricocheted off the four walls, and a disordered bale of curly black hair appeared above the switchboard, followed by a pair of blue eyes, swollen from sleep, an upturned, Irish nose and a full-blown, lower-story brush as thick, curly and black as the upper.

"Jim Mooney, you lazy bum," Will said, "come out from behind that box. So this is the way you've been spending your time when you're supposed to be hitting the ball? No wonder we get so many complaints about the service."

"*Arr-agh.*" Mooney yawned, limping around the instrument and disclosing a thickset body garbed in a red woolen shirt that was wrinkled and streaked with dried mud and an equally battered and dirty pair of blue jeans. "Sorry, Mr. Burke. Must've fell asleep. Had a hard night."

Then I saw that his body list was not caused by a skeletal or muscular impairment. It was due to a self-induced imbalance in dressing. He wore but one boot, while his other foot was protected only by a sock, half on and half off. At this juncture my presence apparently sank into him, for he had been squinting, yawning and shaking his head at Will in the interim, and now he hurriedly began to finger-comb his hair and slap at his clothing.

"Never mind the lady." Will grinned. "Nothing, aside from boiling you in sheep dip, will make you more presentable. This is Miss Margaret Knudsen. She has come to set you free."

"*Ar-k*," Mooney replied, rendering me a bob of his head, an upraised finger in salute, and a dopey, apologetic smile. "G'f'n."

"She's going to take over the switchboard on a permanent basis."

"You're not givin' me a snipe hunt, Mr. Burke?"

"Nope. Gospel truth."

"An' she's gonna do it all alone? None of us has to punch that fool thing no more?"

"That's it."

"Can't believe it," Mooney whispered hoarsely. "None of th' others will either. Nobody c'n be that lucky. If I ain't fevered an' hearin' things c'n I leave right now?"

"Not quite," Will said, "she'll need to get settled. Maybe she can take over the first of the week. Meanwhile you'll have to get your duffle out of the cabin. I expect," he added dryly, "that she'll want to tidy it up a bit. You can find another place to bunk, I suppose?"

"Another place?" Mooney cried, snatching the boot from the floor and pulling it on, "f'r this, I'd sleep on an ant hill!"

The living quarters included in my contract consisted of a sturdy cabin of rough lumber not more than fifty feet behind the telephone office, backed by a lean-to large enough to protect a cord of wood, a small trunk, and, with careful planning, a dog. Several greasy and beclotted iron hooks dangled from the two skinny rafters overhead, indicating that meat had been hung

274

there upon occasion. A board fence drew the line on any inter-mingling of the dance-hall life beyond and Fairbanks' sedate business community.

The inside was as cluttered as the telephone office. The few pieces of furniture were broken at one joint or another and flung about. There were two bunks, but the blankets were piled on the floor, and the place smelled of whisky fumes two days old.

"Pretty bad, isn't it?" Will went to the window and hoisted it open. "Those boys are not good housekeepers except on the trail. And they hate this job. Not that I blame them. It's not much of a hitch for a man."

If there is such a thing as instantaneous evolution, then I grew up right there. Sweat, mud or blood, this was my country, my life and my people. I wanted that cabin, my job, my dog, this beautiful land, my independence and Jack Bartlett—and I didn't care how it all smelled, acted, bathed, ate, bred, breathed or voted.

"Well," Will said, gesturing at the debris, "there must be some furnishings some place in town. You're sure that you want to live here? I can adjust your salary if you would prefer living at a hotel. In fact, I suggest it."

"No. This is fine. Will, I love this country. When Jack comes back, we'll be married, and—"

I could have ground my tongue between my teeth. All day I had avoided any mention of Jack. Now I had put my foot in my mouth, and I didn't know what to think or do or what turn to take. But I needn't have worried. Will was as he always was, strong, understanding and sympathetic.

"I know how you feel, honey," he said. "And you need not feel embarrassed. I can never have your love. But I want your friendship. If you let Jack Bartlett come between us—what have I got left?" He took a cigar from his shirt pocket, lit it, and this time his hands trembled. "That kid Bartlett doesn't like me—but that's beside the point. Please don't deny me your friendship because of Bartlett's dislike of me."

I think I loved him then. But Jack's face floated between us.

"I want to clean this up right now!"

"I'll send you some help."

As usual, his promise was sound as bedrock. I had scarcely rolled up my sleeves and heaved the first broken chair into the back yard, when a couple of Indians showed up carrying buckets, brooms, a bale of rags, bars of lye soap and a can of stinking disinfectant. While they went to the river for water I awoke Jim Mooney again and told him of my decision to take over at once. His answer was to let out a whoop, grab his extra clothing from the cabin and make off up the path at a run.

Since I could hear the buzz of the switchboard from my new living quarters, I was able to keep the Indians working while I listened for calls and answered them, and the delousing, sloshing, rasping and burning progressed at a fair rate of speed. In fact we finished the job around nine o'clock that evening, and when the Indians had guided me to Sheila Wilson's cabin near the Northern Commercial Company, I could sigh with satisfaction for a task well done. The day's labors ended pleasantly, for Sheila had a hot roast waiting and had broken out a bottle of champagne.

"Will asked me to take off tomorrow and help you shop. I know the warehouses hereabouts, and possibly I can unearth some furniture for you," she explained. "I wish I were in your shoes. This hut must have been built by a midget."

After dinner as we sat relaxed and tingling from the wine she told me that prior to her own Alaskan adventure she had been an office hand in a little town in the state of Vermont. She had been married two years when her husband, a high steelworker, had fallen to his death while spidering a job on a bridge above the Connecticut River.

Their marriage had been a love match, and, sick at heart, having no children, no parents living and no other serious ties or responsibilities, she had wandered from city to city, living on her husband's insurance. She had been in Seattle when her nest egg ran out. Forced to look for a job, she had applied to the Northern Commercial Company office there for work as a bookkeeper. The following month she was in Fairbanks and reporting to Will Burke.

"At first I was miserable with the cold and the lack of modern conveniences here," she added. "But now I feel like you do. It's a rough life on a woman. But I've found what I want."

Despite her aloof, almost haughty attitude, I felt a growing affection for her. Then I recalled her appraisal of her dinky cabin, and gave it a closer look. That she was an impossible housekeeper was obvious, and she probably would continue to be so, for the interior looked as if someone had emptied the contents of a grab bag over it months before. However, maintaining an orderly house would never pose a problem for me, even one as large as my present cabin. I had been taught to make a bed, wash up a tubful of clothes, sweep out and do dishes three times a day before I was ten years old, and the routine had become second nature. Because I enjoyed her company and didn't relish the idea of living alone in a raw camp and in a strange society, I invited her to move in with me. She jumped at the suggestion.

"I'm grateful to you. Frankly, I've been lonely. I need to talk with a woman somewhere in my own age bracket. Until you arrived it was impossible. Every white woman in town is at least fifteen years older than I, and they're a pretty closely knit lot. But I'll probably be bad company for you on occasion. Somehow I haven't been able to thaw out since my husband died."

"I can understand that. And don't give it another thought. We'll get along just fine."

Sheila's decision to share my cabin simplified the furnishing of the place, for she owned two living-room chairs covered with sealhide, several wall prints, some fur rugs, plenty of bedding for both bunks, enough tableware for a dozen people, a wooden washtub, towels, lamps, a flatiron and other additions to the necessities required for genteel living in Fairbanks. To these she added a new horsehair sofa dredged from some Fairbanks recess, and as the cabin already stabled four kitchen chairs and a table, all repaired now, we were in the home stretch.

Will, of course, was delighted. The next morning while I was at the board he invaded the area, backed by half an Indian tribe, all toting various articles from Sheila's cabin. Five minutes later one of his troops was repairing the broken cupboards, three were dispatched to the Northern Commercial Company with a grocery list, and the rest were instructed to lug in firewood.

Sheila, it soon became apparent, was a considerate companion and an extraordinarily conscientious and imaginative cook, even if she did not know a broom from a dustpan. She had only one serious rival in Fairbanks, Angelo Ricci, familiarly known as the Tamale Man. Incongruous as it may seem, we had real tamales in Alaska in 1906, and they were not the glutinous blobs that canners pass off as the real thing today. Roly-poly Angelo and his equally fat wife Violetta manufactured them in a shed behind their cabin, grinding their meal by hand from Indian corn, and using only the loin of moose or caribou for filling—deer, rabbit or bear were not considered fit to fill a Ricci tamale.

When I was working at the switchboard in the evenings, I was often called upon to track down the vinous Angelo (in some saloon where he was relaxing) to order tamales for dance-hall girls and their customers; and my reward was customarily a few tamales, courtesy of the house. Since they cost $2 and I could wolf six at a sitting, the extra dividend was welcome. Between Angelo's tamales and Sheila's nourishing food, I began to recapture some weight; in a month I had overcome my susceptibility to colds, and my depression vanished.

About this time a social volcano erupted in Fairbanks, all because of Will's determination to bring civilization to the camp. One morning he telephoned and said, "Margaret, honey, remember I told you we had a judge coming. He's in Fort Gibbon now, and he'll be here in a few days. Name's Britain. Now listen. Before he shows up we'll need to set up a temporary city government to work with him. I'm calling a meeting of the town's senior citizens tomorrow night to set it up, and I'm sending their names and telephone numbers to you. Will you contact them and ask them to be at the community hall at eight o'clock sharp?"

He also suggested that Sheila and I might pitch in and clean the hall, which hadn't been used for some time. So we turned swampers again, with the help of Mrs. McKay, and not only turned out the dirt and debris but decorated the place with colored paper and ribbons that Sheila produced from her mysterious sources of supply. During our labors Will sent in champagne for us and whisky for our male helpers, and we forgot the drudgery of the task until we paid for it later with blistered hands and aching backs.

Fifty-two out of the fifty-four persons on Will's list attended the meeting. Sheila and I served as hostesses, and I realized for the first time what a power Will was in Alaska. The assembly was made up—except for a few trappers and hunters in buckskin —of conservatively dressed businessmen and their modestly caped and gowned wives. It was obvious from their quiet, reserved conversation and the solid topics that they chose that this was the hard core of what Will had called the Fairbanks old guard.

Sheila, who knew most of them, bent every effort to introduce me around, and two of the people I met, Martha Dawson, wife of a bath house owner, and Livy Slater, widow of a wealthy freighter, I'll never forget. At a later date they blunted the point of my social pick with a species of snobbery that shouldn't have been visited on a member of the Bull Moose Party, or a Girl Scout leader.

Will, who attended the session in a black suit, black boots, string tie and white shirt, looking as handsome and wicked as a Spanish freebooter, mounted the platform, picked up a claw hammer, and pounded the table for order. When the accumulated gentry was seated he announced the impending arrival of Judge Britain, the purpose of the conclave, and asked for suggestions.

"For a start," he prompted, "we can probably get by with a mayor, a police chief and his assistant, and three councilmen, one of whom can act as treasurer. We have no fire-fighting equipment, so we won't need a force there. Everything else dealing with the problems of city government can be handled by the council. Later we could hold an election and also add to our official staff."

"Any money in the jobs?" someone asked.

"Sure," Will said, grinning, "any amount you like. Out of your own pocket."

It was agreed that the officials be picked to serve for one year, after which enough taxes would have been collected to make the jobs worth fighting for in elections. So the first city government was formed in Fairbanks, and its officials were appointed by Will Burke.

Bob Ryan, he decreed, would be mayor. Cal Nairn, who owned the New York Jewelry Company, James G. Granning the banker, and Edward A. Paas, proprietor of the Pioneer hotel, were the council. Regular meetings would be held twice a month wherever they chose to deliberate, and they were to be responsible for making laws applicable to the community needs. These statutes would be enforced by Jim O'Connors as chief of police and his brother Joe as assistant and utility flatfoot. Jim was also empowered to conscript additional help in emergencies when and if the need arose.

Naturally I was so proud of Will that the buttons of my blouse strained at their leashes. However, after the meeting ended and I got home, my enthusiasm dimmed. Once a goal was in sight he let no grass grow under his feet, and this occasion was no exception. Sheila and I had barely closed our eyes when lights began flickering through our one window and a frightful racket sounded outside. Torches, stuck in the ground, lit up the jail and courthouse area adjacent to our cabin, and workmen stormed the structures, hammering, sawing and brandishing brooms. Finally Sheila, who was as weary as I, could stand it no longer, and slippers flapping, hair flying and blood in her eye, she went to investigate. She should have saved her breath to cool her porridge.

From Will, who was bossing the jobs, she learned that Judge Britain could be expected at any moment. His Honor's sentencing quarters and watchhouse were to be adequately equipped and in repair for the judicial reign even if the whole of Alaska must suffer from insomnia and pandemonium.

So Benjamin Moseley Britain, late of the Sunland Federal Judiciary District, Washington, D. C., got his reception, and it quickly blossomed into a gala occasion. All of the newly appointed city officials were on hand to greet him, to his real or feigned surprise, and by the time he got to Main Street he was surrounded and admired by half the town. Later, ramrodded by Will, the committee finally extricated him and ensconced him at a table in Art Williams' café, where an early evening of toasts, handshaking and other forms of conviviality followed. Toward seven o'clock, however, the judge, who had been alternately upright when a speech was required, then down when a refresher was indicated, complained that his legs, rendered unsteady by the roll of the boat, were getting worse. Consequently he was registered at the Pioneer Hotel and left to plot his own recovery.

The following morning Will called me and said that a dinner party and dance would be held in honor of the celebrity in the community hall. It would start at six o'clock, and he was sending over another list, this one involving more than a hundred people. The affair would be by invitation only, compliments of the Northern Commercial Company, and all were urged to attend and get acquainted with the new chief criminal officer of Fairbanks' new governmental regime.

Sheila and I were to act as hostesses again, and Will would arrange with the cafés for food and provide the liquor himself. After I had contacted the guest list Sheila and I dug out a couple of enormous packing cases from the company warehouse, had them taken to community hall, and covered them with two dozen tablecloths borrowed from Art Williams. Then we started collecting knives, forks, spoons, tin cups, and plates from everyone within a mile's radius.

With the arrival of Will and the judge we calmly accepted their compliments on our work and sat back and applauded the ensuing oratory. A few minutes before eight a drove of waiters that almost outnumbered the guests arrived, staggering under hampers of food.

Shortly after dinner a fiddler, a guitarist and a harmonica player took the platform and tuned up. Since Will's attentions to me were friendly but discreet and the other males were older and married, I could enjoy myself without fear of any tongue wagging that might reach Jack Bartlett's ears later. I hotfooted it through every square dance, Virginia reel, and schottische that came up, was the last to leave, and went home whistling, resolved always to be sweet to everyone, stay out of trouble and live the good life.

That's what *I* thought. Nothing was ever peaceful for long in the Alaskan camps of my day, and the events of the following week were no exception. It was then that a sociodomestic revolt erupted, growing out of Will's relentless determination to force marriage on men living with Indian squaws—or whites for that matter—and particularly in cases where offspring were concerned. Once he bit at anything he never let go, and he now persuaded Judge Britain to sign an order requiring all unmarried couples living as man and wife to take the yoke. Failure to comply was punishable by a $5,000 fine, a year in jail, or both. The deadline for compliance was the next Monday, and the judge would hitch all couples free of charge.

Will had Sheila run off fifty copies of the order on the old Oliver typewriter that she kept in her office, then had them tacked to every bulletin board in town. The reaction was instantaneous, and as most of the male sinners were illiterate hunters and trappers who lived in a tight little colony east of Main Street, it was also violent and profane.

My board started screaming about noon on the day that the signs went up, and continued unabated for the remainder of the week. The statutory offenders wanted to talk to Will, for his stand on the subject was public knowledge; or if he was unavailable, then to the judge. If neither could be reached they insisted on haranguing me, and the names they called Will and His Honor enriched my vocabulary beyond a mule-skinner's dream.

Then the ruckus died in its tracks. When the deadline had passed and both of the O'Connors had been dispatched to snaffle the culprits, they discovered that the men had moved in together, leaving their wives and children to themselves, save for visits by the recalcitrant breadwinners. This development was a bitter blow to the author and the executor of the order, namely Burke and Britain, for they had no further recourse. The rebels were supporting their families, and the edict read: "All unmarried couples living in residence as man and wife." They were therefore breaking no law, and so far as cohabital inconvenience was concerned, there was little or none. Their cabins were not ten feet apart, so the situation seemed destined to become permanent.

Will's sense of humor helped to lighten his disappointment and chagrin. But His Honor skidded near a stroke, it was reported. In his book, a town without crime was not much of a town. The law was not being enforced properly, he reasoned, and to remedy this he called Police Chief Jim O'Connors to his office and stood him in a corner. Jim's answer was to hurriedly summon Brother Joe to *his* office in the jail.

"The judge give me fits," he told Joe. "He thinks we ain't arresting enough people. I hold with him."

"Arresting enough people?" Joe echoed. "For what?"

"What kind of policeman are you? For things that ain't lawful, that's what. So you get a move on."

"*Me* get a move on? How about yourself? You ain't done so much. Why don't you run in somebody?"

"Because I'm chief—that's why!" Jim bellowed. "I ain't supposed to!"

"Well, I don't see nobody doing nothing."

"Then collar somebody for getting drunk. There's plenty of fist fightin' goin' on, ain't there? Get 'em for things like that."

"Are you nuts?" cried Joe. "When's *that* been a crime?"

"Right now!" howled Jim. "I just made it one! Now look! You get out and pinch somebody! There ain't nobody in jail, and it makes the department look silly!"

So Joe dutifully expanded his catalogue of offenses against society and went after the drunks and the brawlers. As far as I can recall, he made no immediate arrests, although he reportedly came close a couple of times. His failures stemmed from his faith in the honesty of man, for never could he be accused of lacking sincerity and intent.

One of these near misses happened when he saw a man staggering up a path off Main Street. Joe, who was fast on his feet despite his bulk, quickly overhauled the fellow and pounced on him.

"You're under arrest," he announced, "and don't gimme a fight."

"For what?"

"You're drunk. It's against the law."

"I'm not," the man protested, "what I am is sick."

"Yah? You smell like a saloon."

"I'm sick, I tell you. I just saw an ice worm."

"A what? What'n the world's that?"

"Ice worm," the man—who obviously was no fathead—repeated. "The most terrible-looking creature alive. They come down here, you know, from the North Pole. When winter hits up there. Migration, they call it."

"I ain't never seen one. They poison—or anything?"

"Nope." The victim shuddered. "Just terrible looking."

"Good Lord," Joe breathed, "I better git you home."

Joe was working in his shop one day when he heard shouts, curses and sounds of a struggle at the rear of the Northern Lights Saloon next door. Upon investigation he discovered a pair of bravos rolling about and whaling at each other with all four hands. Yanking them up and apart, he told them to prepare for immediate incarceration and added his usual admonition against giving him a fight.

"What charge?" one of them panted.

"Fightin'."

"Fightin'?"

"Yep."

"Why, I was only teaching my friend—here—how to handle himself. Case trouble starts."

"Oh," said Joe, "that's different. Well, it's a good thing you wasn't fightin', I'd a had to clink ya."

Chapter Fourteen

JACK turned up two days ahead of the first snowfall. Aware of his conviction that I was incapable of independent reasoning when a decision concerned both of us, I had steeled myself to a dressing down for ignoring his orders and following him to Fairbanks before he had sent for me. But I had not reckoned on facing a wild man.

Eyes blazing, hair curling below the collar of his torn and dirty mackinaw, cheeks bearded, and fingernails broken and black rimmed, he walked into my office one morning, then slammed the door shut so hard that the whole cabin shuddered.

"All right," he whispered, his voice quivering with rage, "couldn't you stay away from Burke or what?"

"Oh, Jack—Jack, dear!" Scrambling from my stool, I ran to him and tried to embrace him. He answered the gesture by shoving me so hard that I nearly went down. "Jack!"

"Shut your mouth," he snarled, "and sit down—before I knock you down."

I dropped into a chair in a hurry, too well versed in the peculiarities of his rages to make more overtures, much less argue with him. An hour went by before he quit pacing the floor and left off his raving and cursing to become coherent. Not that his insults and abuses were the more bearable. But at last he began to tire, and the threat of violence to my hide was less likely. He had cuffed me in the past and he always swung to hurt. Of course his accusations, to any but himself, would have sounded ridiculous.

"Your attraction to that mealy mouthed Holy Roller promises to become legend," he sneered. "How often do you see him? Every night?"

"Darling, darling, please let's not fight! I've been so lonesome for you! Nome's become a horrid place to live! I just couldn't stand it—without you!"

Noting a flicker of interest in his eyes, I hurriedly outlined the town's present depression, the causes, my run-down condition and the other elements that had led to my decision to get away.

"I asked you about Burke," he interrupted, "doesn't the telephone company belong to the Northern Commercial Company?"

"Yes, but—"

"Then you're working for Burke, aren't you?"

"Of course, only—"

"Will you try to keep your peanut brain on a single, simple question?" he grated. "I want to know if you've been running around with Burke!"

"No—no, Jack, I swear it. I've only seen him in a business way. Ask anybody."

"Well, I don't believe you. You've made a fine laughingstock of me. I've a few friends up here. And they know how I feel about that black-faced grave robber. He'll underwrite a medicine fund for a lot of mangy Indians one week; the next he forecloses on three business houses that can't meet their bills with the celestial Northern Commercial Company. He's a *real* civic leader—this Burke of yours! Now my intended wife's working for him!"

"But I don't see why my meeting Will on business—strict business—would mean anything. A job's a job, dear, and—"

"You see few things, Margaret, because you're too dense to look beyond your nose. I wanted you up here when I could support you. If there were two telephone companies in town, it would be different. But there aren't. Your money-grubbing parson probably has seen to that. You can't do anything else for a living, so far as I know. So it's work for him or nothing, isn't it?"

"No, sir! Not by a long shot!" He had given me an opening in his last remark, and I pounced on it gratefully. "I sold my business, and I've—we have—over six thousand dollars in the bank. I took this job," I lied, "just to make expenses while you were away. Now we'll set up your law practice and I'll get into the freighting end."

"Law office?" he snapped. "Are you crazy? There isn't even a judge in this hole."

"Oh yes, there is." I told him of Judge Britain's coming, the formation of the new city government and of other developments, and while doing so I got out my book of bank drafts and wrote a check in his name for $1,000. "How's that for a start, dear?"

His response indicated that lump sums from my coffers could still cool his temper magically, for he grabbed me, lifted my feet from the floor, kissed me and waltzed us around the room.

"You're right, sweetheart!" he whooped. "What's the use in quarreling over nothing?"

By this time it was near noon and I could expect a respite from my labors. If the town's commercial practices and habits hadn't changed overnight, then the bulk of my clientele would spend two hours at lunch and hence isolated from their telephones. When Sheila came home to whip up a bite for us, as her custom dictated, I made her acquainted with Jack and we went to my cabin. I broke out a bottle of whisky, and while Sheila fired away at the stove, Jack and I took up where we had left off in Nome.

On his side, he hated Fairbanks and most of its people as cordially as he had detested Nome and its citizenry. But he was impelled to admit that, now, he might need to review his opinion of Fairbanks. Where Nome's legal practitioners had frozen him out and he had helped them by spitting on the town, he was currently the only lawyer in Fairbanks, and the community was growing.

"Maybe," he said, "my luck has changed."

Thus far he had earned his bread by gambling, and had preferred to play at a combination dance hall and saloon known as the Cosmopolitan. The place had a touch of class. In addition to enjoying a moneyed trade, it featured the only raised stage, four-piece orchestra and coterie of high-kicking females on honky-tonk row. It was owned by Jim Fredericks and his partner, Byron Morris, a couple of showmen gamblers who had plied their talents over much of the world, and they had welcomed Jack as sort of a bird of a feather.

He had met their wives, and this casual relationship had graduated to an all-around friendship. The association had also helped to line Jack's pockets. Although Fredericks and Morris permitted no sharpery at their poker tables, as proprietors they could steer the poke-heavy and wilder plungers to him, and for a time he had rolled in clover. However, a few months before my arrival he had suffered a bad run of cards, and his assets had slowly floated off. Then Fredericks, whose hobby was shooting wildlife, had formed a hunting party and invited Jack to go along, expenses free. Down to a thin dime and hoping that his absence might discourage his jinx, Jack had accepted. But he had regretted his decision every minute of the days out of town.

"I wasn't cut out for the frontier life," he said. "I've never had such a miserable experience. I'm a mass of welts from insect bites; the sun baked me dry; my bones are broken from sleeping on rocks. Except for the fresh meat we killed, the food would have poisoned a cave man. We had no soap, but that wouldn't have made any difference; the creeks and rivers are so cold you couldn't bathe, anyway. I got to a point where I almost repented and became a Christian."

On that note he gulped the last of his lunch, downed another shot of whisky, and left, after instructing me to meet him in the lobby of the Regus at nine o'clock that night.

After a fidgety afternoon, I fell into such a scatterbrained state by eight o'clock, when I quit my board, that I was ringing wrong numbers by the dozen and barely aware of the irritated mutterings that resulted. In fact I was into Main Street when I noticed that I had forgotten my purse and my wrap. Returning for them, I made myself fifteen minutes late at the hotel and arrived disheveled, out of breath and shiny nosed. But if Jack disapproved of my appearance, he didn't comment. On the contrary, he liked my new hair-do, which he had failed to note earlier in the day, and he loudly approved my recently adopted use of rouge.

"My, my, how Little Eva has grown," he teased. "She's a grown woman. Take my arm, gorgeous."

Fifteen minutes later we stopped before a pair of large, brightly lighted cabins made of milled new lumber, at the north end of Main Street. They stood so close together that a single porch served both, and, stepping to the door of the first, Jack rapped, then took my arm. A statuesque, auburn-haired woman, bejeweled and exquisitely gowned, answered his summons and welcomed us with a smile and a gesture.

Inside the cabin—a gallery of print pictures, crippled furniture and rumpled rugs, all in a state of neglect—were two men and a woman, the latter a blonde whose features and dress matched those of her female companion. The men were of the type that some novelists like to represent as saturnine—tall, spare, dark browed, meticulously barbered and faultlessly dressed; always in command of their faculties and viewing the world with amused smiles of tolerance. I silently congratulated myself, upon being confronted by this sartorial magnificence, that I had worn the green gown Carol had given me, particularly since Jack looked like diamonds, sired by ermine, out of mink. I also hoped that I would put my best foot forward in conversation, for I had never been even remotely adept at the medium, and on this occasion it was obviously a case of do or die. More than anything else I didn't want to let Jack down with his friends. Not at this point. As it came to pass, my concern amounted to another bridge before you come to it.

"Y'avva drink, duck?" Auburn Hair asked.

"S-z'ure, she'll have a drink," the blonde assured her, "what d'you think she is—a cold mug? Jus' 'cause she's dressed in them clothes? She's only a kid—you're only trying to start a fight! Janie, one o' these days—"

"Shut your fly trap!"

"You're drunk again, Janie!"

"I'm only trying to buy this kid a drink! Is that starting a fight? Is it? Is it?"

"You ain't kidding me, old girl! I've known you too long! Just trying to start a fight—I know you!"

Thus I became acquainted with Jim Fredericks and his blond wife Nella and with Byron Morris and Janie. I love them to this moment, for they were instrumental in fashioning a pattern of life for me that helped in a later day. Twelve years afterward Fredericks and Morris sold their place and the foursome moved Outside, where I lost track of them. But never, to that day, did either of their wives so much as hint at their former lives and times, and I could guess the reason. Not that I cared. They were excellent companions, despite their illiteracy and their constant bickering. They watched their manners and their physical appearances closely, and they even had a wistful dignity about them. Money meant nothing to Fredericks and Morris, and since all had healthy appetites for good food and drink, we staged some monumental table bouts during my first winter in Fairbanks. The opening bell sounded that night.

"We have a permanent reservation at the Del Norte," Jack informed me, when I had caught up on the champagne and someone suggested dinner. "I think you've probably never been there. It caters almost exclusively to us gamblers, dance-hall *femmes*, saloonkeepers and other of Fairbanks' unsavory and abandoned element. It's located on the bank of the Tanana, below the last cabin south of here. Thus the stench is less offensive to the nostrils of the clean and the pure in heart."

The Del Norte proved to be appreciably smaller than its sister eateries up town, but it took no back seat in the matter of cuisine and liquors. Like the others, it had a brace of Yukon stoves and a gentlemen's bar. However, there was no lunch counter and the tables were sheathed in white napery and furnished with silver service. The café was kept open around the clock, for the entertainers, members of the wagering fraternity and other laborers by night, rarely ate breakfast before five in the afternoon, lunch at ten at night, and dinner at two in the morning.

As the result, when we dry-docked shortly after eleven, the restaurant was filling with burners of the midnight oil, and when we had found our table, many of them stopped to hail Jack or our hosts. True, the incidents had their irritating overtones. Jack wasn't the only one who could be jealous, and he *did* know a lot of girls by their first names!

However, as the night wore away I forgot that phase of the whirl. After dinner he started drinking, and so presented his old, loud, insulting front to all within reach of his voice. He must have lowered a quart of the hard stuff in straight shots, and at dawn he was helpless in his chair. Jim Fredericks paid a couple of waiters to stagger him to his hotel and another to see me to my cabin. From that moment until the day I saw him last, Jack was never entirely sober.

It was a week before we met again. A blizzard struck the area, leaving a good four feet of snow on the paths, and battling the crusty stuff, waist deep, was hard going. The temperature dropped to thirty, forty-five, then to fifty-five degrees below zero, and inhaling the atmosphere was like breathing needles. But when the snap broke, the town came out from hibernation, spilling dog sleds by the score into the thoroughfares. One had only to step outside for a lift, and it was a relief—after being imprisoned with the dour, tight-lipped Sheila—to spend evenings with Jim, Byron, Nella and Janie, either in their cabins or on our frequent Del Norte raids.

But rougher waters were awaiting me, and before I reached the end of my troubles I felt as though I'd been falsely arrested, tied to the runners of a racing sled, and banished to the North Pole country.

To begin with, Jack's drinking got worse, and even Fredericks and Morris—the most tolerant of men—showed their disapproval. Often I would not see him for days, and when I telephoned his hotel he was inevitably sleeping off a jag, sick and shaky, or taking on a hair of the dog. But his boozing was not the paramount issue. Certain people downtown suddenly put the freeze on me—pronounced enough to discount any stretch of imagination. When Mrs. Slater cut me on the street a week later, I knew for sure that I had been gaffed. Not that I was surprised, considering Jack's deportment and my own unconcealed preference for speedier company. But sniff as I might, I couldn't be happy with the thrusts, and one morning I needed some male backbone to lean on. Unable to locate Jack at his hotel or in any of his troughs, I decided to commit the unpardonable sin—in Jack's book—and talk with Will. But Will gave me no comfort, and I should have recognized the handwriting on the wall even at that stage of the preliminaries. In fact he practically hung up on me.

"You are no longer a child, Margaret," he said. "You've been in Alaska two years. You should understand, by now, the line that separates the liberals and the conservatives."

"But—"

"You spilled the milk. You're not being too adult."

"All right! I like the Fredericks and the people at the Del Norte! Why should those fuddy-duddies treat me like dirt?"

"You're not being treated like dirt. If I thought so, I'd step in. Fact is, you're being criticized, and in a polite way. It's their way of telling you to get in step."

"They're a bunch of narrow-minded buttinskies!"

"Some of them are. Others are honestly anxious to see the type of root in Alaska that doesn't wither and die. If a perennial is damaged in the process, so be it. Somewhere, on every frontier since the world began, there has been a holier-than-thou society. Like it or not, it acts as a draw for men and women of stability. That means roots."

"But I can't see why—why—people like Jim Fredericks and Byron Morris and their wives—they're nice people!"

"Undoubtedly. I don't know them well enough to pass judgment. But they represent an opposing force to the—ah—buttinskies."

"Oh, Will!" The conversation was not going the way that I had anticipated. Always in the past he had dressed my wounds, stood me on my feet, and walked with me in my convalescence. Now his voice even sounded different, and I wished that I had not called him. "I don't want Fairbanks to dislike me! What shall I do?"

"You might persuade Jack Bartlett to act like a man for a change. You could help yourself by calling on the Slaters, the Ryans and the Grannings. The old-guard females have projects going for civic improvement. You might look into that possibility."

"Will, you sound just like one of them! I didn't think you were that way!"

"I am. And then again I'm not. I like my whisky, poker and other forms of night life. But I'm on their side when it comes to making a final decision in the matter of what's good for the country. Why don't you spread yourself out a little?"

He could have ordered me to turn into a tree for all the good that his advice did, even had I wanted to spread myself out. With Jack Bartlett all things were possible, and the following day he set himself up for another letdown. Appearing at my office, he told me that his luck at cards was still bad, and hit me for an additional $1,000. Since his losses had occurred at the Cosmopolitan, where the players and their respective styles were known to each other, he would switch his allegiance to another house. With a fresh crowd to draw from, he figured to do better, perhaps even run up a big stake.

"A stake?" His request was startling, for it meant that he had dropped my last thousand or most of it in a month, although he had not played every night. If the practice kept this pace I would soon be broke. If I honored this demand my bank balance would be less than $4,000. "Jack, I thought we were going to start your law office."

"This isn't the time for it," he wheezed, sinking into a chair. His face was a mottled white and his lips were raw and chapped. But I saw, thankfully, that he was sober. "Business," he continued, "is at its worst this time of the year. We'll do it in the spring."

"But, darling, it'll take awhile to establish yourself. Why not get in a lick early?"

"I don't want to argue. I said spring."

Producing his Bull Durham and papers, he twirled and lit a cigarette, and was immediately convulsed by a combination fit of coughing and gagging. His face turned red and his eyes bulged and watered. Despite my alarm over our finances, I knew a stab of pity for his extravagance and weakness of character. Going to him, I dropped to my knees and rested my head on his chest.

"Jack, dear, what's to become of us? We're not getting anywhere—and you're drinking so much, and—"

"Dry up!" He bounced to his feet so abruptly that I was thrown on my side and lit solidly enough to lose my wind partially. "Do I get the money?" he demanded. "Or don't I? If the weeps go with it, keep it!"

My second bank draft put him on a horse that he couldn't handle. That night at the Arizona he was caught cheating at poker. In St. Michael, the year previous, he had merely been suspected of the crib, but this time he had been pegged red-handed. Drunk, and thus slower in his reflexes, he had flubbed the shuffle, and while six of his opponents simply left the game, the seventh—one Hogjaw Moran, a freighter—called him outside. Jack knocked Moran down several times, then put him out. But he could not be happy with an easy victory. Straddling his unconscious victim, Jack resumed the punishment, and it required the combined efforts of four men, including the burly Jim and Joe O'Connors, to pry him loose and throw him in jail.

But even in this instance his luck stood fast. A few hours later Judge Britain signed an order for his release. Ignoring their contempt for Jack's cheating, witnesses to the fight—upon being interrogated by the O'Connors' testified that Moran had thrown the first punch. But if Jack was clean with the law, he now wore a collar that in one way was more serious. Overnight he was barred from every poker table in Fairbanks.

"That finishes me in Alaska, the ringworm of North America," he said. "I couldn't be happier. I've loathed every minute."

"Don't worry. We have each other, dear." To me, the turn of events represented, in one sense, the most welcome development in our two-year engagement. True, he could not be persuaded to prospect or seek a job. He was through, at least for awhile, as a lawyer. Sharpers were a species that Alaska held in small esteem—even among the ranks of the righteous. Yet Jack had no record as a professional and the Territory was quick, if a man went straight, to excuse and forget. To be sure, I could expect some embarrassment. But I could live with *that*. Now he would need to depend on my earnings and savings exclusively. He would have to tone down his drinking, and that was bound to improve his health and disposition. Suddenly I wanted to sing. "Things are never all bad."

"No? What would you call it?"

"We can live on my salary, darling."

"On two hundred dollars a month? Two people?"

His question suggested a topic that I had promised myself to avoid and had been successful in doing so since my arrival in Fairbanks. Knowing his prejudice against marrying me until he could support me, I had steered wide of the subject. In the past these discussions had triggered his bitterest tirades and I had given him his head. But now the circumstances indicated an ideal condition for reopening the discussions and I decided to risk it.

"We could live more cheaply—if we lived together."

"Good idea. I've been meaning to sound you out on the deal. For some time."

"Jack!" The breath left my lungs and my legs wobbled. "When? When?"

"Soon's we can rent a cabin, I suppose. And get our things packed."

"Should I call Judge Britain now—do you think?"

"Britain? What for?"

"Why for—you said—"

"Ah!" He gave me a quick glance and his lips curled. "The old song. Marriage. Well, my clutching, grabbing little mother, it's not going to work. I said double up. I mentioned nothing about marriage. I won't until the idea appeals to me. If you want to save expenses and keep me in sin, say so. If not, let's talk about something else."

I could feel the blood creeping up my neck and into my face. There was a good deal of Blair, Nebraska, left in me yet. "You know we couldn't do that. The town, and all. How could you suggest such a thing?"

"I didn't. You did. Anyway, I'm going Outside. As soon as the ice breaks. You can come with me or not. Meanwhile, my sticky-fingered pancake, I'll try to survive. Without the benefit of your charms, wifely or otherwise."

He had threatened to leave the country before, in Nome.

However, we had both realized that upon those occasions he had only been belaboring an intransigent peeve. And that had been a time of semiprosperity, too, colored with a fresh new love and far-reaching plans, and at distinct variance with the circumstances of our lives in Fairbanks. This time I knew he would go. He had every reason. Since I still hoped to marry him, my next play was cut out for me, particularly because I didn't want to quit Alaska. I would need to make our living, at least until he got back on his feet, and that would demand more money than my salary provided. In short, I would have to go into business.

Swallowing my pride, I traipsed down to see Will. I found him in his office. I was grateful that he showed no inclination to bring up our late unpleasantness. Encouraged, I laid it all out for him, omitting nothing.

"You *are* in a quandary," he murmured, when I had run through my wailing. "I can appreciate your position. It always takes money to keep a pet."

"Will, I don't expect you to respect me." I was so worried that I lacked the strength to resent his biting inference. In fact I was determined to swallow any insult that he might offer, if only he would let me lean on him once more. "I don't deserve it, after you've put up with so much from me."

"You're jumping to conclusions, Margaret. I do respect you. Probably more so now than ever. I would be proud that a woman could fight that hard for me. It makes no difference that you're pouring sand in a rat hole. To you it's something reasonable—if not to me. That's the main thing."

"I've been miserable, Will. I don't know which way to turn."

"All right, ease off," he said harshly. "I'll help you. I always have, haven't I? We'll start by tearing up your contract. I could raise your salary, but not enough for what you want. My company becomes annoyed when salaries soar. Besides, I'd like to see you make it by yourself. Call it faith in human nature, if you like. This country needs more people who are stubborn, unscrupulous and shamelessly ambitious—such as yourself."

"Will! please don't blister me today! I've never been so unhappy, and—"

"Obviously," he interrupted, "and don't forget, when you're

a grandmother, that you brought it on. But that's not the issue here. Have you an idea of what you want to do?"

"No, I'm in the dark there too. I'd thought of freighting."

"I wouldn't." Slipping from his chair, he reached for a drawer in his file cabinet, took out a cardboard dossier, thumbed through it and extracted a typewritten sheet of paper. "At the last count," he continued, running his finger down the page, "there are seventeen outfits operating out of here. They range from three to six teams apiece, and that's stiff competition for a newcomer."

"But there were a lot of them in Nome too."

"Different—much different. Leonard Dodge controlled the freighting industry down there, and he was your friend. These fellows would cut your throat in a week. We'll think of something else." Replacing the folder, he slid back into his chair, got out a cigar and lit up. "Give me the rest of the week."

"Will! I can't tell you how grateful I am!"

"Get along. I've work to do."

His telephone call two days later was the opening shot for a project that put me on easy street and turned my life upside down.

"How much money do you have?"

"Why, nearly four thousand."

"That should do it. I believe I've got a fish for you."

Two years previously, he explained, one Claude Hoernig had established a machine shop on the Tanana bank, south of the main dock. Shortly thereafter a prospector whom Hoernig had grubstaked hit it on Dome Creek, and Hoernig's share had put him on the velvet. He had immediately sold off his equipment and gone Outside, leaving the building vacant and in fair repair. It was as large as six average-size cabins, and since no one owned the place, it was a case—more or less—of squatters' rights.

"You go over there and start a public kennels," Will directed, "and I'll wager you get rich."

While Fairbanks, he went on, had more dogs than people in town, accommodations for the animals were scarce. The freighters and businessmen, of course, owned private quarters for their teams. But trappers, hunters and miners must dig up

their own shelters for their animals, and there were none available. Visitors were forced to tie their dogs to anything stationary and suffer the added burden of feeding and exercising
them. This sat sourly on the shoulders of men who were in town
for a good time, especially if they were inclined to celebrate
for a month and didn't want to be interrupted at it.

"You will do even better in spring and summer," Will predicted, "when the teams are idle. They've got to stable them
some place."

Hoernig's old shop, he said, would house twenty kennels if
the space were properly budgeted, and he would send a couple
of so-called carpenters to work on it. Their combined salaries
amounted to $25 a day, and I could buy a Yukon stove on which
to cook the dog food. Other accessories would come from the
Northern Commercial Company—on credit. The lumber
needed in construction—also on credit—was available at the
Burke-Boyd lumbermill. I could be in business within the
month. I should charge $10 a week per dog for its food, kennel-
ing and exercise, and an additional $10 a dog for candling.
Pending my grand opening, I could keep my job, thus extending the free use of the company cabin, and have time to look
for new quarters and get settled.

"Wonderful—oh, Will!" I was so excited that I forgot to
thank him, to wonder what Jack would say if he learned of our
dealings, or even to ask whether my dwindling hoard of money
would foot the bill. "I can't wait to get started!"

"Probably." His deep voice, usually so mellow, held a dry,
bitter note that penetrated even through the thick veneer of
my rhapsody. "Very probably."

"Will—I—"

"Don't bother—don't get upset. I suggest that you take in a
partner. The work's going to be hard, and hiring help isn't easy
here. I've a man in mind who can help you—and himself. His
name's Pete Robb. He's a cripple. But he's a worker, and he'll
be happy for a chance. Shall I send him over? He'll grab at ten
percent gross."

"Oh, yes! Yes, Will, of course!"

"Smooth sledding, then."

Robb, a needle-beaked, ragged little offshoot of melancholy,

298

came to my cabin that night, and within ten minutes we made a deal. He was in line for a change of fortune. Two years previously he had lost a leg in a hunting accident and now wore a misshapen peg that made it awkward for him to get around. He had been reduced to swamping jobs and other menial and low-paid tasks. Several months before, his Indian wife had died in childbirth, leaving him three little girls to care for, and if these misfortunes were not enough to satisfy fate, he was going blind in one eye. However, he became one of my richest discoveries and he was out front from the moment he left my cabin.

Under his driving, the carpenters finished the installation of the kennel pens and structural repair in less than three weeks. Two days later we fitted out a little office and received, from the Northern Commercial Company, a thousand pounds of rice and dried salmon, a dozen wooden feeding troughs and a couple of galvanized-iron cooking tubs—the staples for a high-class dog beanery.

Thus the Knudsen Kennels Company was born. It made money from the start and even held its own through three costly expansions. It was fat as a pig when, much later, I sold it to Robb so that I could spend more time with Will, whose business kept him traveling for nine months of the year. I went into mourning when I was forced to give it up. It had been my bulwark against the specter of want, and to lose it was like the death of a benevolent and indulgent guardian.

It was a new showcase for life, and I sat up nights to wallow in its beauty and wonders. Sheila and I were fortunate in finding a rental cabin in the neighborhood of Will's "suburbia" but far enough from his living quarters to mollify Jack. It was owned by an ivory-and-wood carver, one Walter Grossman, who later became Fairbanks' first multimillionaire real-estate developer. Early in December, 1906, I was his first customer. With the kennels contracted for a year in advance, I felt minded to sink another root, and I bought the cabin. It cost me $2,200, and the generosity of my clients encouraged me to cram it with creature comforts.

"Spill a little, Margaret," they would urge, when I weighed out their gold dust in payment for services rendered, "spill a little for yourself." Their wishes never went ungratified.

But the most satisfying aspect of my prosperity was its effect upon Jack. While he laughed at my offer of a partnership and ignored my renewed hints to marry me, he was favorably impressed with our new affluence. He dressed more carefully, kept our dates, and snapped at me less often. His temper toward the public improved too. Before his living had depended upon long, wearying night hours at cards; now he could afford to sleep late. Where previously his winnings had determined the scope of his largess, he could now buy things for the house without such a worrisome handicap. In the past he had been tolerated or merely ignored by a great many people, but now a certain element in Fairbanks was showing interest in him. True, he still drank like a fish, but getting into the money helped him to hold it better. I was elated. We were on our way back.

Then I realized how alone we were. The date was Christmas Eve, 1906. Dressed in our finest, we arrived at the Del Norte. I was floating on air. Sheila had delivered my gift to Will, a handsome watch engraved with his name, and she had returned his present to me, a gold, diamond-studded bracelet. Sheila's gift to me had been a half-dozen satin petticoats, and I had presented her with fox furs. In exchanges with the Frederickses and the Morrises, I came off best with a sable coat and a cameo brooch over matched cedar chests. Understanding Jack's dearest love of possession, I gave him a bank draft for $1,000, traded for a promise of a surprise gift from Outside come spring, and to other acquaintances I scattered a carload of pipes, ivory poker chips, wood carvings and bottles of stuff that passed for cologne water and perfume.

When we went to our table I felt like somebody. However, the attitude of the crowd soon changed my mood. We were scarcely noticed. The people of the night, hurrying down a last-minute drink, were en route to a party from which I was barred by convention. Paradoxically, the people of the day, pausing for a cup prior to a session of respectable conviviality, didn't want me at their parties either. We were in the middle with a vengeance—neither fish nor fowl. While stabbing dully at my food, I was able to understand, fully and at last, Will's patient delineation of Alaskan customs. I decided to do something about it and told Jack so. I should have known him better.

"What d'you care? Why don't you quit turning the other cheek?"

"I'm not, dear. But we've got money now. We've got to take our place."

"Place? Whose place? You take your place!" He choked. "I'll choose my own!"

With that, he stormed out of the restaurant, leaving me to sit and wonder, between sniffles, whether I had ever, in all my life, picked up a jot and tittle of sense. I wondered about that later, too, when it became apparent that our quarrel had started a series of dog falls that got me kicked out of Alaska.

To begin with, my telephone had been out of order, so I couldn't call him. On Christmas Night I could stand his silence no longer and went to his hotel. As I rounded a corner a shadow from an upstairs room attracted my attention. There, silhouetted by the light in back, Jack stood in close embrace with a woman. She was tall, sheathed in a black, shoulder-drop gown, and her hair was redder than mine. I learned something, as I watched, about the art of kissing.

Today I suppose I would have been able to view his lapse with more charity. In 1906, however, my corset was not the most strait-laced article in my make-up. When next I saw him, a day or two later, I cried him an ocean of tears. This emotional release helped me to come out of it, for I had been too numb to toss and roll in my sleep, and my agony had been prolonged and intensified by a feeling that I had failed as a woman, a potential wife and mother. But, mercifully, he was charitable and even sympathetic, for once.

"Get off of it, Margaret. You're acting like a child."

"Jack! Oh, my dear—how could you?"

"Don't you know anything about men at all?"

"I—I thought I did—but this—"

"Blow your nose."

"Who is she? How—how long have you known her?"

"You really want to paw this over? Why can't you be satisfied to squawk your head off and forget it?"

"I want to know."

"All right, I'll tell you."

Luckily for my peace of mind the Del Norte, where we had

met, was deserted, save for a souse or two at the bar. Also I was grateful for the fact that he looked around to anticipate possible eavesdroppers and kept his voice down.

"Month, maybe two, before you got up here."

"What's her name?"

"Honey, you're getting all lathered up. Sure you want to know?"

"I certainly do!"

"Her name's Ann Crampton. She works at the Arizona. I see no reason for not being honest. Not when you so recently climbed into a suit of armor."

"Me? Armor?"

"The suggestion of doubling up. Remember? What have you got to yammer about, honey?"

It was then that I decided to have it out with him—win show or place. He wouldn't work; occasionally he had hit me; he was a heavy drinker. He hated everything and everybody, and beneath it all was the cold fact that I had been working like a horse for nearly two years to put us in one position. Now I wanted marriage. Now it was a case of drink or get away from the well.

"Do you intend to marry me? Did you ever?"

"Oh, that—"

"Yes, that! I want to know—right now!"

"Of course, you know it!" he yelled. "What're you trying to do? Start another fight?"

"You've started plenty of them. I asked you a question and I want an answer, Jack."

"Sure. I'll give it to you." Whistling, he attracted the notice of a waiter, made a motion with his hands to indicate another bottle of champagne and winked at the man, his teeth flashing between the exciting contour of his lips. "Whenever you say."

Goose pimples took over my skin from foot to hairline, and when they had faded out I was hot, then cold—and cold, then hot. When the wine arrived I was thirsting for a big glass and I downed two of them before I got my breath under control.

"Did you say—whenever *I* say?"

"That's what I said, sweetheart."

"And—and you'll give that woman up?"

"Absolutely."

I set the wedding date for a week later. Ordinarily I would have grabbed at the deal the next day. But I was no longer a switchboard operator. Currently I was a businesswoman—one of Alaska's first in the field and proud of it—and I wanted my marriage to be a civic event. Also, I hoped that it would serve to induce the staid and the conservative to look at us more kindly. If I had anything to say, it would be a magnificent wedding. That much I had promised myself. But one day before the wedding, with the announcements out and the town becoming interested, I got another kick in the pants. Judge Britain died of a heart attack, and that left no one in town—except for a couple of Indian medicine men—to marry Jack and me. I kicked over the traces again.

As I recall, we were sitting in my office playing cards. He had been lapping at the bottle, and suddenly he threw down his hand.

"Let's get out of here."

"Well, all right, dear. The Del—"

"The Del Norte! You crazy—let's go somewhere where there's some people!"

"Of course, darling."

"Don't give me that of-course-darling stuff! Get your parka on!"

The place that he chose was the Cosmopolitan, owned by our friends Fredericks and Morris. The place was bursting its brisket when we got there, and for very good reason. Everyone inside was drunk or getting that way, and the excitement of the hour was helped by a row of young females, kicking with genuine appreciation for the enthusiasm of the audience of miners, gamblers and trappers that ringed the stage.

Almost before we were seated, Fredericks showed up and he wasn't friendly.

"Are you crazy, Bartlett? Get her out of here."

"Don' be silly, Fredericks. Giv'us champagne."

"You've had enough."

"Giv'us champagne."

"Get out of here. And take Margaret with you."

The incident left me in a stupor of disbelief. Alaska, all of it, had slammed the door in my face—first the responsible citizenry and now even the so-called seamy side. Both elements had identified me completely with Jack Bartlett, and they wanted no part of Jack Bartlett. For the first time in my life I had no place to turn. Not even Will Burke, for when he returned from Fort Yukon a few days after Jack and I had been expelled from the Cosmopolitan, he closed the final door. I was working on my books when he came into the office, and his voice was so sharp that I jumped.

"Margaret, a word, please, if I may."

"Oh, Will! Sit down."

"No need. Get out of the country."

"What— Will, you're joking."

"No. I'm not. You need a vacation. Go see your people. When the ice breaks, get out."

"But why?"

"To get your feet on the ground. Think things over. Rest a little. You're going off the deep end. I'll let you know when you can come back."

"Come back? Come back! Who are you to order me around, like this, Will, I—"

"This last little escapade of yours did it," he said, and his voice dripped vitriol. "I'm telling you once more, get out of the country. At least until you are old enough to reason from the standpoint of an adult."

"Mr. Burke!" I could afford to employ a cavalier air. I had money. My position in the city was growing. I was no longer his minion. "You're not telling me what to do."

"In many respects, no," he said. He slipped off his parka and flopped it across his arm. "But in this case, yes. Get out."

"Will—why?" His sincerity was scaring me, the more so for the fact that he didn't bite and kick. "Why do you talk like that?"

"You're off on the wrong foot, as I told you. Bartlett's a sadist. He's also a potential killer. On top of that, he's worthless. Well, I don't care about him. But I love you. That makes the difference. Beat it."

"You can't *make* me leave this country."

"You will go Outside on the first boat. Otherwise, you will

not be allowed to buy even a piece of sourdough and no supplies for your kennels nor a shred of clothing in this town. I have only to pass the word. That's all it takes."

"Will, please." By stages, I had been getting his point, and I was becoming frightened. His manner was courteous, but his face was like a thundercloud. "What can I tell Jack?"

"I do not care what you tell him," he bit out as he shrugged on his parka. "That's up to you. Just be gone with the ice break."

"But—for how long, Will?"

"I'll let you know, later."

I tried to reason with him upon several occasions in the ensuing week. But he refused to listen. I was to go Outside and that was that. So to pacify Jack and to keep myself from more trouble, I wrote a fake message to myself stating that my mother was seriously ill. Then, with no one at the dock to see me off, I took the long trail back.

At home in Blair, Nebraska, following the usual uncomfortable ship accommodations, train coaches, and glued shingles that passed for sandwiches, I ate the fatted calf and was looked upon as the loved prodigal. My family had no way of knowing that I had not left Fairbanks and Alaska of my own free will.

I was bursting with bitterness over my exile but I was beginning to see the reason for it. Alaska's solid citizens—people like Will Burke and Al and Lucy Boyd—were anxious to see this beautiful new country get off to the right start. These were the years that would determine its future and they knew it. It could be a place where men and women were responsible, hard-working, civic-minded, and decent, or it could become a hell-hole of con men, cheaters, drifters. Will Burke was determined that the wholesome element in Alaska should gain the upper hand. Will and Al and Lucy had brought me to Alaska and made it possible for me to stay there. Now my association with Jack Bartlett and his friends had placed me on the side of the unsavory element. This not only caused Will great concern over my welfare, but, since I was publicly known to be his protégée, his reputation was at stake, too. The point of my banishment was clearer to me by the minute: give up Jack Bartlett or

keep out of Alaska. But I couldn't give up Jack—I loved him
and wanted to be his wife—and, languishing in Blair, I realized now more than ever that Alaska was my home and I could
never give it up. It wasn't that Blair had changed. I had. I had
known an exciting new land and its vital people. So Blair soon
palled. Bored to a point of no return, I went to visit friends in
Denver. I even camped with Cletus for a time in Los Angeles.
I went to plays. I bought clothes and jewelry for myself and
friends. All in all, I spent $4,000 in trying to get well. But the
free, strong abandon of Alaska had me in slavery. One day in
Yorkshire Hotel I blew up. I sent a telegram to Will in Fairbanks, care of the Army Signal Corps, St. Michael. It had a lot
of tears in it. His reply read: COME HOME. WILL.

Chapter Fifteen

I STARTED back to Fairbanks late in September, after an exile of nearly four months. Regardless of the rigors of my long, boring trip, my sticky, bathless condition and the cold, I felt like a garden in the rain. I was that happy to be going back. Moreover, I was determined to mend some of my ways. The lonely, dragging hours, weeks and months Outside had provided me with plenty of time to think. Jack Bartlett would have to change. Will Burke had been right. Individuality and independence were commendable qualities in anyone. Even a certain amount of pigheadedness could be tolerated. But only to a point. After that, if you want to live in porcupine country and avoid trouble you shouldn't throw quills. Lucy Boyd was to have some shocking things to say to me on this score. I saw her when my trip back to Fairbanks was interrupted by a three-day layover in Nome. I knew that ultimately we would come to the subject of Jack Bartlett, but first she filled me in on all that had happened in Nome since I had left.

"Nome," she told me, "has recovered to some extent. Mainly, I believe, because its sports fever has been broken."

Lumber shipped in from Seattle during the summer had repaired the damage done to the town by the fire of the previous year. A new gold deposit on Salmon Creek had put most of the idle to work, and money was easier to get and to circulate. So far as our mutual friends were concerned, Leonard Dodge was still broke, but making headway back. Barney McCready had rebuilt the Great Northern Saloon, and, encouraged by Nome's new prosperity, was planning on opening another trough. The work among the Indians was going strong, and the coffee at Erickson's Restaurant continued to be weak. The water pipes in the bathhouses were becoming ossified with age and needed replacing. No one had heard from Tex Rickard and his venture in New York. But Rex Beach reportedly was writing a book. Steep, the long arm of the law, had never left off grumbling about the slickness of people like Jack Bartlett and the Messrs. Bridges, Wheatly and Ridgell, and he would cage them one day, "and don't yew jist fergit it, either." A lot of the town still recalled me as that "sweet little girl with such a nice voice on the telephone," and Lucy had several pokes of gold dust addressed to me. They were Christmas gifts from miners who had not learned that I was no longer around.

On other fronts the destruction of Judith and Lew Crouch's horses remained a mystery to plague the most doggedly curious, and a new store had come to Nome. It dealt exclusively in men's footwear; this was distinguished from boots and ordinary shoes by the fact that these had no tops above the ankle, were of grain leather and would take a high, spit polish. The winters, of course, continued to be impossible and the summers worse. But there was talk that the Japanese Current was changing its course. If so, that could mean—in a matter of a hundred years—a more favorable climate for Nome. A number of Indian women had given birth to babies by unknown white fathers, and there was the inevitable wood shortage. Al Boyd, currently in St. Michael on business, was well and still in hot pursuit of the dollar. Prices were rising.

"So goes the encroachment of civilization," Lucy went on, "even here in Nome."

With respect to my own problem, she admitted that Will Burke's nose had a blue tinge, and that he could even be suspect of witch hunting if the occasion demanded such attention.

"He's developed a phobia." She went out back, returned with a fresh bottle of champagne, poured some and sat down. "But at least he's dedicated."

"He certainly is. And he doesn't mind throwing his shoulder into it too."

"Shoulder? Burke?" She drained off the last of her drink and slammed the tin cup down so hard that it bounced off the arm of her chair. "You've never got anything but kindness from him. What've you given him?"

"Why—uh—nothing. He never asked for anything."

"Oh yes, he has!"

"Lucy, please, let's not quarrel! I agree with you! Sometimes I just don't say things right! I'm sorry that—"

"He asked you," she interrupted, "to use your head. You wouldn't do it, so he sent you home. My hat's off to him. Few men would go to so much trouble for any woman." She picked up the wayward cup. "Margaret, once you were a baby. Now you're not. So I'm going to tell you something else—something for adult ears. Perhaps, as the result, we'll speak to each other no more. Want to take that chance?"

"Yes, of course, Lucy."

"You're sure?"

"Yes."

"You invited it. You got what was coming to you. You ran after a rotter, a drunk and a coward. Jack Bartlett is all of those things. Al and I—and your other friends—kept hands off because, I suppose, we lacked the courage to do what Will Burke did. Jerk you up by your bootstraps!"

"Lucy!" Her spurs were biting deep. But I knew that once in the saddle she would ride me out whether I liked it or not. So I sought to appease her while I had some hide left. "I agree with you. Will was right, and I was wrong! But Jack . . ."

". . . is a bum. He's like the rest of his ilk. They're all romantic, handsome and gallant—until they hook you. They don't marry. But, oh, how they love your money! Have you asked yourself, Margaret, why he went to pieces in Fairbanks?"

"Why, I didn't think he did. He was just unhappy. Like he was in Nome."

"I mean recently. Or haven't you listened to the grapevine yet?"

"Lucy, you're holding back something. I don't understand you. Please come out with it." Her cabin, warm and cozy as it was, suddenly seemed cold. "Don't talk in riddles."

"All right, I'll give it to you straight. But first let me ask another question or two. Why didn't Bartlett marry you in Fairbanks? That's what you went up there for, wasn't it?"

"Yes. Yes it was! But what you're suggesting isn't true! We were going to be married. Only Judge Britain died and there was no one else licensed to marry people!"

"And Bartlett's law practice?" she drawled, insultingly. "What happened to that?"

"We were going to start it this spring! Jack thought it best to wait, for economic reasons!"

"He'd have thought of other excuses for not marrying you and for not making a decent living for himself. He'll squander your money and take your love. Then when he tires of you or you get wise—off to greener pastures. He's strictly a cottonmouth, so far as I'm concerned."

"Very well, Lucy. But let's get back to that grapevine that you mentioned." I had expected to learn of new, lawless acts by Jack while I had been gone, or at least fresh transgressions and irresponsibilities. However, in my trusting ignorance, I had left myself unprepared for what followed. "Is he in serious trouble?"

"He's been in jail several times for disturbing the peace. Knowing him, you know what *disturbing* means. And he's been robbing your business blind and spending the money on every strumpet in Fairbanks."

"Oh." Her remark brought a switch in the chemistry of my body. Now my face was cold and my feet—conversely—were hot. "Women?"

"Yes. And he's not trying to hide it either."

"Lucy, are you sure that this is not just a vicious piece of gossip?"

"Get rid of him, Margaret. Before it's too late."

So Ann Crampton was in the picture again. Ann Crampton, and this time, others.

Fortunately by the time I reached Fairbanks my days and nights of mental agony had manufactured a thin but tough callus on the wound in my heart. My head, for once in two years, was ruling the roost. After I disembarked from the Fort Gibbon packet I even was able to pay a businesslike visit to my kennels before continuing on to my cabin.

"Yep," Robb said, sourly. "Things is good. Fer me. But you ain't got much left. You got about eight hundred dollars. Yer boy friend has took the rest. Want receipts? Got 'em fer you."

"But, Robb, why did you give it to him?"

"You never said anythin' about holdin' him off. When you was here last you allus filled his hand. How'd I know?"

"You're right." I was sorry that I had spoken so sharply. "See you tomorrow. Thanks for everything, Robb."

When I reached my cabin, Sheila corroborated Lucy's reports of Jack's boudoir prowling and added some strong observations about his character.

"You're a fool," she ended, her lips—as usual—tight and pinched. "And a fool's got no leg to stand on."

At any rate, I was able to sleep that night. I was up and about early, considerably refreshed in both mind and body. As a first order of business I figured that I should make my peace with Will Burke. Since Jack, if he followed his custom, would sleep until noon, I decided to see Will personally rather than telephone him. So I went to his office. I should have anticipated that he would react just as he did.

"Welcome home." He smiled, waving me into a chair. "You're prettier than ever."

"Will, I'm so sorry. Honestly. I'm going to be a much different woman from this moment on. You'll see."

"I'm glad to hear you say that. It's what I'd hoped for. But let's not hash it over. It's all over and done with."

"Yes, I guess it is. But there seems to be no peace for me. Now a new crop of thistles has grown up."

"Oh? What is it this time?"

"Bartlett." Despite my long rest of the night before, my bones and muscles ached, and as my eyes rested on his right shoulder—its great expanse outlined by the light of the window in back—I wanted, more than anything at the moment, to lay my head on it. It seemed to contain all the power in the world —a bulwark against every threat. "He's been acting up again, hasn't he?"

"So I hear," Will said. "I haven't seen him since you left Fairbanks." Getting to his feet, he went to his liquor cabinet, took out a bottle and tumblers, and gestured. This time I wanted one, and I recall that he poured a stiff one for me. "Why? He's never been much different, has he?"

"But what have you heard?"

"All right, I see no reason for not being honest. I've been told that he's keeping company with Ann Crampton, even living with her. But that's as far as my information goes."

"Will, what—I just don't know what to do."

"It has to be your decision, my dear. This is a man capable of murder. I've seen it in his eyes, in his whole behavior. And he gets worse every day. I'd like to tell you to drop him, but I can't —not as long as you're in love with him." Will poured himself another stiff hooker and downed it. "So all I can tell you is if you want him badly enough, get hold of him. Try to straighten him out. Lay down the law. Tell him to be good or else."

Will might as well have asked me to command the sun to rise in the west, and I knew he saw the look of futility that crossed my face when he continued. "I can whip this man, but what if he goes into one of his insane rages when I'm not around? He'll kill you. Don't doubt it."

Jack came to my cabin that night. He was so drunk that, in grabbing at me, he staggered and fell into a chair. His suit was rumpled, unpressed and soiled. Whisky bloat had added at least ten pounds to his waistline. His eyes were swollen to slits and his lips were cracked and chapped. His face was blotched and there was an ugly, red rash on one side of his neck. I could have cried in my humiliation and anger, but for a far, far removed reason from that which had formerly motivated my similar reactions over his conduct. The woman who sat there watching him as he passed out that night was not the blind, adoring girl of yesterday.

Call me fickle, if you will—even shallow. But at that moment, when he lay in that chair, snoring, slack lipped and slobbering, I saw Jack Bartlett as so many others had seen him—

vain, boastful, useless, arrogant, conscienceless—a dangerous, drunken parasite. I felt no need to question him about his reported infidelities. It was written, silently and glaringly, in the decadence of his face. He would never change. His kind only became worse, until they drank themselves to death, or as Will had said, they killed. Meantime, their very breaths poisoned and debauched.

"Bartlett's a sadist," Will had said. "He's also a potential killer."

"He's a rotter and a coward," Lucy had said.

Suddenly I recalled the expression of animal viciousness that I had seen on Jack's face on the day that he beat and tortured Caw, the big freighter, in Nome, and my hands shook so violently that my shoulders jerked.

A cup of coffee helped me to regain my control, and before the last gulp was down I realized what I must do. Starting with the fact that I wanted Bartlett no more, I would need to get away—simply disappear for awhile. If, not, he would bleed me of my money and marrow until he or I died. Deprived of my money and unable to locate me, he would be forced to go Outside, possibly, and that route could mean an end to our association. Of course there was an alternative. I could have him jailed on charges of forced attentions. However, I realized in the next breath that this would not work out permanently. He would be released sometime. Then we would be back, right where we had started. No, escape was the thing. But I must use caution in the planning. One mistake on my part and the entire project would fall apart. I would have to see Robb, take him into my confidence, cut Jack off from my handouts, and fade out for a year—perhaps a little longer. At midnight I shook him awake.

"S'tart," he mumbled, weaving to his feet, "le's go s'where. Le's go get a drink."

"Jack, I'd rather not. I'm awfully tired. You know, my trip and all."

A half hour after he had lurched up the path toward town I was on the telephone talking to Will. He was at his cabin, preparing for bed.

"Margaret! Why in heaven's name are you calling me at this hour?"

"Will, I've got to talk to you!"

"Where? Here? Margaret, are you insane?"

"Will, I'm scared—I'm scared to death!"

"Scared?" The wire went dead for perhaps ten seconds. Then he cleared his throat and a faint chuckle came across to me. "What of? Had a nightmare?"

"Please, Will! I mean it!"

"Very well." His voice this time was clipped and soberly concerned, decisive. "I'll meet you in my office in fifteen minutes."

His face showed neither surprise or satisfaction when, seated across from his desk again, I outlined my desire to leave Jack and my reasons. At first he couldn't agree that I was choosing the right course, since the application of the law had always been his favorite recourse for the settlement of most problems.

"I suggest that you serve legal notice that you don't want to see him. Then if he persists in annoying you, he can be tossed in jail."

"Will, please, don't you see? He'll just get out. It'll start all over! I'm afraid of him too! You remember what you once said —about his being dangerous?"

"Well," he said harshly, "why don't you let me throw him out of the country then?"

"Don't you see? He'd get some money and come back! Will! He'd make me go with him! I don't want to leave Alaska! Oh! There must be some place that I can go—in this country— where he couldn't find me! That's what I came to you for!"

"Maybe there is. And maybe you're right about this."

Something like a year ago, he explained, he and Al Boyd had bought into some claims in the Kuyokuk country, a primitive section of Alaska in the mountains about 500 miles northeast of Fairbanks. Their partners in the venture, some twenty in all and most of them married to Indian women, had started a village there, currently unnamed and presently almost inaccessible.

In the winter, communications and the delivery of supplies depended upon freighters. At the first heavy snowfall he intended to move out with the necessary stock of medicine and sundries to last the natives for the usual spell.

"I can promise you nothing but hardship," he went on, "but you'll certainly be well hidden. If that's what you want."

There were no orchestras, dancing or restaurants in the camp, he emphasized. In essence, cards were the sole medium of entertainment, unless one could think of new fireside lies, now and then, enjoy shooting animals or trading at the Yukon Trading Company Post. The weather in summer was hot as a pitch-fired griddle. In winter it was so cold that icicles formed in your pockets.

"Want to go along?"

"Yes—I certainly do!"

"What about your business?"

"I've a little money left. Robb can take care of my kennels. He's been doing it."

"All right," he replied. "I hope for once you'll be satisfied. I assume from your tone that you want this transaction kept from Bartlett's ears. So now to the schedule."

After the first blizzard, he outlined, his freighting train would move out. It would consist of two supply sleds pulled by heavy dogs, and his own lighter, trail-breaking team. A minister of the gospel, one Reverend Edward Sheldon, had asked to be included in the retinue. He was new in Fairbanks and had evinced a determination to visit the heathen in the back country, and to attempt some pietistic influence on the whites of the camp.

"He'll ride my sled," Will said, "so that leaves you to be taken care of."

He could put at my disposal, he added, a Northern Commercial Company dog team, and he would press one of his female employees, an Indian, into acting as my chaperone. Meanwhile I should sit still and keep quiet—if, that is, I wanted to keep Bartlett out of my hair.

Winter's first cozy white coverlet tucked us in for two weeks. Darkness was upon us for twenty-four hours a day, and my mood surely matched the elements. With Jack, everything now was in half light or total obscurity. He didn't even concern himself with the satisfaction of hitting me. Night after night I was forced, for appearance's sake, to sit at our table in the Del Norte, picking at my food, smirking at his vulgarities, closing my ears to his insults and trying to be civil to his cronies.

Then Fairbanks' first blizzard hit. It was a howler, and two days later I got a call from Will.

"We'll be on our way at four tomorrow morning. Ready?"

"Yes, yes, Will! Did you take care of everything? What do I need?"

"Just your parka—trail clothes. Your team's ready. So is your chaperone. Meet me at my office."

I was there an hour early. I liked what I saw, despite the fact that it was purple dark and appallingly cold. The Indian girl had a flat face but a wide smile. The preacher looked the way a preacher should look; he was elderly, dreamy eyed, and Kansas stooped. The teams were made up of fine dogs, and the sleds were piled with supplies and camping equipment. The freighters, Jim Thompson and Bill Neff, both employees of Will, were pleasant men topped by fur caps and sheathed in roomy parkas. Will, when his silhouette was visible in the gloom, looked like the leader of a Devil's Island insurrection.

"Our first stop for the night," he explained to me, "will be about forty miles from here at a small camp called Baldy. Most of the way to the Kuyokuk we'll be able to enjoy the hospitality of small camps. However, for a hundred miles beyond the last one we'll be living the life of the true frontier. But don't worry. You'll be taken care of."

As I look across the years the events in the following six hours seem incredible. As we approached Baldy, a mining camp that boasted all of four shacks, I knew somehow that Jack Bartlett was on my trail, and the feeling became so strong that I was actually whimpering to myself in terror. When I had built a roaring fire in the pot-bellied stove of the cabin of a gracious miner who had relinquished it to bunk with a colleague and had sat back to relax with my Indian chaperone, I discovered that my premonition, or whatever it was, had been right.

There was a cacophony of animal coughs and yapping outside, laced with shouts and cursing. Then my door crashed in and Jack Bartlett was there. Beyond him, in the trail, a tall Indian stood beside a panting racing team.

"So—so you and Burke!" Jack's face was that of a murderer's, and his fingers opened and closed. "When did the two of you cook up this little trick?"

If my life had depended upon it, I could not have uttered a word. I was paralyzed with fear.

"Answer me, Margaret," he choked, "before I beat you to death!"

"Jack." That was as far as I could become articulate, and the sound was only a whisper. "Jack."

"Did you imagine that you and your lover had me fooled? It's been going on all the time, hasn't it, you dirty little—did you think I hadn't been watching? Or that I couldn't persuade one of Burke's men to talk?" Peeling off his parka, he threw it on the floor, then reached for me. His clutch tore my blouse to shreds and flung me to my knees. "Get your things together. We're going back. Just as soon as I put Burke in his grave."

He didn't need to look for Will. Suddenly Burke was in the cabin.

"What the—"

Jack's answer was typical of him. Whirling, he threw a right-hand punch. Taken unaware, Will caught it in his left eye, and as he sprawled into a corner of the cabin his brow winked white, then red. Jack was upon him instantly, bludgeoning, hammering and kicking. Somehow Will managed to roll from beneath Jack's feet and stagger upright. But he was too dazed to protect himself properly. A couple of swings later, Will spun about and went down again, and this time he fell into the stove. There was a quick hiss, and when he rose, shreds of skin hung from the spot on his cheek where it had touched the wood burner.

I never shall understand how Will managed to survive the next few minutes. The sound of Jack's blows as they connected with Will's body and head were sickening. Half unconscious and blinded by blood in one eye, there must have been no inch of the cabin floor that he didn't smash into.

Then, as the end seemed near, Jack made his first mistake of the fight. He knocked Will through the door, and in pursuit of him, stumbled and fell into a snowbank off the path to the cabin. When he got up, Will was waiting for him, this time in the middle of the hard-packed trail. Partly revived by the cold air and able to employ his footwork skill from his days as a professional boxer, Will managed—for a minute or two—to ward off Jack's crushing blows. But he was pretty far gone. Another exchange of blows sent him floundering into the center of the Indian driver's team. Excited by the commotion, the dogs began fighting among themselves. The snarls, growls and curses of the miners as they sought to separate the animals provided a din that could have been heard for twenty miles.

I suddenly grew dizzy. The next thing I recall was that I was sitting in the snow outside the cabin and that Will's back was against a tree. Jack, crouched in front of him, was feinting at him with a pickax. Maybe I saved Will's life then. I don't know. In any event, I found my voice and screamed. It was probably the loudest scream ever heard, before or since, in Alaska. As he swung the pick, Jack's head jerked at the sound. Simultaneously, Will ducked and fell flat, and I swear the bit of the pick went into that tree six inches deep.

Then Jack made his second mistake. Tugging at the pick in order to free it, he threw himself off balance. Grappling at his legs, Will threw him, and they rolled into the trail once more. As Jack rose, Will hit him with his first telling punch, and Jack landed on his back. Staggering upright, he ran into another that also dropped him.

I don't know, to this day, whether Jack Bartlett was a coward, as Lucy Boyd had suggested. But when he got up after Will's second punch, his battered face reflected an odd expression—one that I had not seen before. If he was afraid, I do not blame him. Will, smeared with blood, his black hair flying like the tail of a horse in a storm and teeth bared, resembled the Devil's chief torturer.

Jack was finished. Will began knocking him down with ease, and after a half-dozen more trips to the snow, Jack didn't get up. Will fastened his hands in the front of Jack's shirt and stood him on his legs.

"Bartlett," Will gasped, his face an inch from Jack's, "can—can you hear me?"

"U-uh."

"You—get out of—Alaska. First ship. Find you in this country—again—I'll look you up—kill you. Understand?"

Jack nodded. Then he allowed Jack's driver to roll him on his sled and cover him with a blanket. A minute later the outfit was out of sight.

"Sorry."

I looked up and I thought my heart would burst. Will, standing at his sled, had taken a towel from a knapsack and was wiping the blood from his face.

"It was bound to come—sooner or later, Margaret."

Then the great character of his love, the patience, the sacrifices and honest, undemanding friendship, came to rest on my shoulders. All the things that he had done for me crowded home. And now this terrible beating. There were so many things, so many. I ran to him. The great arms opened.